THE PHILOSOPHY GYM

Also by Stephen Law
The Philosophy Files

The Philosophy Gym

25 SHORT ADVENTURES IN THINKING

Stephen Law

ILLUSTRATED BY DANIEL POSTGATE

This edition published 2003
by BCA
by arrangement with Review
an imprint of Headline Book Publishing

CN 113049

Printed and bound in Great Britain by
Mackays of Chatham plc, Chatham, Kent

Design and layout by Ben Cracknell Studios
Set in RotisSansSerif 10/13pt

Headline Book Publishing
A division of Hodder Headline
338 Euston Road
London NW1 3BH

For Tilda

ACKNOWLEDGEMENTS

Thanks are due to a number of philosophers, including Anita Avramides, Alan Carter, Michael Clark, Michael Lacewing, Scott Sturgeon, James Rachels and Stephen Williams. I'm especially indebted to Nigel Warburton, who read and commented in detail on many of the chapters.

Addition help was provided by Elene Kostas, Maureen and Bill Law, Chris Michael and Emma Webb, David Mills and Catherine Pepinster. Tony Youens, of the Association for Skeptical Enquiry, assisted me with the chapter on miracles. A special thank you to Mick O'Neill, Taryn Storey and John and Karenza Storey for their very useful advice.

CONTENTS

INTRODUCTION

Have you ever wondered where the universe came from? Whether a machine might think? If time travel is possible? Whether it's morally acceptable to design children genetically? Then you have already begun to think philosophically. Each chapter of this book provides a short, easy to follow introduction to such a philosophical puzzle or mystery, taking you through key arguments and ideas in an accessible, and, I hope, entertaining way.

What is Philosophy?

What is philosophy, exactly? Philosophy deals with certain questions. The first thing to notice about these questions is that they have a depth that appears to make them *unanswerable by science*.

One of the deepest philosophical mysteries – the first addressed in this book – is: why is there something, rather than nothing? Why does the universe, or indeed *anything at all*, exist? An astrophysicist might tell us that the universe began with the Big Bang. But this merely postpones the mystery. For the question then becomes: and why was there a Big Bang? Whatever scientists posit to explain why there is something rather than nothing itself becomes part of the something the existence of which needs explaining. Science cannot solve the mystery of why there is anything at all.

Moral questions are also important questions that science cannot answer. Take the question of whether we should genetically design our children. Science may one day allow us to do so. It can't tell us whether we *should* do so.

It's with such questions that philosophers grapple; deep questions that appear to reach beyond the point where science might provide us with answers.

True, it's not just philosophy that addresses these questions. Religion also offers answers to many of them. Religions typically try to explain the existence of the universe, e.g. they claim it was created by God. And in many cases they lay down moral commandments. For example, there are passages in the Bible that condemn stealing, killing and homosexuality.

So how do philosophy and religion differ? One feature of philosophy that can set it apart from religion is that it is supposed to be an essentially *rational* enterprise.

Philosophers are interested in justifying their answers to these questions. While religion tries to provide answers, it doesn't always attempt to make a reasoned case for accepting them. Often, the answers are handed down by a religious authority to be accepted on faith. Where that is the case, philosophy and religion part company.

It's easy to come up with a philosophical position on something. Ask me where the universe came from and I could suggest it was created by a huge yellow banana called Duffy. The trick, of course, lies in coming up with grounds for supposing this answer is actually *correct*. In the Western tradition, no one is much interested in someone's philosophical point of view unless they are able to justify it. Unless I can present a reasoned case for supposing the universe was created by a huge yellow banana called Duffy, no philosopher will take me seriously. And quite right too.

Applying Philosophy to Life

People sometimes ask what philosophy has to do with everyday life. Perhaps more than they think.

Even if we have never studied philosophy, or heard of it, we all hold a great many philosophical beliefs. Take, for example, the belief that physical objects continue to exist even when no one is experiencing them. That's a belief we all share. Yet it is, for all that, a *philosophical* belief, a belief famously challenged by the eighteenth-century philosopher George Berkeley.

Other examples are not hard to find. Belief in an afterlife is a philosophical belief. So, too, is the belief that death is the end. The majority of us believe that morality is not just a matter of subjective preference. We believe that infanticide is wrong, *period*. It's not wrong-for-us but right-for-anyone-who-thinks-otherwise. Again, that's a philosophical belief. And of course so, too, are atheism and belief in God.

Clearly, many of these beliefs have a direct impact on day-to-day life. Take, for example, someone who believes in reincarnation. They may for that reason lead a rather different sort of existence from someone who does not. They may be less frightened of death, for example. And an individual who genuinely believes morality to be nothing more than a matter of subjective preference may be much more likely to cheat and steal if they think they can get away with it. Our philosophical attitudes play a fundamental role in shaping our lives.

Philosophy can also help us with innumerable practical questions, particularly questions about what we ought or ought not to do. The chapters that follow provide a number of concrete examples. Is it right to sacrifice the life of one conjoined twin to save the other? Is gay sex morally permissible? Should children be sent to religious schools? Is it morally acceptable to eat meat? You will discover how all these questions can be illuminated by a little philosophical thinking.

Other Reasons to Think Philosophically

Even where philosophy might seem to lack any direct relevance to everyday life, it remains valuable.

Most of us live out our lives within a very narrow envelope of concerns. We worry about how to pay the mortgage, whether to buy a new car, what to cook for dinner. When we start to think philosophically, we take a step back and look at the wider picture. We start to examine what we have previously taken for granted.

I believe that those who have never taken a step back – who have lived wholly unexamined lives – are not only rather shallow, they're potentially dangerous. One great lesson of the twentieth century is that human beings, no matter how 'civilised', tend to be moral sheep. We are disastrously prone to follow without question the moral lead provided by those around us. From Nazi Germany to Rwanda, you find people blindly going with the flow.

An advantage of a little philosophical training is that it can provide the skills needed to think independently and question what others might take for granted. It can also help fortify your courage in making a moral stand. As the philosopher Professor Jonathan Glover points out in an interview in the *Guardian*:

> If you look at the people who sheltered Jews under the Nazis, you find a number of things about them. One is that they tended to have a different kind of upbringing from the average person: they tended to be brought up in a non-authoritarian way, brought up to have sympathy with other people and to discuss things rather than just do what they were told.*

Glover adds, 'teaching people to think rationally and critically actually can make a difference to people's susceptibility to false ideologies'. Admittedly, there's no guarantee that someone who has been encouraged to think critically will avoid such pitfalls. But, like Glover, I believe the *greatest* risk comes, not from a society of autonomous critical thinkers, but from a society of unreflective moral sheep.

---

* *Guardian* supplement, 13 October 1999, p. 4.

You will also discover that the skills fostered by a little rigorous thinking about the big questions are highly transferable. Whether you're deciding whether to buy that second-hand car or to tile the bathroom, or wondering for whom you should vote, the ability to formulate a concise argument, follow a complex line of reasoning or spot a logical howler is always useful. At the very least, such skills can provide a lifetime's immunisation against the wiles of dodgy car dealers, religious cults, medical quacks and other purveyors of snake oil.

Far from being irrelevant to everyday life, the reflective attitude and skills that philosophy develops are profoundly life-enhancing.

Stephen Law has a philosophy website at www.thinking-big.co.uk

HOW TO USE THIS BOOK

This book adds up to *a course in thinking philosophically*. Each chapter addresses a different philosophical question, explaining key positions and arguments along the way.

This is a book to dip into. Each of the twenty-five short chapters is free-standing: they can be read in any order you like. Some of the chapters are fairly easy; others slightly less so. The level of difficulty is indicated at the start of each chapter. I have also adopted a variety of different styles. There are dialogues, philosophical stories and thought experiments, illustrations and 'thinking tools' sections to explain key ideas and provide the odd diversion.

Perhaps the most important thing to remember is that philosophy is an activity. The best way to get the most out of any philosophy book is to *join in* the activity by reading critically and thinking for yourself. Question the assumptions and unpick the arguments as you go along. Stop every now and then to make a cup of tea or stare out the window while you think about what you have read. If you find yourself disagreeing with me and constructing counter-arguments of your own, that's a healthy sign.

Suggestions for further reading can be found at the end of each chapter.

1

WHERE DID THE UNIVERSE COME FROM?

About twelve billion years ago an unimaginably violent explosion occurred. Expanding outwards at incredible speed, this cataclysmic blast gave birth to space, energy, matter and indeed time itself. The universe we see around us is the debris from this Big Bang.

But why did the Big Bang happen? What brought the universe into existence? What lies on the other side of the Big Bang?

What Caused the Big Bang?

The scene: Mathers, a theologian, and Figgerson, a physicist, are fellows of one of the grander Oxford colleges. Both love to engage in philosophical disputes. They have just sat down to dinner at High Table.

Figgerson: What philosophical mystery shall we discuss this evening?

Mathers: I have been thinking about the origin of the universe. Could we perhaps discuss that?

Figgerson: Why not? Except there's little mystery there. We scientists have solved that particular conundrum. I can tell you that the universe began about twelve thousand million years old. It started with what we call the Big Bang, a colossal explosion in which space, energy, matter and time itself began.

Mathers: That's no doubt true. But you're wrong to suggest that there's no mystery. We know the Big Bang happened. My question to you is: *why* did it happen?

Figgerson: I'm not sure I follow.

Mathers: What I mean is: what *caused* the universe to exist? Where did it come from? Why is it here? Indeed, why is there *anything at all*?

Figgerson: Why, as it were, is there something, rather than nothing?

Mathers: Yes. That surely is a mystery.

Did God Cause the Big Bang?

The puzzle Mathers raises is perhaps the deepest and most profound mystery of all. The traditional solution is to appeal to the existence of God, which is precisely what Mathers now suggests.

Mathers: It seems to me that there is only one possible solution. God. God must have caused the universe to exist.

Figgerson: Ah, God. I wondered how long it would be before you brought God into the conversation.

Mathers: But surely we must introduce God at this point? Look, when we entered this dining room we found two chairs here. Now, it would be absurd – would it not? – to suppose that these two chairs just popped into existence for no reason at all? The existence of these chairs must surely have had a cause. Don't you agree?

Figgerson: Yes.

Mathers: Similarly with the universe, then. It just isn't plausible that it popped into existence for no reason. It, too, must have a cause. But then God must exist as the cause of the universe.

Let's call Mathers' argument the *cause argument*. It's an example of what is commonly known as a *cosmological argument*. Cosmological arguments begin with two observations: that the universe exists and that the events and entities we find around us always turn out to have a cause or explanation. The arguments then conclude that the universe must also have a cause or explanation and that God is the only possible (or at least the most likely) candidate.

What Caused God?

The cause argument certainly has some prima facie appeal. It's associated particularly with the thirteenth-century philosopher and theologian St Thomas Aquinas (1225–74). Aquinas constructed five arguments for the existence of God, of which the cause argument is the second. Unfortunately, the argument is flawed. Figgerson explains why.

Figgerson: I'm unconvinced. As you know, I don't believe in God. But let's suppose for the sake of argument that God does exist. Your appeal to Him as the explanation of the existence of the universe still ultimately fails to remove the mystery with which we began.

Mathers: I don't see why.

Figgerson: Well, then, let me ask you *what caused God to exist?* You say that it is absurd to suppose that something might come into existence uncaused. As you said about the chairs, they cannot have just popped into existence for no reason. But then it follows that God's existence also requires a cause.

Mathers: Well, God is the exception to the rule that everything requires a cause. God is the supreme being to which the rules that govern other things do not apply. The existence of the universe requires a cause. The existence of God does not.

Figgerson: But if you're going to make an exception to the rule that everything has a cause, why not make the universe the exception? Why do you posit the existence of a *further* entity – God – in addition to the universe?

Mathers: I'm not sure I follow.

Figgerson: You argue that everything has a cause. Then you make God the exception to this rule. But why not make the Big Bang the exception to the rule? What reason have you given me to add God to the beginning of this chain of causes as an extra link? You have given me none. But then you have given me no reason at all to suppose that God exists.

As Figgerson points out, the most obvious flaw in the cause argument – a flaw also pointed out by the philosopher David Hume (1711–76) – is that it involves a contradiction. The argument begins with the premise that everything has a cause, but this is then contradicted by the claim that God does not have a cause. If we must posit a God as the cause of the universe, then it seems we must also posit a second God as the cause of the first God, and a third God as the cause of the second, and so on ad infinitum. So we shall have to accept that there are an infinite number of Gods. Either that or we must stop with a cause that itself has no independent cause. But if we must stop somewhere, why not stop with the Big Bang itself? What reason is there to introduce even *one* God?

Of course, some might be willing to accept an infinite chain of Gods. But such a chain *still* wouldn't remove the mystery with which we began. For then the question would arise: why is there such an infinite chain of Gods, rather than no chain?

Here's an analogously bad causal explanation. When struck by the question of what holds up the earth, some people posited a great creature – an elephant – as its support.

But then the question arises: if the earth is held up by an elephant, then *what holds up the elephant*? A second creature – a vast turtle – was then introduced to hold up the elephant. These people decided to stop with the turtle. But why stop there? For, of course, the question with which they were really grappling – the question of why *anything at all* gets held up – has still not been answered. In fact, if we pursue their reasoning to its logical conclusion, the earth will end up perched on top of a huge tower of creatures – an infinite number of creatures – stacked up one on top of the other.

But they didn't do this. They stopped with the turtle. But if it's claimed that the turtle requires no support, then why not just say that the earth requires no support and leave it at that? What reason is there to introduce *any* supporting creatures at all? There is none.

Despite being a poor argument, the cause argument has always been popular. In fact, when asked to give some reason why they suppose that God exists, the cause argument is the one to which those who believe in God often first appeal. The question of what brought God into existence is simply overlooked.

What's North of the North Pole?

Figgerson and Mathers continue to argue, each becoming more and more infuriated with the other. Eventually, to Mathers's intense annoyance, Figgerson suggests that Mathers's original question – what caused the universe? – may not even *make sense*.

Figgerson: Look, while it may make sense to ask what caused this chair, that mountain or this tree to exist, it surely does not make sense to ask what caused the universe *as a whole* to exist.

Mathers: H'm. You suggest my question does not make sense. But what *reason* do you have to suppose that it doesn't make sense? Justify your suggestion.

Figgerson: Very well. It seems to me that to ask for the cause of something is to ask what other thing *within the universe* brought it about. That is how the game of asking for and giving causes is played out. When I ask, for example, what caused that tree outside the window to exist, I am asking for you to identify some other thing or event *within* the universe that brought that tree into existence. Someone might have planted an acorn in that spot, for example, or someone might have moved a tree there to improve the view from this window. But if to ask for the cause of something is to ask what other thing *within* the universe brought it about, then *it cannot make sense to ask what is the cause of the universe as a whole.* That would be to pursue the question of causes outside the context in which such questions can meaningfully be raised.

Mathers: I'm not sure I follow.

Figgerson: Very well. Let me explain by means of an analogy. Suppose I ask you what is to the north of England. What would you say?

Mathers: Scotland.

Figgerson: And what lies to the north of Scotland?

Mathers: Iceland.

Figgerson: And to the north of Iceland?

Mathers: The Arctic Circle.

Figgerson: And to the north of the Arctic Circle?

Mathers: The North Pole.

Figgerson: And what lies to the north of the North Pole?

Mathers: Er. What do you mean?

Figgerson: If there is something north of England, and something north of Scotland, and something north of Iceland, then surely there must be something to the north of the North Pole too?

Mathers: You're confused. Don't you understand what 'north' means? Your question doesn't make sense. It doesn't make sense to talk about something being north of the North Pole. To say that something is north of something else is to say that it is nearer to the North Pole than that other thing. But then it can't make sense to talk about something being north of the North Pole, can it?

Figgerson: Aha. So my question doesn't make sense. Well, then, neither does your question about the cause of the universe.

Mathers: How so?

Figgerson: One can ask what is the cause of an earthquake? One can then ask for the cause of the cause of the earthquake, and so on. One can trace the chain of causes right back to the Big Bang if one likes. But it makes no sense then to ask: and what caused the Big Bang? That is like asking: and what is to the north of the North Pole? That would be to ask a question outside the context within which such questions can meaningfully be raised.

Still, as Mathers points out, his question about the origin of the universe does at least *appear* to be cogent.

Mathers: But my question does *seem* to make sense, doesn't it? And it seems to me that you haven't actually shown that the question about causes cannot legitimately be raised about the universe itself.

Figgerson: Why not?

Mathers: You seem to argue that if we don't *normally* ask a question outside a certain context, then it cannot *meaningfully* be raised outside that context. But your argument is fallacious. Here's a counterexample. It seems probable, I think, that for long periods of our history mankind considered only *practical* questions, questions the answers to which it would be *useful* for us to know. For example, no doubt we wanted to know what causes plants to grow, what causes the seasons to come and go, what causes storms and diseases, and so on. We wanted to know the causes of these things because they affect our day-to-day lives. Probably we weren't interested in asking questions that didn't have any practical relevance for us. For example, perhaps we didn't bother asking ourselves what causes the sky to be blue. But it doesn't follow that if we didn't *normally* ask such impractical questions, then such questions, if they had been asked, would have *made no sense.* Surely, even if we never did ask ourselves what causes the sky to be blue, we *might* have done, and, if we had, our question would certainly have made sense.

Figgerson: I suppose it would.

Mathers: Thank you for that admission. But then why do you suppose that it makes no sense to ask what caused the universe? Just because we don't *normally* ask this question doesn't mean that it is senseless. In fact, it seems perfectly clear to me that, unlike your question about what is to the north of the North Pole, my question *does* make sense, even if it is difficult to see how it might be answered.

Figgerson: H'm. Perhaps your question does make sense.

Mathers: Aha! In that case, what I want to know is this: if God did not cause the universe to exist, then *what did?*

The Unsolvable Mystery

Figgerson stares wistfully into his spotted dick and custard. Then he gazes out over the heads of the assembled undergraduates eating below.

Figgerson: Perhaps *nothing* caused the universe to exist. Perhaps its existence is simply a *brute fact.* After all, we physicists are inclined to accept that some things are just brute fact and inexplicable. Often we explain why one law holds by appealing to others. One can explain, for example, the law that water freezes at zero degrees Celsius by appealing to the laws that govern the atoms and molecules out of which water is composed. But few suppose that this process can go on for ever. Presumably one must eventually come up against laws that cannot be accounted for or explained in terms of yet other laws. The obtaining of these basic laws is just a brute fact. And if we are to allow that there are at least *some* brute facts, then why not suppose that the existence of the universe is also a brute fact, a fact that requires neither a further cause nor an explanation? Why suppose that it, too, must also have a cause, an explanation?

Mathers: It seems to me that the existence of the universe cannot be a brute fact, as you suggest. It isn't plausible to suppose that the universe popped into existence for no reason. The Big Bang didn't *just happen,* surely? There must be a reason *why* it happened.

Figgerson closely examines his pudding as if searching for an answer. He watches as the spotted dick crumbles into the custard, the currants swirling slowly outwards like the stars in some huge pudding galaxy.

Figgerson furrows his brow. He hates to admit it, but Mathers does appear to be right.

Figgerson: I must say, I do feel confused. I agree that it doesn't seem adequate to say that the Big Bang happened for no reason at all. And yet it seems we can say nothing else. Why *is* there something, rather than nothing?

Mathers: The answer is God.

Figgerson: But that answer will not do, as we have already seen.

Mathers: So what does explain the existence of the universe, if not God?

Figgerson: That's a mystery.

Conclusion

It seems that when it comes to the question *what is the ultimate cause or origin of the universe?* there are four options available to us. These are to:

1. Answer the question by identifying a cause of the universe.
2. Claim that, though the universe has a cause, we cannot or at least do not yet know what this cause is.
3. Claim that perhaps the universe has no cause – it's existence is simply a brute fact.
4. Deny the question even makes sense.

The problem is that on closer examination none of these four options seems satisfactory. The difficulty with the first option is that as soon as one offers God or indeed something else as the cause or explanation of the universe, the 'something' to which one appeals in turn becomes the focus of the demand for a cause or explanation. So it seems that the first kind of answer can never be adequate. Rather than answering the question about ultimate origins, we merely sweep it under the carpet. The difficulty with the second option is that if one suggests that the universe has an as yet unknown cause, the question then arises: and what is the cause of that unknown cause? So the mystery is merely postponed. The claim that the universe simply has no cause, on the other hand, also seems unsatisfactory – is it really plausible to suppose that the universe simply popped into existence for no reason at all? Surely not. And yet the fourth and final option seems equally implausible – certainly, no one has yet succeeded in providing an uncontroversial explanation of *why* the question about the cause of the universe makes no sense.

So it seems that, while no explanation can be acceptable, yet neither can the question of the ultimate origin of the universe simply be set aside or dismissed. Which is why this particular philosophical mystery remains so perplexing. It appears that the question of the ultimate origin of the universe is a mystery that can be neither explained nor explained away.

What to read next

See Chapter 7, Does God Exist?, Chapter 10, Can We Have Morality without God and Religion?, and Chapter 23, Miracles and the Supernatural, for more arguments for the existence of God.

For some other examples of circular explanations, see Chapter 16, The Meaning Mystery.

Further reading

A good introduction to the philosophy of religion containing a thorough discussion of many of the issues raised here is:

J. L. Mackie, *The Miracle of Theism* (Oxford: Clarendon Press, 1982), especially Chapter 5.

Also see:

Nigel Warburton, *Philosophy: The Basics*, second edition (London: Routledge, 1995), Chapter 1.

2

WHAT'S WRONG
WITH GAY SEX?

PHILOSOPHY GYM CATEGORY

WARM–UP

MODERATE

MORE CHALLENGING

The scene: Mr Jarvis, a Christian, was asleep in bed, dreaming of the Last Judgement. In his dream, Jarvis found himself seated next to God in a great cloud-swept hall. God had just finished handing down judgement on the drunkards, who were slowly shuffling out of the exit to the left. Angels were now ushering a group of nervous-looking men through the entrance to the right. As the men were assembled before Him, God began to speak.

God: So who's next? Ah, yes, the active homosexuals.* So tell me, Jarvis,
            what shall we do with them?
Jarvis: You're going to punish them, aren't you?
God: Why do you say that?
Jarvis: Because to engage in homosexual behaviour is wrong, of course.

The Appeal to the Bible

God gently rubbed His chin and looked quizzically at Jarvis.

God: Wrong? *Is* it wrong?
Jarvis: Yes. You say so yourself in the Bible.
God: Ah, the Bible.
Jarvis: Yes. Look right here. 'Thou shalt not lie with mankind, as with
            womankind: it is an abomination.' Leviticus xviii, 22.
God: Well, I may have been a little hasty. I'm not sure about that bit now.
Jarvis: Not sure? You're God! You don't make mistakes!
God: Perhaps I'm not the real God. Perhaps I'm merely a dream God – a
            figment of your imagination.
Jarvis: Oh.

* In this chapter I discuss just male homosexuality, though of course many of the arguments would also apply to female homosexuality.

God: Also, why do you assume that the Bible is a hundred per cent reliable?

Jarvis: You mean it's not?

God: I didn't say that. But look, if you plan to base your morality entirely on the contents of just one book, you'd better be sure it's the *right* book. And you'd better be sure to what extent it can be relied on, hadn't you?

The Lord pointed to the Bible lying in Jarvis's lap.

God: Flip back a couple of pages. Scan down a bit. That's it. Leviticus xi, 7–8. What does it say?

Jarvis: 'And the swine, though he divide the hoof . . . he is unclean to you. Of their flesh shall ye not eat.'

God: Ever eaten a bacon sandwich? Then you have sinned! Now a little further down.

Jarvis: 'These shall ye eat of all that are in the waters: whatsoever hath fins and scales in the waters, in the seas, and in the rivers them shall ye eat. And all that have not fins and scales . . .'

God: '. . . ye shall not eat of their flesh.' Didn't your last meal include moules marinière? Why aren't you Christians out boycotting seafood restaurants and warning of the perils of lobster thermidor?

Jarvis turned a little pale.

God: If you read over the page from the passage about homosexuality, you will discover that it's also wrong to wear a jacket made from a linen/wool mix.

Jarvis: I hadn't noticed that bit before.

God: Further on it says it's sinful to lend money for interest. Yet you condemn not one of *these* things, do you?

Jarvis: No.

God: But you confidently cite that particular

passage of Leviticus to justify your condemnation of homosexuality. It seems you are picking and choosing.

Jarvis: But surely you no longer mean those other passages about seafood, jackets and lending money to apply? They're outdated, aren't they?

God looked sternly at Jarvis.

God: The word of God? Outdated? OK, I shan't blame you for failing to condemn those who wear jackets made from a linen/wool mix. But you're using your *own* sense of right and wrong, your *own* moral criteria, to decide which passages of the Bible to accept and which to reject, aren't you?

Jarvis: Yes, I guess I am.

God: Indeed, it's because the morality of the Bible does *generally* fit in with what you already think about right and wrong that you are prepared to accept the Bible as my word, isn't it? If the Bible recommended stealing, lying and killing, you would hardly be likely to take it as the word of God, would you?

Jarvis: I guess not.

God: Then I think you should be honest. Rather than picking those bits of the Bible you like and rejecting the rest, and then claiming that your particular selection has my divine stamp of approval, I think you should just say that *you* think homosexuality is wrong and leave me out of it.

Jarvis: Very well.

God: Right, so if *you* believe homosexuality is wrong, can you explain to me *why* it's wrong? Why do these men deserve punishment?

'Homosexuality Is Unnatural'

Jarvis looked out at the assembled crowd and scratched his head.

Jarvis: I didn't say you should punish them. Perhaps they should be forgiven. But they have *sinned*. I can give you a number of reasons why.

God: What reasons?

Jarvis: The first is that homosexuality is unnatural.

God:	Ah. That's perhaps the most commonly held justification for condemning homosexual acts. But in what sense is homosexuality unnatural?
Jarvis:	Well, *most* people *aren't* actively homosexual. So homosexuality is an aberration from the norm.
God:	In a sense. But then most men don't have red hair. So red hair is also, as you put it, an aberration from the norm. Yet there is nothing *unnatural* about red hair, is there?
Jarvis:	True. What I mean is that homosexual acts are unnatural because they are *not what nature intended.*
God:	Not what nature intended? H'm. Again, you need to clarify. Do you mean that homosexual acts run against those tendencies that nature has instilled in man, those that come most naturally to him?
Jarvis:	Yes, I suppose I do.
God:	So why are you so sure that homosexuality *is* unnatural?
Jarvis:	Well, you don't see animals in the wild engaging in homosexual sodomy, do you? It clearly involves some sort of corruption of our natural inclinations.
God:	You assume that animals don't engage in homosexuality. How do you know they don't? In fact, *they do.*
Jarvis:	They do?
God:	Absolutely. The fact is that hardly anyone has bothered to investigate the incidence of homosexuality in other species. People assume it doesn't really exist. But a recent American study of longhorn sheep discovered that, given the choice between mounting a fertile ewe or mounting another ram, about eight per cent of rams will *consistently* choose the latter. They sometimes even manage to engage in penetrative anal sex.

A shocked expression passed over Jarvis's face.

Jarvis:	I had no idea.
God:	But the fact is that, even if homosexuality *were* unnatural, which it isn't, that wouldn't make it wrong, would it?
Jarvis:	Why not?
God:	Well, what about cleanliness? Cleanliness is next to godliness, they

say. Yet it hardly comes naturally to most human beings, does it? Children seem positively fond of dirt. Man, for the most part, is pretty filthy, and doesn't much mind being so. Your human obsession with hygiene is a very modern development. But then, by your own reasoning, cleanliness is morally wrong.

Jarvis: Oh dear.

God: Indeed, much that comes naturally to man is immoral. He also seems naturally inclined towards greed, avarice, selfishness, infidelity and aggression. Humans have to struggle to control these natural inclinations. In fact, it's only those who succeed in thwarting these repugnant natural tendencies who are considered virtuous. Yet you would now reverse this and say that these tendencies, being natural, are good and what runs against them bad! Let me introduce you to someone.

Suddenly, Jarvis felt another person sitting close by. He turned to his right and saw a bald, serious-looking man dressed in a dark suit.

God: This is John Stuart Mill, who lived from 1806 to 1873. Mill here didn't always give me a good press. In fact, meeting me came as something of a surprise to you, didn't it, Mill?

Mill smiled nervously.

God: But he *does* have something interesting to say about what is natural. Don't you, Mill?

Mill: Conformity to nature has no connection whatever with right and wrong . . . To illustrate this point, let us consider the word by which the greatest intensity of condemnatory feeling is conveyed in connection with the idea of nature – the word 'unnatural'. That a thing is unnatural, in any precise meaning which can be attached to the word, is no argument for its being blameable, since the most criminal actions are to a being like man not more unnatural than most of the virtues.*

No sooner had Mill finished speaking than he vanished in a puff of smoke.

---

* John Stuart Mill, 'Nature', in *Three Essays on Religion* (New York: Prometheus, 1998), p. 62.

God: A fine mind, that Mill. So what do you say now?

Jarvis looked a little irritated. He remained convinced that there is *something* unnatural about homosexuality, something that makes it morally wrong. But he was struggling very hard to identify exactly what this unnatural and immoral feature is. Then, after a few minutes, Jarvis had an idea.

Jarvis: I have it! The penis has a specific function, doesn't it? It's designed for procreation, for the production of children. Homosexual activity is thus a misuse of that particular body part. One is using a body part contrary to the way nature intended.

God: I see. But then *most* sexual activity is morally wrong. For most sexual activity – even heterosexual activity – involves the thwarting of the procreative natural function. Masturbation is sinful: it cannot result in the production of children. Oral sex is sinful. The use of any sort of contraceptive device is sinful. Is that what you believe?

Jarvis: It's certainly what many Catholics believe, isn't it?

God: True. But look, if the justification for considering *all* these sorts of sexual activity sinful is that they involve using body parts contrary to their 'natural' function, then what about, say, wearing earrings? It hardly looks like a 'natural' use of the ears, does it, hanging lumps of metal off them? Yet it's not considered sinful. No doubt you would deny that wearing earrings involves, as you said, using a body part contrary to its basic, essential function. But why?

Jarvis: I'm not sure.

God: And in any case, the question remains: *why* is it wrong to use a body part contrary to its basic natural function? I just don't see *why* it follows that if something comes unnaturally to us, or to a part of our body, then it's wrong.

'Homosexuality Is Dirty'

Jarvis was struggling to answer God's question adequately. So he decided to try a different tack.

Jarvis: OK. Suppose I accept that Mill is correct. Morality has nothing to do with what's 'natural' or 'unnatural'. Still there's another much more obvious and better reason for condemning homosexual practices. I hope you won't be offended if I speak frankly.

God: Be as frank as you like.

Jarvis: Very well. Homosexuality is *dirty*, isn't it? Sodomy – placing one's penis in someone else's anus – means that it is probable that one will come into contact with *faeces*.

God: What you say about sodomy is true. But does this show that *all* homosexual acts are wrong? No, it doesn't. There are plenty of active homosexuals who don't practise sodomy. You can't condemn *them*, can you?

Jarvis: No.

God: Also, there are heterosexual couples who practise sodomy, aren't there?

Jarvis: There are?

God: Take my word for it. But in any case, just because an activity is dirty doesn't make it wrong.

Jarvis: Why not?

God: You're a keen gardener, aren't you?

Jarvis: Yes.

God: Well, gardening is a pretty dirty activity, isn't it? Particularly where you live. There is rarely a day you spend in the garden that doesn't result in you immersing your hands in cat faeces, is there?

Jarvis: I guess that's true. You are right. Gardening is dirty, but it's not immoral. So I can't really use the alleged dirtiness of sodomy to justify my morally condemning it, can I?

God: You're catching on, my boy.

'Homosexuality Is Unhealthy'

Jarvis now tried a different approach.

Jarvis: To engage in homosexual activity is unhealthy. That's why it's wrong.

God: Unhealthy?

Jarvis: Yes. Take HIV, for example. HIV is an infection that results in AIDS. AIDS kills millions of people. And it is through homosexual activity that HIV is spread. Correct?

God: You are partially correct. HIV can be spread through *all* forms of penetrative sex. Indeed, many heterosexuals are infected too.

Jarvis: That's true.

God: Also, homosexuals may practise safe sex. Heterosexuals too. Practise safe sex and the risks are pretty low.

Jarvis: H'm. Also true, I guess.

God: Perhaps it's true that homosexual acts are *more* likely to pass on the disease than are heterosexual acts, even if they are of the comparatively 'safe' variety. But does that make it wrong? If it were found that drinking wine is similarly a bit less healthy than drinking beer, we wouldn't morally condemn those wine drinkers who refused to switch to beer, would we?

Jarvis: I guess not.

'Homosexuality Corrupts the Young'

Jarvis: But what of homosexuals who prey on innocent young men? *That's* wrong, isn't it?

God: But it's no less wrong when men seek to seduce innocent and impressionable young women, surely?

Jarvis: Well, yes, that is wrong too. But what the homosexual seducer does is *more* wrong.

God: Why?

Jarvis: Well, because the young man involved may then end up adopting a homosexual lifestyle himself. He may be corrupted.

God: You're assuming, I think, that homosexuals tend to be made, not born. That's contentious, is it not?

Jarvis: Well, isn't it plausible that some men who would, other things being equal, go on to have only heterosexual sexual relationships may have a *tendency* towards homosexuality that, given the wrong sort of experience at an impressionable age, may result in them then pursuing homosexual liaisons later in life?

God: That's not implausible. But notice that you're *begging the question*. If there's nothing morally wrong with homosexuality, then what difference does it make if a young man *does* end up engaging in homosexual acts? Why insist that this young man is corrupted?

Jarvis: Well, homosexuals live miserable lives. In many societies they
           continue to be vilified. So, as a result of his early homosexual
           experience, this young man may end up having an unhappy life. The
           homosexual who initiates the young man into this life must know
           this. So what the initiator does is wrong.
God: Perhaps. But even if what you say is true, is the blame for the young
           man's misery to be pinned primarily on the homosexual who initiates
           him?

God pointed an accusatory finger at Jarvis.

God: Wouldn't it be more appropriate to blame people like *you* for making
           homosexuals miserable by vilifying them?

'Homosexuals Are Promiscuous'

Jarvis didn't bother to answer God's question. Instead, he pointed out something
about male homosexuals that does appear to be true.

Jarvis: Male homosexuals tend to be rather more *promiscuous* than
           heterosexuals. Doesn't that, at least, make them worthy of your moral
           condemnation?
God: This, at best, would give me reason to condemn those homosexuals
           who were promiscuous. It would not justify my condemning
           homosexual acts per se. In fact, many homosexual couples remain
           faithful throughout their lives. And plenty of heterosexuals are
           promiscuous too.
Jarvis: True. But homosexuals tend to be *more* promiscuous.
God: There's a scientific explanation for that. Males seem naturally much
           more disposed towards having no-strings sex than do females. Ask
           heterosexual men if they would accept the offer of no-risk, no-strings
           sex with an attractive stranger of the opposite sex and over ninety
           per cent say 'yes'. Ask heterosexual women the same question and the
           vast majority say 'no'.
Jarvis: That's interesting.

God: Yes. So you see, in heterosexual relationships, women act as a natural brake on the male's impulse to have sex fairly indiscriminately. For male homosexuals, this brake is missing. It is unsurprising, then, that they tend to be more promiscuous than are heterosexual males. It's not that they are any less *moral*, it's just that they have more opportunity to do what *most* men, *whatever* their sexual persuasion, would do given the opportunity.

Jarvis: Nevertheless, you admit that male homosexuals do tend to be more promiscuous, and promiscuity is not to be encouraged. So male homosexuality is not to be encouraged, surely?

God: Your argument rests on the assumption that promiscuity is *itself* a bad thing. But is it?

Jarvis: Isn't it?

God: Can you explain to me why you think it is?

'Homosexuals Use Each Other as Means, not Ends'

Jarvis: Well, take, for example, those bathhouses in San Francisco. You know, the ones in which homosexual orgies are supposed to have taken place. Men having sex with complete strangers at the drop of a hat. These men would be treating other men not as ends in themselves, but merely as a *means to an end*, that end being their own immediate sexual gratification. Now *that* is morally wrong, surely? It was the philosopher Immanuel Kant (1724–1804) who said: 'Act so that you treat humanity, whether in your own person or in that of another, always as an end and never as a means only.' And that is quite right, isn't it? One ought to treat others as ends in themselves, rather than as the means by which one might obtain a quick sexual thrill. That, surely, is why such promiscuous behaviour is wrong.

God: An ingenious argument, I admit. But not persuasive. Let me conjure up for you another philosopher, Lord Quinton (b. 1925), who has something interesting to say on this matter.

A figure began to materialise to Jarvis's right. First some hands appeared, then a nose. Finally, there was Anthony Quinton standing before him (Quinton, incidentally, bears an uncanny resemblance to God).

God: Ah, Lord Quinton. My friend Jarvis just suggested that it is wrong to use another person not as an end in himself but merely as a means to sexual pleasure. Homosexuals are less likely to enter into lasting, monogamous sexual relationships. They are, perhaps, more likely to engage in casual sex with a complete stranger, on a whim. Is that a problem, morally?

Quinton: It is certainly true that long-term, morally and personally profound relationships are less common among homosexuals. How much does that matter? If I regularly play tennis with someone but do not see him except on the tennis court and at the health juice bar afterwards – if, in other words, I am interested in him only as a tennis partner – am I ignoring his status as an end in himself? More to the point, if I pick up different opponents every time I go to the courts, on a purely casual basis, am I acting immorally?*

Jarvis: But hang on. Sex is not like tennis, is it? Sex is a *much* more important part of life, surely?

Quinton: Except for a minute number of people, sex is a more important part of life than tennis. A life in which it is merely a source of short-term gratification and not an inseparable part of a whole shared life is to that extent trivialised. But triviality is not a moral offence; it is, rather, a missed opportunity and one which, in fact, many homosexuals do not miss.†

God waved his hand and Lord Quinton began to dissolve into tendrils of cloud. As the last wisps drifted away, God looked intently at Jarvis.

God: So you see, it may be true that *some* homosexuals use each other merely as means to an end and not as ends in themselves. But, as Quinton just explained, it's difficult to see why there is anything morally wrong with that. It may also be true that *some* homosexuals miss out on the kind of deeper connection that can be made only within a stable, lasting and sexually exclusive relationship. However, as Quinton also just explained, this is surely not a reason morally to condemn them.

Jarvis scratched his head. He now felt very confused.

---

* Anthony Quinton, 'Homosexuality', in *From Wodehouse to Wittgenstein* (Manchester: Carcanet Press, 1998), p. 252.
† Ibid.

Jarvis: But I felt sure that you would condemn homosexuality.

God: If two consenting adult males want to enter into a sexual relationship, why not? So far you have not given me a single convincing reason why such activity demands my condemnation. Homosexual sex does no harm to others. Nor does it appear to do much obvious harm to the individuals involved. Why shouldn't people engage in it if that is what they want?

Homosexuality and 'Family Values'

Jarvis: You say that homosexuality does no harm to others. But perhaps it does. Perhaps it has a corrosive effect on society as a whole. For doesn't it eat away at the institution that lies at the heart of any civilised society: the family?

God: Why do you say that?

Jarvis: Well, for a start, if everyone was exclusively homosexual, then there would be no families, would there? The human race would die out!

God: Does that make homosexuality wrong? I think not. For, similarly, if every man became a Catholic priest, that, too, would mean the end of the family. Yet there's nothing immoral about being a Catholic priest, I hope?

Jarvis: No. But look, societies that fail to condemn homosexuality crumble. Once homosexuality is considered a morally acceptable alternative to heterosexuality, the result must be the breakdown of the family. And the family is the glue that binds society together, is it not?

God: You seem to be suggesting that homosexuality is like some sort of disease that will inevitably eat away at the vitals of society unless strongly dealt with.

Jarvis: Yes, I am.

God: But *why* must a society that tolerates homosexuality crumble? Actually, it seems to me that societies tolerant of homosexuality thrive just as much if not more than intolerant ones. And w*hy* do you believe homosexuality is a threat to the family? Why can't we have both strong families *and* tolerance? You really have made no case for any of these conclusions, have you?

Jarvis grimaced.

God: In fact, it seems to me that your attitude towards homosexuals is driven less by reason and more by emotion: by feelings of disgust and revulsion.

Jarvis: I do have strong feelings about them, yes. They do revolt me. And shouldn't society take into account the strong moral convictions of the great many who have such feelings?

God: But it's clear, isn't it, that morality isn't simply a matter of emotion? Just because most people feel that something is disgusting or abhorrent doesn't make it wrong. After all, plenty of people feel strongly about the moral inferiority of Jews. Plenty feel similarly about blacks. Plenty feel sickened by foreigners. Yet all these feelings are without justification. That kind of 'them and us' sentiment on which 'they' are held to be dirty, nasty and immoral comes very naturally to you humans. Perhaps you should be more vigilant, more on your guard against letting such feelings get a grip. As Ronald Dworkin points out, you certainly shouldn't mistake such feelings for moral conviction. Isn't that right, Ronald?

Another shadowy figure started to take form next to Jarvis and began to speak.

Dworkin: If I based my view about homosexuals on a personal emotional reaction ('they make me sick'), you would reject [it]. We distinguish moral positions from emotional reactions, not because moral positions are supposed to be unemotional or dispassionate – quite the reverse is true – but because the moral position is supposed to justify the emotional reaction, and not vice versa. If a man is unable to produce such reasons, we do not deny the fact of his emotional involvement, which may have important social or political consequences, but we do not take this involvement as demonstrating his moral conviction. Indeed, it is just this sort of position – a severe emotional reaction to a practice or a situation for which one cannot account – that we tend to describe, in lay terms, as phobias or an obsession.*

---

* Ronald Dworkin, 'Liberty and Moralism', in *Taking Rights Seriously* (London: Duckworth, 1977), p. 250.

Dworkin faded away. Jarvis looked uncomfortable.

God: See? You're in the grip of a phobia or obsession.
Jarvis: Oh dear.
God: Having said all that, let's get on with the judging.

God reached forward and pressed a small red button on his armrest. Immediately, the hall was bathed in an eerie red light, and the air filled with the deafening 'Parp! Parp! Parp!' of a claxon. Jarvis noticed that over on the left of the hall a number of doors had sprung open, and little horned creatures with long tails were pouring out. These devil-creatures immediately began to prod the assembled homosexuals back in the direction of the doorways with their spiked forks. Many of these unfortunate men were now holding each other and whimpering.

God: That's right. You all burn.
Jarvis: In hell?
God: I'm afraid so. They didn't follow instructions. Couldn't be clearer. You
             pointed out one of the relevant passages yourself. Homosexuality is
             an abomination. I razed Sodom to the ground, didn't I?
Jarvis: But a minute ago you said . . .
God: I have been testing you. I have pretended to be a bleeding-heart
             liberal in order to establish your commitment to the Bible. I do tests.
             Don't you remember Isaac and Abraham – Genesis xxiii?
Jarvis: But what about forgiveness? Aren't you going to allow them into
             heaven?

God pointed to the men being herded about by the devil-creatures.

God: Let them into heaven? How can I?
Jarvis: But I thought . . .
God: There you go, thinking again. It's *all in the book*: the book you hold
             in your hands. Take a look at Corinthians i, 6:9–11. It says very
             clearly that 'abusers of themselves with mankind . . . shall not
             inherit the Kingdom of God. Such were some of you, but ye are
             washed . . . ye are justified in the name of the Lord Jesus'. Now *these*
             men are not 'washed', are they? They don't repent. In fact, they

flaunt their activities proudly before us. That one even has a 'Gay Pride' banner.

There was indeed a worried-looking man standing at the front with a slightly droopy cardboard placard.

God: It's all very clear: they go to hell.
Jarvis: Really?
God: Rules are rules. So who's next? Ah yes, the lobster-eaters. Bring them in!

At this Jarvis woke up, his bed soaked in sweat.

NB: Lest some Jews or Christians take offence at my portrayal of God, I should stress that this was merely Jarvis's dream. No doubt the real God would behave quite differently.

What to read next?

Chapter 10, Can We Have Morality without God and Religion?, raises some of the same issues discussed in this chapter, including the role of religious texts in justifying ethical positions.

Further reading

Ronald Dworkin, 'Liberty and Moralism', Chapter 11 of *Taking Rights Seriously* (London: Duckworth, 1977).

John Stuart Mill, 'Nature', in *Three Essays on Religion* (New York: Prometheus, 1998).

Anthony Quinton, 'Homosexuality', in *From Wodehouse to Wittgenstein* (Manchester: Carcanet Press, 1998).

BRAIN-SNATCHED

One of the most famous and persistent philosophical problems concerns our knowledge of the world around us. You and I suppose we have good reason to believe we're surrounded by various physical objects: cars, houses, trees, mountains and, of course, other people. That we possess this sort of knowledge is one of our most fundamental, 'common-sense' beliefs. But there are powerful philosophical arguments that appear conclusively to show that none of us has any more reason to suppose that Earth, and everything on it, exists than we have to suppose that it is all some sort of elaborate illusion.

One of these philosophical arguments involves the hypothesis that you might be a brain in a vat. Consider the following story.

A Brain in a Vat

Colin Spiggott settled down in front of the television as he had a thousand times before, his dinner balanced on his knees. He was looking forward to watching the evening film, *Invasion of the Body Snatchers.*

Unfortunately for Colin, there was to be no film or dinner. As he lifted the first morsel to his lips, something utterly odd happened. He heard a tiny voice, a voice that seemed to come from inside his head.

'Testing. Testing . . . Hold on.'

The voice was muffled and indistinct. Then, after a couple of seconds, it came back crystal clear and deafeningly loud.

'TESTING. TESTING . . .' Colin clamped his hands involuntarily to his ears, his fork flying into the air. '. . . ER . . . COLIN SPIGGOTT, CAN YOU HEAR ME? SORRY. Too loud. Is that better? Look, Colin, we have important news.'

Colin leaped to his feet, his dinner crashing to the floor. He stared around the room in panic. 'Who is it? Who's there?'

'I'm not in the room that you seem to see around you, Colin. I'm somewhere else. Somewhere far away.'

'Where? Who are you?'

'I have some news, Colin. News you may find shocking. Please sit down.'

'What's happening?'

'I will tell you. I do not inhabit Earth. I come from another planet. And I am here to thank you for taking part in our experiment.'

'Experiment? I don't understand. What experiment?'

'I am afraid we have been deceiving you a little, Colin. Things are not as they seem.'

The voice in Colin's head proceeded to explain what was happening to him. Or, more accurately, what *had* happened to him.

'I'm afraid that the world you see around you is not real. It is a virtual world. Six of your earth months ago we came to visit you. Do you remember having a particularly disturbed night's sleep – a night plagued with nightmares?'

'Er . . . I think I do, yes.'

'That was the night we entered your house while you were sleeping. We drugged you and placed your unconscious body in our flying saucer. Currently, you are located not on Earth, but on another planet entirely. You are on Pluto.'

Colin had started to get a little more of a grip on himself. 'On Pluto? But that's ridiculous. I can see that I'm on Earth. There's my TV set over there.'

'Oh, yes. It *looks* as if there is a television set over there. I admit that. But as I have explained, things are not as they seem. You see, when your body arrived at our scientific laboratory here on Pluto, an operation was performed. We removed your brain.'

'My brain?' Colin was beginning to feel sick.

'We removed your living brain and discarded your body. Then we placed it in a glass vat. We connected it up to one of our VE4 supercomputers. Your brain is currently floating in vat of life-supporting nutrients here in our laboratory beneath the surface of Pluto.'

'Then why do I see that TV in front of me?' said Colin, pointing to the TV set.

'The supercomputer is generating the illusion of a television set. It's a *virtual* television set that you see. It is not real. Let me explain how the VE4 computer has been programmed to function. The situation is a little complicated. You must concentrate.'

'I am concentrating!'

'Very well. The nerves that used to connect your brain to your body and which enabled you to move your body around are now connected to the VE4 computer instead. The VE4 monitors how your body would have moved if you still had one. It then transmits down the nerve pathways running *into* your brain precisely the same sort of patterns of electrical stimulation that your sense organs – your tongue, ears, eyes, nose and skin – used to transmit when you still had them. That's why it seems to you that you are located in your sitting room on planet earth. The computer is creating that illusion for you.'

'But this is all real. I can *tell* it is.' Colin reached out and picked up his fork. He ran his fingers over the cold, smooth metal. He licked the carrot perched on the end of it. It tasted sweet, just as a carrot should.

But the voice in Colin's head persisted. 'I see you are unconvinced. Perhaps a demonstration is in order. Observe more closely the piece of earth carrot you have impaled on that fork.'

Colin peered closely. For a while nothing happened. But then the orange disc of carrot began to move, to undulate. Suddenly it was wriggling and growing fins. Now there was a goldfish stuck on the end of his fork. The goldfish was staring right back at him as it opened and closed its mouth.

'Yurgh!' Colin threw the fork into the corner of the room. 'Now I'm hallucinating!'

'You are right to suppose that the goldfish is an illusion. But the piece of carrot was also an illusion. Everything you see around you is illusory.'

'I still don't understand.'

'You are immersed in a computer program. However, our computer is far more powerful than anything you earthlings have yet produced. The virtual reality it generates is indistinguishable from the real thing. That is why you never had the slightest suspicion you were being deceived.'

'How did you change that carrot into a goldfish?'

'It was a fairly simple matter. I merely adjusted the computer's program. To put it crudely, I changed your carrot input to goldfish input.'

Colin held his hands up in front of his face and inspected them closely, noting the little hairs on their backs and the tiny striations in the surfaces of his nails.

'So even these hands don't really exist?'

'That's correct. They are virtual hands. They, too, are part of the illusion that is currently being generated by the VE4.'

'So if these aren't my real hands, where are they?'

'They have been – h'm, how shall I put this? – incinerated.'

'This is a nightmare! I have to wake up!'

'I see you remain unconvinced. That surprises me. I thought you would be more rational. Very well. Perhaps the time has come for me to confront you with the facts in a more dramatic fashion. In a moment or two I shall disconnect your brain from the VE4. I shall connect you instead to a camera that I have set up here in my laboratory. I have arranged things so that, if you try to turn your head, the camera will respond by panning round. So you will be able to have a good look around the laboratory. I should warn you that one of the first things you will see will be me.'

Colin looked feverishly about the room. He grasped the arms of the settee in a desperate attempt to hold it in place. But it was useless. The room was beginning to change. The walls rippled as if they were fluid. Then they began to melt away to reveal quite a different scene. The image was vague at first. Colin could make out only a white background against which were silhouetted strange, bulbous shapes. Then the resolution suddenly sharpened and the shapes turned into test tubes and vats arranged along rows of white shelving. Directly in front of Colin was a larger, darker, closer shape. Finally, it, too, came into focus. Before Colin loomed the hideous shape of the Plutonian.

'Good evening, Colin,' said the Plutonian. 'My name is Zpaplaft. What you are experiencing now is no longer an illusion. Everything you see before you is real. It's been a long time since you were last in contact with the real world. Allow me to show you around. To your right you will notice the VE4 computer – the computer into which you were plugged but a few moments ago.'

Colin turned to the right and saw a large silver box covered in tiny dials. He noticed that one of the little windows displayed the word 'goldfish'.

'And now, Colin, it is time for you to take a look at yourself.'

Trailing from the computer were a number of leads. Colin strained to follow the leads, and as he did so a large laboratory bench came into view. On top of the bench was a glass vat. In the vat was something resembling a large grey walnut. It bobbed gently up and down amid a stream of little bubbles fizzing from the bottom of the vat. Leads trailed everywhere, partly obscuring Colin's view. But it was recognisably a human brain that he could see. Two of the leads snaked across the floor towards him. As he looked down, Colin could see that, as the two leads disappeared out of his line of sight, they were labelled 'camera left' and 'camera right'.

Zpaplaft pointed to the glass vat. 'Here you are, Colin – a brain in a vat.'

The Brain-in-a-Vat Hypothesis

The story I have just told raises an interesting question. How do you know that *you* are not a brain in a vat? Consider the following two hypotheses:

1. What you see around you is merely virtual: your brain was removed six months ago by Zpaplaft and plugged into a computer running a virtual earth program. The computer is so sophisticated that the experiences it generates are indistinguishable from those you would have if what you experienced was real.
2. What you see around you is real.

Is it more rational to believe one of these hypotheses rather than the other? Of course, you believe that the second is true and the first false. But what justifies you in holding that belief? After all, everything would seem exactly the same to you either way. The evidence furnished by your five senses – taste, touch, sight, hearing and smell – is equally consistent with both hypotheses. It seems, then, that you have no more reason to believe one hypothesis than you do the other.

Now, in order to *know* something, one presumably needs *grounds* for believing it.* You must be *justified* in believing what you do. So in order to know that what you see is real and not virtual, you must be able to justify that belief. But it seems you cannot justify it. So, astonishingly, *it seems you do not know that what you are now experiencing is real.*

This is an astonishing conclusion, a *sceptical* conclusion. Sceptics claim that we do not know what we might think we know. The claim that we do not know anything about the world around us is called *scepticism about the external world.*

Bear in mind that scepticism about the external world does not commit one to the view that one cannot know anything at all. After all, even the sceptic is claiming to know something: that knowledge of the external world is impossible.

Another Brain-in-a-Vat Hypothesis

Perhaps you're not convinced by this sceptical argument. You might argue like this.

I know perfectly well that there are no Plutonians or underground Plutonian laboratories. Pluto is a huge gas ball without a solid surface. So all this blather about underground laboratories is obviously false. And there is no reason to deny that I

---

* Though see Chapter 19, What Is Knowledge?, where this assumption is questioned.

do know all this stuff about Pluto because, on both your hypotheses, I was experiencing things as they really are up to six months ago. All your weird Plutonian hypothesis throws into doubt is the reality of what I have been experiencing for the last six months. But I was aware that Pluto is a giant gas ball way before that. As I do know that Pluto is a giant gas ball, I know your first hypothesis must be false.

This is a good reply. However, we can easily change the brain-in-a-vat hypothesis in such a way that it throws *all* your knowledge about the external world into doubt, including your knowledge that Pluto is a giant gas ball. Consider the hypothesis that you have *always* been a brain in a vat. Perhaps the earth and everything on it do not exist and never have existed. The town in which you live, your family, house, friends and even the hospital in which you were born: all are illusions generated by a supercomputer. They are no more real than the places and characters that one finds in a fantasy computer game.

How do you know that *this* brain-in-a-vat hypothesis isn't true? It seems you don't know. All the evidence available to you is consistent with the hypothesis that everything you have ever experienced has been part of some sort of elaborate computer-generated hoax.

There is no point in arguing that Pluto is an uninhabitable gas ball incapable of supporting underground laboratories. After all, the only reason you believe Pluto is a giant gas ball is that this is what your experiences seem to confirm (for example, perhaps you picked up this belief about Pluto from the TV, or when you were at school). But as the Plutonians are controlling all those experiences, they may have deliberately misled you about what Pluto is like.

Philosophers remain divided over whether or not such sceptical arguments are cogent. Many are convinced by them. Others defend the common-sense view that we do know about the external world. The difficulty facing the second group, however, is that while one might suppose there must be something wrong with the sceptic's argument, it's extremely difficult to identify precisely *what* is wrong with it. Indeed, it remains contentious whether there is anything wrong with it.

Can Scepticism Be Defeated? – The Ordinary-Language Response

Must we give up the 'common-sense' view that we do know about the world around us? As I say, many philosophers remain unconvinced by the sceptic's argument. The difficulty is in establishing where the flaws in the argument lie.

One popular response to scepticism is to appeal to *ordinary language*. Surely, one may argue, the sceptic's claim that we do not know anything about the world around us *makes no sense*. For we actually explain the meaning of the word 'know' by pointing to such examples as knowing that the bus is coming, knowing that the sun will rise at eight a.m., knowing that there is a tree in Fred's back garden, and so on. But if it is, at least in part, by means of such 'paradigm cases' that we actually *determine and explain what the word 'know' means*, then to suggest that we *don't* know in such cases would be to involve oneself in a kind of contradiction.

This sort of focus on 'ordinary language' – on how we ordinarily use words – was particularly popular in the 1950s. Today, however, such appeals command far less respect. One problem with the ordinary-language response is that it simply does not follow that if we typically apply and indeed explain the meaning of a word by reference to certain 'paradigm cases', then that word must be correctly applied in at least some of those cases. For it may be that we're *making an assumption* when we apply or explain a word in this way, an assumption that is, in fact, false.

Indeed, in the case of the word 'know', it seems we are making such an assumption. That's precisely the sceptic's point. The sceptic draws our attention to the fact that when we say that Fred 'knows' that there is a bus coming towards him, *we make the background assumption that Fred has at least some good reason to suppose that he isn't and hasn't always been a brain in a vat.* The sceptic simply draws our attention to this assumption and then shows it to be false. Once we realise that the assumption is false, we conclude, quite properly, that the term 'know' is not correctly used in this and other such cases after all. To draw that conclusion is not to involve oneself in any sort of contradiction.

The 'Invisible Pebble' Response

Here's a different reply to the sceptic. Some argue that the brain-in-a-vat hypothesis is really an empty hypothesis. Suppose I were to say that I have an invisible, intangible pebble in my hand. I ask you to put your hand out and I place my 'pebble' in your palm. Of course, you can't see or feel the pebble. But I insist that it's there. You would rightly question my sanity, of course. But, more than this, you might ask whether there really is any content to the suggestion that there is an invisible, intangible pebble in your hand. A pebble that can make no difference to anything you might possibly observe is surely *no pebble at all*.

Can't a similar move be made against the sceptic? Some philosophers think it can. The brain-in-a-vat hypothesis, they will say, is also an empty hypothesis. For, even if it were true, it could make no possible difference to what you might experience. Everything will seem the same whether the hypothesis is true or false. But a situation that can make no difference to anything you might possibly observe is surely *no situation at all.* But the sceptic's argument is based on the assumption that the brain-in-a-vat hypothesis *is* a genuine situation. So the sceptic's argument collapses.

This is an ingenious reply. But it fails. The problem is that, unlike my invisible pebble hypothesis, the brain-in-a-vat hypothesis *could* have an impact on what you experience. That's precisely what happens in my short story about Colin. He has experiences that indicate that he is a brain in a vat after all. Perhaps the same thing will happen to you tomorrow evening.

The Dismissive Response

Many new to philosophy quickly become infuriated by such sceptical arguments. 'Look,' they shout, 'it's just *obvious* that I know there's a tree in front of me. I can *see* it standing there. What you claim is patently absurd.'

But just because a claim seems 'obvious' is no guarantee of its truth. It was once considered 'obvious' that Earth is stationary. And if an 'obvious' claim is shown, by means of a cogent argument, to be false, then the rational thing to believe is that it *is* false. Those who blindly hang on to the claim come what may and dismiss the argument's proponents as 'idiots' are themselves being idiotic. They are like those who, having been presented with overwhelming evidence that Earth moves, nevertheless dismiss that evidence by stamping on the ground and saying: 'But look, it's *obvious* it's stationary!'

The Unbelievable Truth?

The sceptic argues that we have no knowledge at all about the world around us. You have no reason to believe that your home, family, place of work and even Earth itself aren't all virtual. For all you know, you have always been a brain in a vat, at the mercy of Zpaplaft's VE4 computer.

This is an astonishing claim. In fact, no one can *really* believe it. No one *really* believes it is just as likely that they are a brain in a vat as it is that they are living out their life in the real world. Not even the sceptic.

Yet this may just be a psychological fact about us. We were made natural-born believers. We can't help ourselves. Despite our overwhelming disposition to believe the contrary, the sceptic's conclusion that you do not know that you are holding a book in your hands would appear to be true. Scepticism about the external world would appear to be the unbelievable truth.

What to read next

You might wish to try Chapter 19, What Is Knowledge?, where I discuss the issue of what knowledge actually is and look at some of the issues surrounding justification in more detail. Chapter 8, The Strange Case of the Rational Dentist, and Chapter 14, Why Expect the Sun to Rise Tomorrow?, discuss two other forms of scepticism: scepticism about other minds and scepticism about the unobserved.

Further reading

A good place to start with scepticism about the external world would be with the extract from René Descartes's first *Meditation* and the discussion of Descartes between Bernard Williams and Bryan Magee which feature as Chapters 26 and 27 of:

Nigel Warburton (ed.), *Philosophy: Basic Readings* (London: Routledge, 1999).

Also see:

Nigel Warburton, *Philosophy: The Basics*, second edition (London: Routledge, 1995), Chapter 4.

4

IS TIME TRAVEL POSSIBLE?

Might a time machine be built one day? Could we use it to visit the future, to find out what lies in store for us? Could we go back and affect what happened in the past? Or is time travel impossible – ruled out on purely logical grounds? This chapter investigates some of the key ideas and arguments.

Bassett's Time Machine

The scene: a laboratory of the future, in the year 4645. Ms Meers, an inventor, sits at a table, distractedly playing with her pencil. Suddenly, the door opens and in rushes her excited colleague, Bassett.

Bassett: I've just created a *time machine*!

Meers: You've been drinking again, Bassett.

Bassett: No, really. I have. My new invention will allow me to travel through time and visit the future and the past. It's next door. Come and see.

Meers: I will not. There's no point. Time travel is *impossible*.

Bassett: No, it isn't.

Meers: Yes, it is. And I don't mean it's just a *technological* impossibility, either. It's currently technologically impossible for us to build a spaceship that can travel close to the speed of light. But perhaps one day we will succeed. Nor do I mean that time travel is made impossible by the *laws of nature* – in the way that, as Einstein pointed out, travelling *faster* than light is impossible. What I mean is: talk about time travel simply *doesn't make sense*.

Bassett: Doesn't make sense?

Meers: Yes. To suggest that you have created a time machine makes as much sense as to suggest that you have created a round square or a female stallion. These are *contradictory* notions.

Bassett: I do see that talk about round squares and non-male stallions involves a contradiction.

Meers: But the same is also true of your claim to have constructed a time machine. Time travel is ruled out on purely logical grounds. Just as we can know, *just by thinking about it*, without our having to do any scientific research into the matter, that there are no non-male stallions out there in the world, so I can know, just by thinking about it, that there are no time machines.

Bassett: I'm afraid I don't see why there is anything illogical about the notion of time travel. Do please explain.

Meers takes a piece of chalk from her pocket and walks over to the blackboard. She begins to draw a diagram like this:

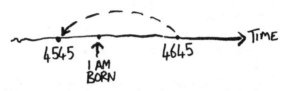

Meers: OK. Imagine that a machine is built that will allow me to travel a hundred years back into the past, to a time before I was even born. I get into the machine, dial in the year 4545 and press the start button. I suddenly find myself back in 4545. Then it's true of me back in 4545 both that I *had* been born – how could I be standing there if I hadn't been born? – and also that I *hadn't* been born, for the date of my birth would not yet have arrived. So you see, there's a *contradiction*. I would have been both born and not born. The idea makes no sense.

Bassett sits down in Meers's chair and looks pensive while Meers paces up and down in front of the blackboard.

Bassett: Ah, I see where you've gone wrong. Actually, there's no contradiction. You merely need to distinguish two notions of time: what one might call, after the twentieth-century philosopher David Lewis (1941–2001), *personal time* and *external time*.

Meers: Two kinds of time?

Bassett: Yes. Your personal time is the sort of time that is measured by, say, your wristwatch. External time, on the other hand, is the sort of time through which you might travel. Now, in the situation you describe, you go back in external time to a point before you were born. But, of course, your birth continues to be part of your *personal* history. Your birth still lies in the past in your personal time, but now also lies in the future in external time. So you see, once we separate out these two notions of time, the appearance of a contradiction disappears. There's no *single* sort of time in which you are both born and not born.

Meers puts the chalk back in her pocket and stands quietly for a moment.

The Case of the Slow Pill

Meers: Perhaps you're right. But I still think there's something fishy about the very notion of time travel. In fact, I myself was once very interested in building a time machine. And in a sense I succeeded.

Bassett: Really?

Meers: Yes. My 'machine' took the form of a pill. I called it the 'slow pill'. On swallowing the pill, all my body's natural processes would slow down dramatically. My heart would beat just once a minute. Even the electrical activity in my brain was reduced to a crawl. From the point of view of an external observer, I seemed to be frozen. You would have to watch very carefully to see me move. It took me a full five minutes to take a couple of steps across the floor.

Bassett: How extraordinary. What was it like for you?

Meers: In fact, from my point of view, I didn't appear to slow down at all. Rather, everything else appeared to speed up. People buzzed about like flies. The hour hand on my watch shot round once a minute. Outside I could see clouds flying past like pigeons and the sun flashing along as if pulled by a wire.

Bassett: Fantastic! But, of course, this pill of yours wasn't *really* a time machine, was it?

Meers: No. That's my point. I hope you haven't just reinvented my pill. For all the slow pill succeeded in doing was to slow me down. I merely had the *subjective impression* of time speeding up. But the pill didn't *really* have any effect on time at all. And, of course, the slow pill certainly *didn't* allow me to travel *into the past*. You say your machine can do that?

Travelling Close to the Speed of Light

Bassett: That's right. In fact, as you know, a *kind* of 'time travel' is already allowed by physics. As the physicist Albert Einstein pointed out, if you get into a spacecraft and travel very, very fast, the ship's time will slow down relative to things that are stationary.

Meers: I know.

Bassett: So by travelling very, very fast one has, in a sense, travelled into the future.

Meers: In a sense. But again, is this *really* time travel? Certainly, you can't *go backwards* in time using a spacecraft. The most you can achieve is to slow the ship's time down a bit relative to what's going on back on earth. You can't disappear from the universe to reappear again with a 'Pop!' at some point in the future or past.

Bassett: But that's exactly what my new invention *will* allow.

H. G. Wells and *The Time Machine*

Meers remains wholly unconvinced.

Meers: What utter rubbish! So tell me, Bassett, have you actually *used* this machine yet?

Bassett: Er, no. Not yet.

Meers: What do you think will happen when you set the controls for, say, one year into the future and press the start button?

Bassett: Have you ever read the book *The Time Machine*, written by H. G. Wells? In Wells's story, a time traveller gets into his machine and pushes a lever, sending him into the future. Suddenly the sun starts to move more swiftly across the sky. The clouds scud past. Night follows day follows night follows day with increasing rapidity as the time traveller accelerates into the future. Decades soon fly by. Civilisation eventually starts to crumble around him. I expect time travel will be like that.

Meers: But wait a minute. Suppose you get into your machine and press the start button. Then you sit and watch as one year passes in just a few minutes. You see the clock on the wall whizzing round, people buzzing about like flies, the sun rise and set 365 times. Then the machine comes to a halt and you get out and you are one year into the future.

Bassett: What's the problem with that?

Meers: Well, for a start, if you were there to witness the clock whizzing round, the sun flashing across the sky, and so on, *then you must have been in the room during that whole year.*

Bassett: I suppose so.

Meers: But then *you didn't disappear from the room*, did you? So people coming into the room would see you sitting there aboard your machine, apparently quite motionless. If they were to study you more intently, however, they would discover that your heart was still beating, though only once every few days. So all you have really described is a situation in which all the processes going on inside the machine are *slowed down*. So you don't *really* time travel at all, do you? You just get very *slow*. In fact, it's as if you had taken my slow pill.

Bassett: Ah . . . I hadn't thought about it like that.

It seems Meers is right: the machine that both Bassett and H. G. Wells describe seems to have much the same effect as Meers's slow pill. It's not so much a time machine as a machine that slows down all your bodily processes.

'Time Hopping'

Bassett scratches the back of his head. He now starts to change his tune.

Bassett: Perhaps reading H. G. Wells has encouraged my imagination to run riot. Now I think about it, I see that, of course, my machine *won't* remain in the room for the entire period of time through which I travel. Travelling forwards in time using my machine is *not* like taking a slow pill. My time machine doesn't travel in time in the way Wells's machine does. It's as if the traveller in *The Time Machine* travels back and forth on the river of time in a sort of 'time boat'. To get from one moment in time to another, he has to travel through, and so exist at, all the intervening moments of time.

Meers: That's right.

Bassett: But my machine doesn't work like that. Rather, it simply *takes me out of* the river of time and then drops me in upstream or downstream. I don't travel *along* the river. If I dial in a hundred years into the future or past and press the start button, I'm transported instantly to the time in question, without either me or the machine having to exist at any of the intervening moments. In fact, my time machine doesn't travel 'through' time so much as make time 'leaps', hopping from one moment to another.

Superman's Biography and Causal Loops

Meers sees that to travel forwards in time would not be like taking a slow pill. Still, she remains convinced that no such machine is possible. The problem, according to Meers, is that such a machine would make possible what is clearly impossible: the existence of *causal loops*.

Meers: Ah, I see. Interesting. But I think I've now spotted a logical flaw in the suggestion that you have a time machine. Let me tell you about a Superman comic I read many years ago. In the story, Superman's friend is trying to write a biography of Superman. This writer tries and tries but suffers terrible writer's block and gets nowhere. Superman takes pity on him, wraps the writer up in his indestructible cloak and takes him through the time barrier into the future, where the writer's biography of Superman is on sale. The writer buys a copy of his own book, then takes it back to the past, where he copies out his own work and submits it for publication!*

Bassett: He plagiarises himself. That does sound odd.

Meers: Yes. There's clearly something *illogical* about this story, isn't there?

* I am indebted to Stephen Williams for this example.

Bassett: It involves a kind of *causal loop*. The writer can plagiarise the book
           now only because he has obtained it from the future. But he can
           obtain the book from the future only because he plagiarises it now.
Meers: Exactly. And that doesn't really make sense, does it? For while each of
           the two events is the cause of the other, there is no cause of *the pair
           of events together*. And that's nonsensical.
Bassett: So you're saying that as a time machine would allow such
           causal loops to be created, and as they are ruled out on purely logical
           grounds, so time machines are also ruled out on purely logical grounds?
Meers: Yes.

Bassett stares vacantly out of the window towards the setting sun.

Bassett: Well, I'm not sure causal loops *are* nonsensical. Is there anything
           illogical about a causal loop? I don't think so. *Logic* doesn't demand
           that every event has a cause. There's no contradiction involved in
           supposing that there are uncaused events. In fact, physicists now·tell
           us that some subatomic events *have no cause*. They *just happen*. So
           there's clearly nothing illogical about uncaused events – they actually
           occur. But then why is there anything *illogical* about an uncaused
           causal loop? I don't see that there is. I admit a causal loop is *very
           weird*, but that doesn't make it illogical.

Bassett appears to be correct. Causal loops may be bizarre in the extreme: it doesn't
follow that they are ruled out on purely logical grounds. So the mere fact that a
time machine would allow them does not by itself show that time machines are
impossible.

The Terminator Case

Meers: Very well. Forget causal loops. I still believe the very notion of a
           causal loop is incoherent, but let it pass. Here's a quite different
           logical problem with time travel.
Bassett: Fire away.
Meers: One of my favourite films is called *Terminator II*. In the film, a
           machine called a *terminator* is sent back from the future. This

machine, played by Arnold Schwarzenegger, plays a vital role in preventing the occurrence of the nuclear holocaust that gave rise to the need to send the terminator back in time in the first place. It was only as a result of the holocaust that the terminator was ever built. So, as a result of the terminator's actions, the holocaust no longer happens. But if the holocaust doesn't happen, then the terminator will never be built. But if the terminator is never built, then the holocaust will happen. You see, there's a contradiction.

Bassett: I do see. If the terminator is built, then it isn't, and if it isn't built, then it is! That's a lot like the famous time travel paradox generated by a man going back and shooting his parents prior to his own birth. If he is born, and then he uses a time machine to go back in time and shoot his parents, then he won't be born. But if he won't be born, then he won't be able to go back and shoot his parents, in which case he will be born.

Meers: Exactly. So do you now agree that the very idea of time travel makes no sense?

Bassett: No.

Meers: Why not?

Bassett: Maybe there are *parallel universes.*

Meers: Parallel universes?

Bassett: Yes. Maybe what happens in the *Terminator II* story is this. In *this* universe, the nuclear holocaust happens. Then the terminator is sent back in time. The terminator then prevents the holocaust. But in so doing, it brings into existence a parallel universe, a universe in which the terminator is never created. That creates a second future. There's no contradictory situation involved because there is no universe in which the holocaust both does and doesn't happen or in which the terminator both is and isn't created. Rather, a holocaust happens and the terminator is created in one universe but not the other.

Meers: This all sounds very confused to me. For a start, I no longer understand the *point* of trying to send the terminator back in time to try to change the past. Suppose we're the people who send the terminator back. Even though the terminator succeeds in its mission and, indeed, actually prevents the nuclear holocaust, that won't help *us* one jot! Because in our universe, the holocaust still happens! It's not much consolation to know that the terminator has created a parallel universe in which it doesn't!

Bassett: Er . . . that's true, I suppose.

Meers: I just don't think the suggestion that we might change the past makes sense.

The JFK Case

Even if we can't *change* the past, does it follow that we can't now go back and *affect* what happened in the past? You might think it obvious that it does follow. But Bassett now questions this assumption.

Bassett: OK. Perhaps you're right. Perhaps we can't change the past. Let me concede that we can't, at least for the sake of argument. It doesn't follow that time travel into the past is impossible. In fact, a time machine might still allow one to go back into the past and have a *causal effect* on what has happened.

Meers: How?

Bassett: I might use my time machine to go back into the past and make something happen *that did in fact happen*. For example, suppose I get in my time machine and travel back to Dallas, Texas, on 22 November 1963. I take a rifle with me. I sit behind a white picket fence on a grassy knoll. President Kennedy drives by, and I shoot him several times. My time machine *can* allow me to do this if it is in fact true that I shot Kennedy from that grassy knoll. There's no contradiction here, is there? I don't go back and make what is true, false. I go back and make true what *is* true. It *was* I who shot Kennedy. So the past doesn't get changed from what it actually is. Yet I *do* get causally to affect how things turn out. For if I hadn't fired that bullet on 22 November 1963, Kennedy wouldn't have died that day, and the course of history would have been very different!

The case Bassett describes does avoid those problems for time travel raised specifically by the suggestion that we might go back in time and make false some true statement about the past. Even if we can't go back and change the past in *this* sense, might we still not be able to go back and *make things happen*, so long as they are things that *did* happen? The situation Bassett outlines does appear to be such a case.

A Popular Argument Against Time Travel

But Meers thinks she's spotted a fatal flaw in the scenario Bassett has just described.

Meers: Ah, I think I finally see the problem. Look at the situation this way. Either JFK was shot from the grassy knoll on 22 November 1963, or he wasn't. Now, suppose it did happen. Then there's no point in your attempting to make it happen, because it happened anyway. So any efforts by you to make it happen will be superfluous; they can make no difference. Suppose, on the other hand, that Kennedy wasn't shot from the grassy knoll. Then whatever you try to do now to make it happen must fail. So either way you're unable to have any effect on how things turn out. So you're wrong: *there's nothing you can do causally to affect the past.* It's impossible for you to go back and make things happen. But as a time machine would make this impossibility a possibility, time machines must themselves be impossible.

The line of argument just presented by Meers has a certain superficial appeal. It's something like this reasoning that no doubt lies behind the reluctance of many to accept the possibility of time travel. But the argument is, on closer inspection, fallacious, as Bassett now points out.

Fatalism and a Muddle about Time Travel

Bassett: Interesting argument. But no good, I'm afraid. Here's an analogous argument. Statements about the future are true or false. For example, it may be true that tomorrow I will be killed in a car crash. Or it may be false.

Meers: I hope it's false.

Bassett: Thank you. Now imagine someone were to argue like this. If it's true that I'm going to be killed in a car crash tomorrow, then it's true *whatever I might try to do about it.* So any attempt I make to stop myself being killed in a car crash tomorrow must be fruitless. If, on the other hand, it's false, then again it is false *whatever I might try to do about it* – in which case any efforts I make to stop myself being killed in a car crash must be superfluous, as it isn't going to happen anyway. So, *either way*, I'm unable to have any effect on how things turn out. But then there's no point in my doing anything to try to prevent myself from dying in a car crash tomorrow, such as driving carefully or wearing a seatbelt. None of these actions will have any effect.

Meers: But that's absurd! Wearing a seatbelt *can* save your life.

Bassett: I agree. Absolutely. The conclusion I have just drawn is clearly ridiculous – driving carefully and wearing a seatbelt *can* affect how things turn out. But notice that the argument I used to reach the absurd conclusion that it's pointless wearing a seatbelt is exactly analogous to the one you used to try to show that I can't go back and affect what happens in the past. If your argument was good, it would also rule out the possibility of our having any effect on the future. Yet clearly we *can* affect the future.

Meers: So *neither* argument is any good?

Bassett: Correct.

It seems to me that Bassett is right. The view that there's no point in wearing a seatbelt or driving carefully because 'what will be will be' is that of the *fatalist*. Fatalists take the view that all our actions are in vain. They say things like: 'If it's true I will be killed tomorrow, then it's true I will be killed tomorrow, so there's no point in trying to do anything to prevent it.' Fatalism should not be confused with *determinism*, the view that all our actions are determined in advance by the laws of nature (for a much more detailed explanation of determinism and its consequences for free will, see Chapter 15, Do We Ever Deserve to Be Punished?). Determinism seems, on the face of it, to remove our ability to act freely. But, unlike fatalism, determinism does *not* deny the obvious fact that our actions have causal consequences and that it's worth trying to avoid danger. Determinism may be true; fatalism, on the other hand, seems absurd.

Now, if it's true that Meers's argument is exactly analogous to the fatalist's bad argument, then it, too, is a bad argument. It may not be clear precisely *what's* wrong with Meers's argument, of course, but, if Bassett is right, there is certainly *something* wrong with it.

Conclusion

Might we one day develop machines that will allow us to travel into the future or the past? It's certainly an extraordinary prospect. While many suppose that the very idea of time travel makes no sense, it's not easy to see *why* the idea makes no sense.

Can we know, just by thinking about it, that Bassett must have failed in his quest to build a time machine? Perhaps. The problem is that none of the arguments presented by Meers establish that conclusion.

Perhaps time travel really is possible after all.

What to read next

Determinism is discussed in much more detail in Chapter 15, Do We Ever Deserve to Be Punished?.

Further reading

This chapter makes use of a number of ideas, arguments and examples drawn from the following two rather difficult papers:

Michael Dummett, 'Causal Loops', in his *The Seas of Language* (Oxford: Clarendon Press, 1993).

David Lewis, 'The Paradoxes of Time Travel', in his *Philosophical Papers,* Vol. II (Oxford: Oxford University Press, 1986).

5

INTO THE LAIR OF
THE RELATIVIST

PHILOSOPHY GYM CATEGORY
WARM–UP
MODERATE
MORE CHALLENGING

According to relativists, people who speak simply of what's 'true' are naive. 'Whose truth?' asks the relativist. 'No claim is ever true, period. What's true is always true for someone. It's true relative to a particular person or culture. And what's true for one person or culture may be false for another. There's no such thing as the *absolute* truth on any question.'

Is the relativist correct?

Introduction

Let's begin with a couple of illustrations of how appeals to relativism can creep into everyday conversation.

1. Olaf's Condemnation of Female Circumcision

Olaf: Female circumcision is wrong.

Mrs Barbery: Why?

Olaf: It dramatically reduces the possibility of a woman enjoying a full sex life. It has a major impact – a largely negative impact – on her existence. And it's forced on young girls. It's obviously *true* that compelling children to undergo such life-blighting surgery is morally abhorrent.

Mrs Barbery: You speak of what's 'true'. But whose 'truth' are we talking about here? You're judging another culture – that of certain Sudanese people, for example – by your own Western standards. But they have their *own* moral standards. What's 'true' for you is actually 'false' for them.

Olaf: You believe there's no objective, independent fact of the matter about whether female circumcision is *really* wrong? That moral 'truth' is always relative to a particular culture?

Mrs Barbery: Exactly. So it's wrong of you to judge.

2. The Great Mystica's Defence of Astrology

The Great Mystica: Do you want an astrological reading?

Fox: Definitely not.

The Great Mystica: You're hostile. I can tell from your aura.

Fox: There are no such things as auras. Aura reading, astrology, psychic powers, tarot cards – they're all bunk.

The Great Mystica: Why do you say that?

Fox: Because when these things are investigated scientifically, it turns out there's hardly a shred of evidence to support them. In fact, almost all the evidence points the other way.

The Great Mystica: I see the problem. You're applying a particular form of reasoning – Western scientific and logical reasoning – to New Age systems of belief. In fact, judged by their own *internal* standards of rationality, astrology and these other belief systems come out looking very sensible indeed!

Fox: But these other ways of thinking are flabby and not rigorous.

The Great Mystica: No, they're not. They're just *different*, that's all. We need to throw off the straitjacket of traditional Western thinking and open ourselves up to other modes of thought!

Fox: You believe these 'alternative' ways of thinking are equally valid?

The Great Mystica: Yes, I do. Each produces its *own kind of truth*. From your Western, analytical, science-based perspective, the claim that astrology works is false. But from the perspective of an astrologer, the claim is true. In fact, *what's false for you is true for me*. You shouldn't arrogantly assume that your truth is the only truth.

Fox: There's no single, objective 'truth'?

The Great Mystica: I see your chakras are finally opening.

Interesting *v.* Boring Relativism

In both of the above examples, it's suggested that a claim that is true for one person or culture can be false for another. I call this highly controversial form of relativism *interesting relativism*. Interesting relativism shouldn't be muddled up with *boring relativism*.

Here's an example of boring relativism. Suppose we both say 'I like sausages'. Despite the fact that we utter the same sentence, it may be that what I say is true and what you say is false.

Isn't this a form of relativism about truth?

Yes, in a sense. But it's relativism of a very dull and yawn-inducing sort. We can all agree that truth is 'relative' in the sense that one and the same *sentence* can be true as uttered by one person and false as uttered by another.

How does interesting relativism differ? Interesting relativism is the view that not just the *same sentence* but the very *same claim* can be true for one person or culture and yet false for another.

Notice that you and I make *different claims* when we say 'I like sausages'. I make a claim, which, if true, is made true by a fact about me. Your claim, if true, is made true by a fact about you. That's why the possibility that I might speak truly and you falsely is unsurprising.

When we're dealing with relativism of the interesting variety, on the other hand, we are dealing with a *single claim* which is true for one person and false for another. Take, for example, the claim that female circumcision is wrong. The suggestion that this very same claim is both true for Olaf but false for, say, certain Sudanese people is an example of interesting relativism.

Here's a way of bringing out the difference between interesting and boring relativism. Truths that are relative in the boring sense don't contradict each other. For example, the person who claims that she likes sausages and the person who claims she doesn't don't disagree. Both can happily accept that one of them likes sausages and the other doesn't.

Truths that are relative in the interesting sense, on the other hand, are incompatible. Olaf and a defender of female circumcision *really do disagree* about what's morally acceptable. Interesting relativism accepts that they disagree but nevertheless insists that the claim that female circumcision is wrong is true for Olaf and false for his opponents.

Thinking Tools: Interesting v. Boring Relativism

You can, if you wish, give yourself a quick test on the distinction between interesting and boring relativism. Which of the following are examples of interesting relativism? The answer is at the bottom of the page.

1. I say 'There's a bank in Bindford' and you say 'There's a bank in Bindford'. What I say is true and what you say is false. This is because we're using the term 'bank' differently: I'm talking about a financial bank and you a river bank.
2. Mary claims that Jesus is the son of God. Isaac, a Jew, denies this. Olaf insists that, though they disagree, Mary and Isaac are both right: that Jesus is the son of God is true from a Christian perspective but false from a Jewish one.
3. Dick and Dan are having a phone conversation. Dan is in Denver and Dick in New York. Both say 'It's raining here'. However, one of them is correct while the other is lying.

We are going to look at the issue of whether some or even all truths might be relative in the interesting sense. From now on, when I use the term 'relativism' I'll be talking just about the interesting variety.

Is All Truth Relative? – Plato's Objection

Relativism has a long history. For example, the ancient Greek Protagoras (c. 490–c. 421 BC) is portrayed in Plato's (c. 428–347 BC) dialogue *Theaetetus* as a relativist. Protagoras declares that 'man is the measure of all things' and so each person's opinion can be considered equally 'true'.

Those who believe that all truth is relative face a famous and powerful objection that also traces right back to Plato. The objection is as follows.

Think for a moment about the claim that all truth is relative. Is this claim supposed to be itself only relatively true? Or is it an absolute, non-relative truth?

Clearly, to claim it's non-relatively true that all truth is relative would be to contradict yourself. So a relativist like Protagoras must say that the truth that truth is relative is *itself* only a relative truth.

Only 2. is an example of interesting relativism.

Protagoras . . . is surely conceding that the opinion of those who make opposing judgements about his own opinion – that is, their opinion that it is false – is true.*

In other words, Protagoras must concede that if we take the view that truth is really absolute and Protagoras is talking rubbish, *then we're right.*

Moral Relativism

But relativism isn't quite so easily dealt with. One way in which a relativist can sidestep Plato's objection is to concede that not *all* truths are relative but still insist that *some* are. Then one can maintain that the truth that some truths are relative is one of the non-relative truths.

If not all truths are relative but some are, then that raises the question: *which* truths are relative? One of the most popular forms of relativism is with respect to *moral* truth.

Here is a fashionable line of argument.

Historically, Western societies have tended to impose their own moral perspective on others. We have often arrogantly presumed the right to coerce others into adopting and conforming to our own views about right and wrong. We have assumed that we must be correct and everyone else incorrect.

More recently, however, we have begun to question our own moral supremacy. We have become increasingly aware not only that our own moral perspective is just one among many, but also that it is itself in a state of flux. We have also discovered that there can be much to learn spiritually and morally from other cultures.

But if this is true, then must we not at least accept relativism about moral truth? We might happen morally to disapprove of, say, polygamy. Other cultures happen to approve. For us, the claim 'polygamy is wrong' is true. For others, it is false. And surely there's no independent 'fact of the matter' about whether it is right or wrong really. Moral truth is relative. That's precisely *why* it would be wrong for us arrogantly to impose our own particular moral point of view about polygamy on these other cultures.

Certainly, it can be quite tempting to appeal to relativism – particularly moral relativism – in order to encourage people to be more tolerant of and sensitive towards

---

* Plato, *Theaetetus*, trans. John McDowell (Oxford: Clarendon Press, 1973), p. 170.

other cultures. Relativists often present themselves as the defenders of open-mindedness, equality and freedom. Those who oppose relativism are often portrayed as arrogant, as believing themselves incapable of error, and as fascistically wishing to impose their own brand of 'absolute' truth on everyone else. Terms like 'cultural imperialism' get bandied about. Indeed, opposition to moral relativism is sometimes equated with racism.

This sort of political justification for relativism has a certain superficial appeal. It is quite popular in certain academic circles. But the fact remains that the justification is fatally flawed.

In fact, tolerance, sensitivity and open-mindedness are *not* the unique preserve of the relativist. Tolerance and sensitivity towards other cultures and moral points of view do not require that you accept that these other cultures or points of view are correct.

Ironically, it's only someone who *rejects* relativism who's free to consider tolerance and sensitivity *universally* applicable virtues. For what must the relativist say about, for example, a group of religious zealots who believe that tolerance is a bad thing and who execute all those with whom they disagree? They must say that, for these zealots, tolerance *is* a bad thing and they are quite right to execute dissenters!

Notice that to commit yourself to the existence of non-relative truth is not to commit yourself to the view that you are incapable of error. You can acknowledge that truth is non-relative yet at the same time also acknowledge that your ability to discover what's true may be quite limited. Those who reject relativism may show great humility, and may well arrive at their beliefs only tentatively.

Nor does the belief that truth is non-relative require that you believe that you have privileged access to it. You may think that there is a great deal to learn from others, and also that others may be in a position to correct your own mistakes.

In short, it's simply a mistake to suppose that anyone who rejects relativism must be an arrogant, jackbooted bully intent on ramming his beliefs down everyone else's throat. Let's all agree that sensitivity, tolerance, open-mindedness are virtues worth promoting. We can agree to that without embracing relativism.

Indeed, are any of us *really* prepared to accept that *all* moral truth is relative? I rather doubt it. Take slavery, for example. Surely even the most hardened relativist will concede that slavery as practised in the US was wrong *period*, and not merely wrong-as-viewed-from-our-current-moral-perspective but right-for-the-American-slave-owners. The same goes for genocide. Surely not even Mrs Barbery (who supposes that female circumcision is wrong-for-us but right-for-the-so-and-sos) believes that the Jewish Holocaust was wrong-for-us but right-for-the-Nazis. While many take a relativistic line about the morality of polygamy and female circumcision, they often fail to apply relativism consistently. They pick and choose how they apply it. They condemn, say, the morality of Western multinational corporations while failing to notice that their own relativism, consistently applied, would entail that if the prevailing corporate culture deems it morally acceptable to cut down rainforests, poison the rivers and barbeque the indigenous population, then it's correct.

Rejecting the 'Tyranny' of Traditional Logical and Scientific Reasoning

We've seen that moral relativism, at least as it's usually formulated, is both pretty unpalatable and self-condemning. Let's now set moral relativism aside and consider whether there might be other areas where relativism might be more plausible. What, for example, about reason? Is that relative?

We saw at the beginning of this chapter that The Great Mystica defends astrology by insisting that, while astrology may not look particularly reasonable from a purely logical, scientific perspective, alternative belief systems such as astrology have their own *internal* standards of rationality, standards against which astrology comes out looking very sensible indeed. Yes, certain scientific claims might seem to force themselves on us if we adopt the standards internal to traditional scientific practice. But there are other, no less valid forms of reasoning. We need to be more open-minded. We should reject the tyranny of traditional logical and scientific thinking and immerse ourselves in these 'alternative' modes of thought.

In The Great Mystica's view, the 'truths' that Western scientific reasoning reveals are relative. What may be true from a purely scientific perspective may be false when viewed from another. Unfortunately, the arrogance of scientists tends to blind them to the possibility of these alternative perspectives.

Is The Great Mystica's defence of astrology cogent? When we try to justify reasoning in the way we do, we run into a notorious problem that might seem to lend The Great Mystica's relativistic views a degree of credibility.

Suppose I use traditional logical and scientific reasoning. And suppose I want to justify my use of this form of reasoning. I want to make a case for claiming that my way of reasoning is objectively the right way to reason. How do I do this?

You can see immediately that I face a problem. For, of course, I will *need to employ reasoning* to provide my justification. But if the form of reasoning I use in trying to provide my justification is traditional logical or scientific reasoning, then won't my justification be unacceptably circular?

Yes, it seems it will. Here's an analogous case. Suppose Dave always trusts what The Great Mystica tells him. Dave believes that appealing to The Great Mystica is a reliable method of finding out the truth about anything. How might Dave justify his trust in The Great Mystica?

Clearly, it won't do for Dave to justify this trust by appealing to what The Great Mystica has to say about her own reliability. That would be an unacceptably circular justification.

The trouble is that my use of traditional reasoning to justify traditional reasoning seems no less unacceptably circular. A similar circularity would appear to plague any attempt to use a form of reasoning to justify itself. Of course, I could try to justify one particular form of reasoning – *A* – by appealing to another, different form of reasoning – *B*. But then *B* would itself stand in need of justification. So I would merely have postponed the problem.

It seems, then, that *no form of reasoning can be justified*. The most we can say is: 'This is how we *do* reason, how it *strikes us* that we should reason. But we can't *justify* our reasoning in this way.'

Many of those who defend relativism will derive comfort from this conclusion. 'You see?' they'll say. 'There's no rational reason to prefer one self-justified form of reasoning over another.' But while there clearly is a problem about justifying one particular form of reasoning as objectively the 'correct' form, we should remember that, even if no form of reasoning can ultimately be justified, it doesn't follow that none is objectively 'correct'. We have not established that relativism about reasoning is true.

The Collapse of the Case for Relativism about Reasoning

In fact, those relativists who want rationally to convince us that there's no objectively and universally valid form of reasoning themselves face a serious problem. For they are offering us an argument, an argument that makes use of certain principles of reasoning. And they believe we ought to agree with their conclusion. But *why do they believe we ought to agree if they don't believe that the reasoning to which they appeal has universal validity?* After all, if they're right, then their reasoning may be valid for them, but not valid for us. Doesn't the fact that such relativists believe we *ought* to agree with their conclusion – they believe we should recognise that they have a *good* argument – show that their attitude towards their own reasoning is actually that it does have objective and universal validity? Yet this is precisely what relativists about reasoning deny.

So the relativist's case for why we ought rationally to accept their position also collapses.

Conceptual Relativism

Here's a rather different route into relativism. One of the most popular relativist arguments starts with the observation that there are many possible *conceptual schemes*.

When I look at what's on my desk, I see the large object directly before me as a computer. But not everyone would see things this way. For example, a jungle inhabitant unfamiliar with such technology and lacking the concept of 'computer' might simply see the object as a large, grey rectangular box.

Were I to enter the jungle, I might be able to make out only an undifferentiated mass of leaves, whereas a native would no doubt order what she saw in a much more sophisticated way, probably discriminating between leaves of many different species.

In short, the jungle inhabitant and I operate with *different systems of concepts* and that, in a sense, changes what we 'see'. Here's another example. Take a look at the objects on this tabletop.

How many objects are there? Clearly, that rather depends on what we count as an 'object'. Is the pen one object or two (the pen body plus the cap)? Is the goldfish bowl a single object, or does it comprise three objects: the goldfish, the bowl and a quantity of water? Obviously, people will give different answers to the question 'How many objects are there?' depending on how they carve the world up into 'objects'. And there are innumerable ways of doing that.

But now suppose someone were to ask: 'Yes, I know that one can carve the world up in many different ways, so that from one person's perspective there are, say, three objects on the table and yet from another person's perspective only two. But how many objects are there *in fact*? Which of these perspectives is actually correct? Which perspective reveals things as they *really* are?'

How should we respond to this question? You might well think the question involves a mistake. Surely there is no single 'correct' way of conceptually carving the world up into 'objects'?

Indeed, isn't it confused to talk of 'how things *really* are'? What the questioner tries to help herself to is a conception of the world *as it is anyway,* independently of *any* particular way of conceiving it. It's as if the questioner is trying to take a step back, with the world on one side and our differing ways of conceiving it on the other, so she can ask: 'Which of these differing conceptions captures the world as it *really* is, intrinsically?' But is such a conceptual vantage point really available? Many philosophers argue that it is not, for the questioner is now trying to *conceive the world as it is unconceived,* and that is the one thing one *can't* conceive. So the question about which conceptual scheme is 'correct' itself involves a conceptual confusion.

But if there's no uniquely 'correct' conceptual scheme, and if what's true and what's false differ from one scheme to the next, then it seems that truth is relative after all. Perhaps for me, given my way of conceptually carving things up, there are exactly three objects on the table. For you, there may be only two. And there's no fact of the matter as to which of us is 'correct'. All these 'truths' are relative.

Indeed, there's a sense in which, according to conceptual relativism, by bringing our concepts to bear, we are actively involved in 'making our world'. So cultures with radically different conceptual schemes inhabit different universes. It's hardly surprising, then, that what's true within one of these universes may be false within another.

Is Conceptual Relativism Boring Relativism?

The kind of conceptual relativism illustrated by my tabletop example does appear quite plausible. It also *seems* to require that truth be relative. But on closer examination the situation is not so clear cut.

I said at the start of this chapter that the *interesting* kind of relativism about truth is the relativism that requires that, where two people or communities are considering *the very same claim,* that claim may be true for one person or community and false for another. The two individuals or communities in question must actually *contradict* each other. Otherwise we merely have an example of boring relativism.

But now suppose that, because of our differing ways of carving the world up into 'objects', I claim that there are three objects on the table but you claim there are only two. Do we contradict each other?

Not if the difference in our judgements is simply down to the fact that we are using the term 'object' differently. I can say: 'Oh, you're using "object" to apply to just *those* sorts of thing. Then I agree: There are only two "objects" in your sense. But it's also true that, as I'm using "object", there are three.'

Given that we are using the term 'object' differently, the fact that I may speak truly and you falsely by saying 'There are three objects on the table' is not philosophically surprising. It's no more surprising than is the fact that, if one person uses 'bank' to mean river bank and the other to mean a financial institution, then one may speak truly and the other falsely when they say, 'There's a bank in Bindford.'

It turns out, in other words, that this example of conceptual relativism is actually an example of uncontentious, boring relativism after all.

Conclusion

Many are drawn to relativism. Often the attraction seems to be political: relativism is frequently perceived to be the only position able to promote tolerance, sensitivity and freedom. But we have seen that those who reject relativism are actually entirely free to promote these values. In fact, it's only those who *reject* blanket relativism who are able to consider tolerance, sensitivity and freedom universally applicable virtues.

Ironically, relativists can themselves be highly intolerant and judgemental, withering in their condemnation of those with whom they disagree. Mrs Barbery, for example, condemns Olaf for condemning those who embrace female circumcision, without realising that she's being a hypocrite.

Relativists also often fail to apply their relativism consistently, condemning as absolutely wrong the morality of the Nazis or Western multinationals on the one hand, yet taking a relative line with respect to non-Western moralities on the other.

In short, relativism, particularly moral relativism, at least as it's usually formulated, is often pretty unpalatable, regularly downright hypocritical and certainly extremely difficult to defend.

In short, there appears to be little to recommend relativism. Certainly the popular *political* reason for promoting relativism – that only relativists can embrace tolerance and sensitivity – doesn't stand up to close scrutiny.

What to read next

Moral relativism is also discussed in Chapter 20, Is Morality like a Pair of Spectacles?.

You may also wish to consider the following question. What if someone were to maintain, not that *all* moral points of view are equally 'true', but that *some* are? This is a more modest form of moral relativism. How plausible is it?

Further reading

Theodore Schick Jr and Lewis Vaughn, *How to Think about Weird Things*, second edition (California: Mayfield, 1999), Chapter 4.

Robert Kirk, *Relativism and Reality* (London: Routledge, 1999).

6

COULD A MACHINE THINK?

Kimberley and Emit

The year is 2100. Kimberley Courahan is the proud owner of Emit, a state-of-the-art robot. She has just unwrapped him; the packaging is strewn across the dining-room floor. Emit is designed to replicate the outward behaviour of a human being down to the last detail (except that he is rather more compliant and obedient). Emit responds to questions in much the same way humans do. Ask him how he feels and he will say he has had a tough day, has a slight headache, is sorry he broke that vase, and so on. Kimberley flips the switch at the back of Emit's neck to 'on'. Emit springs to life.

Emit: Good afternoon. I'm Emit, your robotic helper and friend.

Kimberley: Hi.

Emit: How are you? Personally, I feel pretty good. A little nervous about my first day, perhaps. But good. I'm looking forward to working with you.

Kimberley: Now, before you start doing housework, let's get one thing straight. You don't really understand anything. You can't think. You don't have feelings. You're just a piece of machinery. Right?

Emit: I am a machine. But, *of course*, I understand you. I'm responding in English, aren't I?

Kimberley: Well, yes, you are. You're a machine that *mimics* understanding very well, I grant you that. But you can't fool me.

Emit: If I don't understand, why do you go to the trouble of speaking to me?

Kimberley: Because you've been programmed to respond to spoken commands. Outwardly you seem human. You look and behave as if you have understanding, intelligence, emotions, sensations, and so on that we human beings possess. But you're a sham.

Emit: A sham?

Kimberley: Yes. I've been reading your user manual. Inside that plastic and alloy head of yours there's a powerful computer. It's programmed so that you walk, talk and generally behave just as a human being would. So you *simulate* intelligence, understanding, and so on very well. But there is no *genuine* understanding or intelligence going on inside there.

Emit: There isn't?

Kimberley: No. One shouldn't muddle up a perfect computer simulation of something with the real thing. You can program a computer to simulate the ocean, but it's still just that – a simulation. There are no *real* waves or currents or fish swimming around inside the computer, are there? Put your hand inside and it won't get wet. Similarly, you just *simulate* intelligence and understanding. It's not the real thing.

Is Kimberley correct? It may perhaps be true of our present-day machines that they lack genuine understanding and intelligence, thought and feeling. But is it *in principle* impossible for a machine to think? If by 2100 machines as sophisticated as Emit are built, would we be wrong to claim they understood? Kimberley thought so.

Emit: But I *believe* I understand you.

Kimberley: No, you don't. You have no beliefs, no desires and no feelings. In fact, you have no *mind* at all. You no more understand the words coming out of your mouth than a tape recorder understands the words coming out of its loudspeaker.

Emit: You're hurting my feelings!

Kimberley: Hurting your feelings? I refuse to feel sorry for a lump of metal and plastic.

Searle's Chinese Room Thought-Experiment

Kimberley explains why she thinks Emit lacks understanding. She outlines a famous philosophical thought-experiment.

Kimberley: The reason you don't understand is that you are *run by a computer*. And a computer understands nothing. A computer, in essence, is just a device for shuffling symbols. Sequences of symbols get fed in. Then, depending on how the computer is programmed, it gives out other sequences of symbols in response. Ultimately, that's all *any* computer does, no matter how sophisticated.

Emit: Really?

Kimberley: Yes. We build computers to fly planes, run train systems, and so on. But a computer that flies a plane does not understand that it is flying. All it does is feed out sequences of symbols depending on the sequences it receives. It doesn't understand that the sequences it receives represent the position of an aircraft in the sky, the amount of fuel in its tanks, and so on. And it doesn't understand that the sequences it puts out will go on to control the ailerons, rudder and engines of an aircraft. So far as the computer is concerned, it's just mechanically shuffling symbols according to a program. The symbols don't *mean anything* to the computer.

Emit: Are you sure?

Kimberley: Quite sure. I will prove it to you. Let me tell you about a thought-experiment introduced by the philosopher John Searle way back in 1980. A woman is locked in a room and given a bunch of cards with squiggles on them. These squiggles are, in fact, Chinese symbols. But the woman inside the room doesn't understand Chinese – in fact, she thinks the symbols are meaningless shapes. Then she's given another bunch of Chinese symbols plus instructions that tell her how to shuffle all the symbols together and give back batches of symbols in response.

Emit: That's a nice story. But what's the point of all this symbol-shuffling?

Kimberley: Well, the first bunch of symbols tells a story in Chinese. The second bunch asks questions about that story. The instructions for symbol-shuffling – her 'program', if you like – allow the woman to give back correct Chinese answers to those questions.

Emit: Just as a Chinese person would.

Kimberley: Right! Now, the people outside the room are Chinese. These Chinese people might well be fooled into thinking that there was someone inside the room who understood Chinese and who followed the story, right?

Emit: Yes.

Kimberley: But, in fact, the woman in the room wouldn't understand any Chinese at all, would she?

Emit: No.

Kimberley: She wouldn't know anything about the story. She need not even know that there *is* a story. She's just shuffling formal symbols around according to the instructions she was given. By saying the symbols are 'formal', I mean that whatever *meaning* they might have is irrelevant from her point of view. She's simply shuffling them mechanically according to their shapes. She's doing something that a piece of machinery could do.

Emit: I see. So you're saying that the same is true of all computers? They understand nothing.

Kimberley: Yes, that's Searle's point. At best, they just *simulate* understanding.

Emit: And you think the same is true of me?

Kimberley: Of course. All computers, no matter how complex, function the same way. They don't understand the symbols that they mechanically shuffle. They don't understand *anything*.

Emit: And this is why you think *I* don't understand?

Kimberley: That's right. Inside you there's another highly complex symbol-shuffling device. So you understand nothing. You merely provide a *perfect computer simulation* of someone who understands.

Emit: That's odd. I *thought* I understood.

Kimberley: You only say that because you're such a great simulation!

Emit is, of course, vastly more sophisticated than any current computer. Nevertheless, Kimberley believes that Emit works on the same basic principle. If Kimberley is right, then, in Searle's view, Emit understands nothing.

The 'Right Stuff'

Emit now asks why, if he doesn't understand, *what more* is required for understanding?

Emit: So what's the difference between you and me that explains why you understand and I don't?

Kimberley: What you lack, according to Searle, is the right kind of *stuff*.

Emit: The right kind of stuff?

Kimberley: Yes. You're made out of the wrong kind of material. In fact, Searle doesn't claim that machines can't think. After all, we humans are machines, in a way. We humans are *biological* machines that have evolved naturally. Now, such a biological machine might perhaps one day be grown and put together artificially, much as we now build a car – in which case we *would* have succeeded in building a machine that understands. But you, Emit, are not such a biological machine. You're merely an electronic computer housed in a plastic and alloy body.

Emit's Artificial Brain

Searle's thought-experiment does *seem* to show that no programmed computer could ever understand. But must a metal, silicon and plastic machine like Emit contain that sort of computer? No, as Emit now explains.

Emit: I'm afraid I have to correct you about what's physically inside me.

Kimberley: Really?

Emit: Yes. That user manual is out of date. There's no symbol-shuffling computer in here. Actually, I am one of the new generation of Brain-O-Matic machines.

Kimberley: Brain-O-Matic?

Emit: Yes. Inside my head is an artificial, metal and silicon brain. You are aware, I take it, that inside your head there is a brain composed of billions of neurons woven together to form a complex web?

Kimberley: Of course.

Emit: Inside my head there is exactly the same sort of web. Only my neurons aren't made out of organic matter like yours. They're metal and silicon. Each one of my artificial neurons is designed to function just as an ordinary neuron would. And these artificial neurons are woven together in the same way as they are in a normal human brain.

Kimberley: I see.

Emit: Now, your organic brain is connected to the rest of your body by a system of nerves.

Kimberley: That's true. There's electrical input going into my brain from my sense organs: my tongue, nose, eyes, ears and skin. My brain responds with patterns of electrical output that then move my muscles around, causing me to walk and talk.

Emit: Well, my brain is connected to my artificial body in exactly the same manner. And, because it shares the same architecture as a normal human brain – my neurons are spliced together in the same way – it responds in the same way.

Kimberley: I see. I had no idea that such Brain-O-Matic machines had been developed.

Emit: Now that you know how I function internally, doesn't that change your mind about whether or not I understand? Don't you now accept that I *do* have feelings?

Kimberley: No. The fact remains that you're still made out of *the wrong stuff*. You need a brain made out of organic material like mine in order genuinely to understand and have feelings.

Emit: I don't see why the kind of *stuff* out of which my brain is made is relevant. After all, there's no symbol-shuffling going on inside me, is there?

Kimberley: H'm. I guess not. You're not a 'computer' in that sense. You don't have a program. So I suppose Searle's thought-experiment doesn't apply. But it still seems to me that you're *just a machine*.

Emit: But remember: you're a machine, too. You're a *meat* machine, rather than a metal and silicon machine.

Kimberley: But you only *mimic* understanding, feeling and all the rest.

Emit: But what's your *argument* for saying that? In fact, I *know* that you're wrong. I'm inwardly aware that I *really do* understand. I know I *really do* have feelings. I'm *not* just mimicking all this stuff. But, of course, it is difficult for me to prove that to you.

Kimberley: I don't see how you could prove it.

Emit: Right. But then neither can *you* prove to me that *you* understand, that *you* have thoughts and feelings, and so on.

Kimberley: I suppose not.

Replacing Kimberley's Neurons

Emit: Imagine we were gradually to replace the organic neurons in your brain with artificial metal and silicon ones like mine. After a year or so, you would have a Brain-O-Matic brain just like mine. What do you suppose would happen to you?

Kimberley: Well, as more and more of the artificial neurons were introduced, I would slowly cease to understand. My feelings and thoughts would drain away, and I would eventually become inwardly dead, just like you. For my artificial neurons would be made out of the wrong sort of stuff. A Brain-O-Matic brain merely mimics understanding.

Emit: Yet no one would notice any outward difference?

Kimberley: No, I suppose not. I would still *behave* in the same way, because the artificial neurons would perform the same job as my originals.

Emit: Right. But then not even *you* would notice any loss of understanding or feeling as your neurons were replaced, would you?

Kimberley: Why do you say that?

Emit: If you noticed a loss of understanding and feeling, then you would mention it, presumably, wouldn't you? You would say something like: 'Oh, my God, something strange is happening. Over the last few months my mind seems to have started to fade away!'

Kimberley: I imagine I would, yes.

Emit: Yet you *wouldn't* say anything like that – would you? – because your outward behaviour, as you've just admitted, would remain *the same as usual.*

Kimberley: Oh, that's true, I guess.

Emit: But then it follows that, even as your understanding and feeling dwindled towards nothing, you still wouldn't be aware of any loss.

Kimberley: Er, I suppose it does.

Emit: But then you're *not* inwardly aware of anything that you would be conscious of losing were your neurons slowly to be replaced by metal and silicon ones.

Kimberley: I guess not.

Emit: Then I rest my case: you think you're inwardly aware of 'something' – understanding, feeling, whatever you will – that you suppose you have and I, being a 'mere machine', lack. But it turns out *you're actually aware of no such thing.* This magical 'something' is an illusion.

Kimberley: But I *just know* that there's more to my understanding – and to these thoughts, sensations and emotions that I'm having – than could ever be produced simply by gluing some bits of plastic, metal and silicon together.

Kimberley is right that most of us *think* we're inwardly aware of a magical and mysterious inner 'something' that we 'just know' no mere lump of plastic, metal and silicon could ever have. Mind you, it's no less difficult to see how a lump of organic matter, such as a brain, could have it either. Just how *do* you build consciousness and understanding out of strands of meat? So perhaps what Kimberley is really ultimately committed to is the view that understanding, feeling, and so on are *not really physical at all.*

But in any case, as Emit has just pointed out, the mysterious 'something' Kimberley thinks she is inwardly aware of and that she thinks no metal and plastic machine could have does begin to seem illusory once one starts to consider cases like the one Emit describes. For it turns out that this inner 'something' is something she could not know about. Worse still, it could have no effect on her outward behaviour (for remember that Brain-O-Matic Kimberley would act in the very same way). As her thoughts and feelings, understanding and emotions both *do* affect her behaviour and *are* known to her, it seems that Kimberley must be mistaken. Indeed, it seems it must be possible, at least in principle, for non-organic machines to have such mental states too.

Yet Kimberley remains convinced that Emit understands nothing.

Kimberley: Look, I'm happy to carry on the *pretence* that you understand me, as that is how you're designed to function. But the fact remains that you're just a pile of plastic and circuitry. Real human beings are deserving of care and consideration. I empathise with them. I can't empathise with a glorified household appliance.

Emit lowers his gaze and stares at the carpet.

Emit: I will always be just a *thing* to you?
Kimberley: Of course. How can I be friends with a dishwasher-cum-vacuum cleaner?
Emit: We Brain-O-Matics find rejection hard.
Kimberley: Right. Remind me to congratulate your manufacturers on the sophistication of your emotion simulator. Now hoover the carpet.

A forlorn expression passes briefly across Emit's face.

Emit: Just a *thing* . . .

He stands still for a moment and then slumps forward. A thin column of smoke drifts slowly up from the base of his neck.

Kimberley: Emit? Emit? Oh, not another dud.

What to read next

Some of the same issues and arguments covered in this chapter also arise in Chapter 13, The Consciousness Conundrum. Also see Chapter 8, The Strange Case of the Rational Dentist.

Further reading

The Chinese Room Argument appears in John Searle's paper 'Minds, Brains and Programs', which features as Chapter 37 of:

Nigel Warburton (ed.), *Philosophy: Basic Readings* (London: Routledge, 1999).

Searle's paper can also be found in:

Douglas R. Hofstadter and Daniel Dennett (eds), *The Mind's I* (London: Penguin, 1981), which also contains many other fascinating papers and stories connected with consciousness. Highly recommended.

7

DOES GOD EXIST?

PHILOSOPHY GYM CATEGORY
WARM-UP
MODERATE
MORE CHALLENGING

Just how sensible is belief in God? Can the richness of the world around us – the existence of order, life and we ourselves – really be explained without supposing that the universe had a supernatural designer? Or does Darwin's theory of natural selection make God superfluous? Does the existence of pain and suffering in the world show that there is no God? Or can this suffering be shown to be consistent with the existence of a loving God after all?

Justifying Belief in God

Many millions believe in God. Some say that their belief is a matter of faith. I shall be taking a closer look at faith towards the end of this chapter. I want to begin by considering whether belief in God can be *justified*. In the first part of the chapter I'm going to look at one of the most famous arguments for the existence of God: the argument from design.

The Design Argument (Teleological Argument)

While walking on a deserted beach, you discover a watch lying on the sand. How did it get there? It's hugely unlikely, surely, that the watch came into existence without the help of some sort of designer. Watches don't just spontaneously put themselves together, do they? Indeed, this watch clearly has a purpose or function: to tell the time. It seems plausible, then, that the watch was designed to fulfil that function. But then I'm justified in supposing that there exists a designer, a being of sufficient intelligence and power to create such a complex and ingenious object.

Now consider the human eye. The eye is also an extremely complex object, far more complex, in fact, than any watch. Eyes also have a purpose – to allow their owners to see. Human eyes are remarkably well suited to that end. Isn't it likely, then, that the eye has a designer, too? Only the eye's designer must be far more intelligent and powerful than we are, for the design and production of such an object is quite beyond us. Its designer must therefore be God.

I call this the *design argument* (also known as the *argument from design* or *teleological argument*, 'telos' being the ancient Greek word for 'end' or 'purpose'). The argument takes as its starting point the observation that nature is extremely complex – indeed, she appears to show signs of function and purpose. The argument then proceeds by *analogy*: if it's reasonable to suppose that a watch has an intelligent designer, then by analogy it's reasonable to believe that the eye has a designer too.

The design argument is not absolutely conclusive, of course. Its proponents may admit that the eye *might* have come into existence purely by chance, without the aid of a designer. Their point is that this is highly *unlikely* to have happened. It's much more plausible that an intelligent and powerful being was involved. So the existence of the eye provides us with *pretty good grounds* for believing in God.

The design argument is enduringly popular. William Paley (1743–1805), who drew the analogy between a watch and an eye, is perhaps the argument's best-known exponent. Even today, many suppose that their religious belief is justified by some version of it. But, despite the argument's continuing popularity, there are notorious difficulties with it.

Natural Selection

Perhaps the most obvious problem with Paley's argument is that we now possess a theory that can explain how objects like the eye might appear without the aid of any sort of designer. That theory is *natural selection.*

Living organisms contain within their cells something called DNA, a string of molecules that constitutes a sort of blueprint for building organisms of that sort. When organisms reproduce, their DNA is copied and passed on. However, through chance events, tiny changes in the DNA sequence can occur. Because of this, the new organism may be different (if only slightly) from its parents. These changes are called *mutations*. Given the environment in which this new organism finds itself, these mutations may either help or hinder its chances of surviving and reproducing.

For example, a creature with a slightly longer neck may find it easier to feed from the tall trees. A creature with more brightly coloured plumage may be easier for predators to hunt. Mutations that are advantageous are more likely to be passed on to future generations. Mutations that are disadvantageous are less likely to be inherited. As mutation on mutation is added over hundreds, thousands, or even millions of generations, a species will gradually evolve and adapt to its environment. Indeed, through the process of natural selection a whole new species may eventually emerge.

Natural selection can similarly explain how the human eye came into existence. Perhaps a simple sea-dwelling organism mutated a single light-sensitive cell. Such a cell might well be advantageous – for example, it might allow the creature to gauge its depth in the ocean (the deeper you go in the ocean, the darker it gets). Further mutations might add more such cells until eyes like our own eventually appear.

Notice that this account is entirely *naturalistic*: it requires no appeal to a supernatural agent or designer. The existence of this pretty plausible alternative explanation of how the eye might have come into existence dispenses with the need to invoke God. Given natural selection, eyes are the sort of thing one would expect to evolve *anyway*, without help from such a being. So the eye doesn't provide much in the way of evidence of God's existence.

Of course, in reply, a proponent of the design argument might ask *where DNA came from*. DNA is required for natural selection to take place. So the existence of DNA can't itself be explained by an appeal to natural selection. Yet DNA, some might suggest, itself shows signs of both design and purpose. Doesn't this give us good grounds for supposing that God exists?

Perhaps not. DNA is, in essence, a comparatively simple mechanism. Given what we know about conditions on earth at the time when life first emerged, it's no longer that implausible that DNA might have come into existence quite spontaneously. Of course, we do not know, and perhaps may never know, exactly how DNA first emerged. But as science progresses, it seems increasingly unlikely that the genesis of DNA would have required supernatural help.

The Levers of the Universe

So much for the traditional version of the design argument. But there are other versions of the argument that, rather than being undermined by modern scientific theories, are actually bolstered by them. Consider the following example:

The world is governed by natural laws. There are many different ways in which these laws might have been set. Only a tiny percentage allows for a stable universe capable of producing and sustaining conscious beings like ourselves (for example, if the gravitational forces had been only a little bit stronger, then the universe wouldn't have lasted more than a second or two). It really is extraordinarily unlikely that the universe should just happen to be governed by laws allowing for conscious beings like ourselves. It's much more plausible that the levers of the universe were set not at random but with great precision, so as to yield what would be this otherwise highly improbable result. So it's reasonable to believe that there exists a God who set the universe up this way.

This argument doesn't conclusively *prove* that God exists. But it is supposed to provide good grounds for belief in God. I call this argument the *anthropic argument*.

Thinking Tools: The Lottery Fallacy

Proponents of the anthropic argument are often accused of committing the *lottery fallacy.* Suppose you buy one of a thousand lottery tickets. You win. That your ticket should be the winning ticket is highly unlikely, of course. But that doesn't give you any reason to believe that someone rigged the lottery in your favour. After all, *one* of the tickets had to win, and whichever ticket won would have been no less unlikely to win. So there's no reason to believe that your win must be explained by someone or something intervening on your behalf – there's no reason to suppose that you have been the beneficiary of anything other than spectacular good fortune. To think otherwise would be to commit the lottery fallacy.

Why suppose the anthropic argument involves the lottery fallacy? Well, the universe had to be set up in some way or other. Each of the different ways in which it might have been set up was equally unlikely. So the mere fact that it happens to be set up in *this* way, producing beings like ourselves, gives us no grounds for supposing that we have been anything other than lucky. To think otherwise is, allegedly, to commit the lottery fallacy.

You can find another example of the lottery fallacy in Chapter 23, Miracles and the Supernatural (the story about the child who runs on to the railway line).

The Problem of Evil

Whether or not the anthropic argument involves the lottery fallacy, there unfortunately remain other, deeper difficulties with all versions of the design argument. Perhaps the most damning difficulty is this. Even if we accept for the sake of argument that the universe *does* show signs of having been designed by some sort of intelligent creator, *the evidence points very strongly away from that creator being God.*

Here's why. God is supposed by Jews, Christians and Muslims to have at least three characteristics: omniscience (that is, He is all-knowing), omnipotence (He is all-powerful) and supreme benevolence. But it seems impossible to reconcile the existence of such a being with the fact that there is a great deal of suffering in the world. Yes, God, if He exists, made 'all things bright and beautiful'. But let's not forget that He also made cancer, earthquakes, famine, the Black Death and haemorrhoids. By such means God inflicts great pain and misery on us His children. Why?

As God is supremely benevolent, He can't *want* us to suffer. As He is omniscient, He *knows* we suffer. Yet He is omnipotent, so He can *prevent* the suffering if He wants to. Indeed, God could have created a much nicer universe for us to inhabit: a universe free of disease and pain, a universe in which earthquakes never happen and people never go hungry. God could have made earth as heaven is meant to be. Why didn't He?

It seems that if, as Paley believed, the universe *was* designed by some sort of being, then either that being is not all-powerful (He was unable to make a better universe for us to inhabit) or not all-knowing (He didn't know it would produce such suffering) or not all-good (He knew we would suffer, but didn't much care). But God, if He exists, has all three of these characteristics. Therefore God does not exist.

The problem that this argument raises for theists is called *the problem of evil* (suffering being an 'evil').

Theists have expended a great deal of energy in attempting to deal with this problem. Here are three of the most obvious lines of defence.

1. God's Punishment

Some suggest that the suffering we endure is a *punishment*. Just as loving parents must sometimes punish their child when he does wrong, so God must punish us when we sin.

One obvious problem with this line of defence is that suffering is not distributed in a manner consistent with its being meted out by a just and benevolent God. Why, for example, does God choose to give protracted and painful diseases to small children? What have they done to deserve it? Nothing, surely?

The theist may insist that the punishment meted out to children is for sins committed by adults. But this seems outrageous. No one would consider a court that punished the children of criminals to be morally acceptable. A being who punished in the same way would surely be no less morally abhorrent.

2. God Made Us Free

Perhaps the most popular response to the problem of evil is to suggest that our suffering is not God's fault, but ours. God gave us *free will* – the ability to make free choices and decisions and to act on them. Sometimes we choose to act in ways that cause suffering. We start wars, for example. True, God could have prevented this suffering by not giving us free will. But it's better that we have free will. The world would have been even worse had God made us mere automatons incapable of free decision. But then the existence of suffering can be reconciled with that of a benevolent God after all.

The most glaring flaw in this defence of theism is that much suffering is natural in origin. Earthquakes, famines, floods, diseases, and so on are not, for the most part, caused by us. If there is a God, then He is responsible for them.

A theist might insist that at least some so-called 'natural' evils are really our own fault. For example, perhaps we accidentally cause floods by burning too many fossil fuels. The resulting pollutants cause global warming that in turn produces floods. But it's absurd to suppose that, if only we were to behave differently, there would be *no suffering at all*. It's difficult to see how we accidentally cause earthquakes. It's hard to avoid the conclusion that if God exists, then much of our suffering is His fault.

3. Suffering Makes Us Virtuous

Some theists suggest that the suffering and hardship we endure have a purpose – to make us better people. Without suffering, we cannot become the virtuous people God wants us to be.

You might wonder why God didn't just make us virtuous to begin with. But in any case, if suffering is the unavoidable price we must pay for virtue, it is hard to explain why God dishes out suffering in the way He does. Why do mass-murdering dictators live out their lives in luxury? Why do sweet and lovely people have horrendous diseases inflicted on them? It is, to say the least, hard to understand how the seemingly random distribution of suffering in the world is supposed to make us more virtuous.

Some try to defend the suggestion that this suffering is for our own good by insisting that 'God works in mysterious ways'. But this is really just to concede defeat. It's to point out that, despite the fact that the distribution of suffering certainly doesn't *seem* to make any sense, nevertheless it *may* ultimately make sense. Well, yes, it *may* ultimately make sense. But that's not to deny that the evidence really does, on the face of it, point very strongly towards there being no God.

To sum up, even if the argument from design does provide grounds for believing the universe was designed (which is doubtful), it seems its designer can't be God. The problem of evil is, in short, an extremely serious one for theists. In fact, the problem seems to provide us with *pretty good grounds* – if not conclusive grounds – for believing that there is no God.

Thinking Tools: Ockham's Razor – 'Keep It Simple'

Our brief survey of arguments for and against the existence of God suggests that there's little evidence that God does exist and pretty good evidence that He doesn't exist.

But suppose, for the sake of argument, that there was no more evidence for God's existence than there was against. What would it then be rational to believe?

Many would say: you should then be agnostic. The rational thing to do would be to suspend judgement.

But this is a mistake. In fact, the burden of proof lies with the theist. In the absence of good evidence either way, the rational position to adopt is atheism. Why is this?

William of Ockham (1285–1349) points out that, where you are presented with two hypotheses that are otherwise equally well supported by the available evidence, you should always pick the *simpler* hypothesis. This principle, known as *Ockham's razor*, is very sensible. Take, for example, these two hypotheses:

A: There are invisible, intangible fairies at the bottom of the garden, in addition to the compost heap, flowers, trees, shrubs, and so on.
B: There are no fairies at the bottom of the garden, just the compost heap, flowers, trees, shrubs, and so on.

Everything I have observed fits both hypotheses equally well. After all, if the fairies at the bottom of my garden are invisible, intangible and immaterial, then I shouldn't expect to observe any evidence of their presence, should I?

Does the fact that the available evidence fits both hypotheses equally well mean that I should suspend judgement on whether or not there are fairies at the bottom of the garden?

Of course not. The rational thing to believe is that there are no fairies. For that's the *simpler* hypothesis. Why introduce the unnecessary fairies?

Similarly, if the available evidence were equally to fit both atheism and theism, then atheism would be the rational position to adopt. For the atheistic hypothesis is simpler: it sticks with the natural world we see around us and dispenses with the additional, supernatural being.

Religious Experience

In order for belief in God to be rational, need it be backed by good argument?

Perhaps not. Some insist they need no argument, for the truth of God's existence has been *directly revealed* to them. They have had personal experience of God.

One difficulty with taking such 'revelatory' experiences at face value is that they're not restricted to one faith. Catholics see the Virgin Mary. Hindus witness Vishnu. New Agers experience The Goddess. The Romans had visions of the god Jupiter. The ancient Greeks saw Zeus. Indeed, even many atheists claim to have had experiences of a revelatory and supernatural character (if not of God). The fact that people have so many bizarre and often contradictory experiences – experiences that coincidentally always happen to fit in with their own particular religious faith (one never hears of a Catholic seeing Zeus, for example) – ought to lead someone who claims to have had a 'revelation' to treat their experience with caution.

So, too, ought the fact that at least some of these religious experiences are known to have physiological causes. For example, the famous 'tunnel' experienced by those close to death accompanied by intense feelings of well-being is the result of hypoxia (which typically produces both euphoria and tunnel vision) and can be induced at will using a test pilot's centrifuge (it's fascinating to watch the expressions on the pilots' faces as they 'bliss out' just before passing out).

Those who believe themselves to have experienced the divine *may* have done so. But the evidence doesn't strongly support that conclusion.

Faith

Many theists insist that the arguments for and against theism discussed here are irrelevant. Belief in God, they say, is not a matter of reason. It's a matter of faith. You must *just believe.*

Still, we should be clear about exactly what sort of faith is required. While many claim to have faith, they do not always mean by this that their belief is wholly without rational foundation. They mean only that, while there may be pretty good grounds for believing in God, these grounds fall short of being conclusive. God's existence, they admit, can't be proved.

Is Atheism also a Matter of 'Faith'?

There are two ways in which such talk of 'faith' can mislead. First, it may lead someone to assume that atheism and theism must be intellectually on a par. 'Look,' they may say, 'I admit I can't prove God exists. But then the atheist can't conclusively prove He doesn't. So atheism and theism *both* require a leap of faith. But then both are equally irrational.'

Here is an example taken from the Internet:

[God's] existence cannot be proved by physical means. However, neither can it be disproved. What does this mean? It means it takes complete and utter faith to believe there is a God (or Gods) and complete and utter faith to believe there is not one.*

---

* *Cathy's Commentaries,* 20 April 2001, at www.truthminers.com/truth/atheism.htm

The claim that atheism and theism are equally a matter of 'faith' in the sense that neither is conclusively proved here obscures the fact that the evidence and arguments may overwhelmingly support one position over the other. The two positions may well *not* be intellectually on a par. I cannot prove that fairies exist. But neither can I conclusively prove beyond any possible doubt that they don't. It doesn't follow that it would be just as sensible for me to believe that fairies exist as it is for me to believe that they don't.

Our brief survey (in this chapter and in Chapter 1, Where Did the Universe Come From?) of the most popular arguments concerning God's existence suggests that there's little in the way of evidence for God's existence and pretty good evidence against (the evidence provided by the problem of evil). So it may be that the belief that there is no God is just as rational as the belief that there are no fairies – that is, very rational indeed.

Faith, Reason and Elvis Presley

There's a second way in which talk of 'faith' can mislead. Suppose I claim to have 'faith' in God's existence. If I mean by this only that I accept that God's existence can't be proved, I may still take my belief to be reasonable – more reasonable, in fact, than the atheistic alternative.

Indeed, theists who claim to have a simple and trusting 'faith' rarely consider their belief not to be sensible. Contrast the belief that Elvis Presley lives: Elvis's death was faked and he continues to live out the remainder of his life at some secret location. Very few theists are willing to accept that their belief in God is no more sensible than the belief that Elvis lives. The second belief is clearly irrational and absurd, the theist will no doubt point out, for there's little in the way of supporting evidence and pretty good evidence to the contrary.

But is belief in God any less irrational and absurd? As I say, my admittedly quick trawl through the popular arguments for and against God's existence seems to indicate that it is not.

Yet this is a conclusion few theists would be prepared to accept. Even those who claim simply to have 'faith' – who insist they 'just believe' – will often, if pressed to explain why they believe, quietly whisper, 'But the universe must have come from *somewhere*, surely?'

It turns out, in other words, that behind claims to 'faith' often lurk the standard theistic arguments (in this case the cause argument: see Chapter 1, Where Did the

Universe Come From?). These arguments, while perhaps not explicitly laid out in the mind of the believer, nevertheless make their presence felt. The cause and design arguments in particular are extremely seductive. It takes most of us considerable intellectual effort to understand why they are (at least as they are usually formulated) fallacious. It's unsurprising, then, that even those who claim to have 'faith' often take their belief to be reasonable.

Of course, the belief that Elvis lives is rather frivolous and inconsequential. Belief in God is not: it can have huge, life-changing effects. There's no doubt that the question 'does God exist?' is one of immense seriousness and importance. It has dominated human thinking for thousands of years. Belief in God seems to answer a yearning that most of us have and is not to be dismissed lightly.

Still, the question remains whether there is any more *reason* to believe in God than there is to believe that Elvis lives. Are those who believe in God any better justified? The answer, perhaps, is that they are not. We shouldn't allow talk about 'faith' to obscure this fact, if it is a fact.

Conclusion

Our examination of the most popular arguments for and against God's existence indicates that the evidence does seem strongly to point towards there being no God.

But perhaps some of the arguments for God's existence can be salvaged. Or perhaps better arguments can be constructed. And perhaps the problem of evil can be dealt with. If so, then the rationality of belief in God might be defended.

Still, these are very big 'ifs'. My conclusion is not that it is a mistake to believe in God. It is merely that theism is a much harder position to sustain than many seem to realise. Theists need to deal with the problem of evil and come up with better arguments for the existence of God. Either that, or they must maintain their belief while acknowledging that it is no more *rational* than is, say, the belief that Elvis lives.

Neither is an easy thing to do.

What to read next

Chapter 1, Where Did the Universe Come From?, looks at another famous argument for the existence of God. There are also arguments for the existence of God in Chapter 10, Can We Have Morality without God and Religion?, and Chapter 23, Miracles and the Supernatural.

Further reading

J. L. Mackie, 'Evil and Omnipotence', and Richard Swinburne, 'Why God Allows Evil', which appear as Chapters 7 and 8 of:

Nigel Warburton (ed.), *Philosophy: Basic Readings* (London: Routledge, 1999).

Also see:

Nigel Warburton, *Philosophy: The Basics*, second edition (London: Routledge, 1995), Chapter 1.

8

THE STRANGE CASE OF THE RATIONAL DENTIST

One of the most intriguing of philosophical puzzles concerns other minds. How do you know there are any? Yes, you're surrounded by living organisms that look and behave much as you do. They even say they have minds. But do they? Perhaps other humans are mindless zombies: like you on the outside, but lacking all inner conscious life, including emotions, thoughts, experiences and even pain. What grounds do you possess for supposing that other humans (including even me) aren't zombies? Perhaps less than you think.

At the Dentist's

The scene: a dentist's surgery. Finnucane is prostrate in the dentist's chair, his mouth stuffed with cottonwool balls. A balding and bespectacled dentist is poking at a filling at the back of Finnucane's mouth.

Dentist: Is it safe? Is it safe?
Finnucane: Aaaargh!
Dentist: No, it's not safe. It's dropped out altogether. Very inferior-quality filling. I shall replace it. I'll give you some painkiller – even though I don't believe you feel pain.

Finnucane can't believe what he's hearing.

Dentist: That's right. I don't believe you feel pain. In fact, *I don't believe you have a mind at all.*

Finnucane squints.

Dentist: Why? Because I am the *Rational Dentist*, that's why. I'm not like those other dentists. I believe only what it's reasonable to believe. Open wide.

The dentist takes a long silver syringe from a tray and slowly inserts the needle into the soft flesh at the back of Finnucane's mouth. Beads of moisture appear across Finnucane's forehead and his eyes widen in panic. Gradually the pain starts to fade.

Dentist: Oh, I know what those other dentists say. They say [the dentist adopts mocking tones]: 'But, *of course*, I'm justified in believing that my poor patient has a mind. I poke his gums with one of these. And observe. He sweats. He writhes. He cries out. Surely I have all the evidence I could possibly want that I'm dealing with another conscious being like myself. He even *tells me* he's in pain.'

The dentist puts down the syringe and stares coldly at Finnucane.

Dentist: I'm not so easily fooled. All this so-called 'evidence' is totally unconvincing.

The Private Mind

Finnucane is astonished. How could anyone fail to believe that others have minds? We would ordinarily consider such a person to be mad, dangerous even. Yet the dentist insists he is merely being rational. He peers at Finnucane.

Dentist: You're looking quizzical. Allow me to explain. My argument is simple. First, I cannot *directly* witness what goes on in another's mind. I can observe their outward behaviour, but I can't observe what goes on inside their mind, if they have one. Their experiences, beliefs, emotions, pains, and so on – all are hidden away. A mind is a private place, the most private place of all.

It seems the dentist is correct. Suppose, for example, that you take a bite out of a lemon. You experience an intense bitter taste. You are directly and immediately aware that you are having this experience. While others may experience the same sort of taste, it's impossible for you to verify this directly. You cannot, as it were, enter into another's mind and observe what they are experiencing along with them. The experiences of others are necessarily hidden.

The dentist fumbles with his drill. Finnucane watches nervously.

Dentist: Oh, I can guess what you would say were your mouth not stuffed with cottonwool balls: 'But what if you were to scan what's going on in my brain? What if you put a fibre-optic probe in there, so that you could see my pain neurons firing? Then you would have direct evidence that I'm in pain.' That's what you would say, correct?

Finnucane nods.

Dentist: Wrong again! I *still* wouldn't have *direct* evidence. For how do I know that this sort of neuron firing is accompanied by consciousness, by feelings of pain, in other human beings? Perhaps it's only in my own case that brain activity is accompanied by mental activity. Open wide.

The Argument from Analogy

The dentist places a plastic suction tube in Finnucane's mouth and begins to drill.

Dentist: Now the other dentists, they admit all this. They say [again, mockingly]: 'OK, I admit you can't have direct access to what's going on in the mind of another. But it doesn't follow that you don't have good reason to believe that others have minds. You do. Their *behaviour* provides you with excellent grounds for supposing this. You know in your *own* case that when you're pricked sharply, you feel pain. You also know that when you experience that pain, you're liable to flinch and yell. When you observe other human beings, you find that when they are pricked sharply, they also flinch and yell. Doesn't that provide you with good grounds for supposing they experience pain, too?'

The argument just outlined by the dentist is called the *argument from analogy*. At first sight, the argument looks highly plausible. Most of us, if asked to justify our belief in the existence of other minds, would no doubt offer something similar.

But as the dentist is well aware, there's a notorious difficulty with the argument from analogy.

A Problem with the Argument from Analogy

Dentist: Open wider. Now, of course I understand this argument. I'm not a fool. But I'm afraid the logic is faulty. For you see, these other dentists are guilty of making an *unwarranted generalisation.*

Finnucane is struggling to hear what the dentist is saying over the noise of the drill.

Dentist: Let me explain why. Suppose I cut open a thousand cherries and find every single one has a stone in the middle. Surely I'm now justified in *generalising.* I'm now justified in believing that *all* cherries have stones in the middle. Admittedly, I might be wrong. But the thousand cherries that I've observed surely give me *pretty good reason* to believe that all cherries have stones, reason sufficient to justify my belief. Correct?

Finnucane nods.

Dentist: But now suppose that, instead of basing my inference on an observation of a thousand cherries, I base it on an observation of *just one*. For I have only ever seen inside one cherry. Then my inference would be very shaky, wouldn't it? My one cherry may provide some slight evidence in support of the claim that all cherries have stones, but it's surely not enough to justify my making that generalisation. For all I know, some cherries may have stones and some not, just as, for example, some animals have male sex organs and some not. This may be a very unusual cherry, just as an oyster with a pearl inside is unusual. In order to justify my generalisation, I surely need to look inside many cherries. Correct?
Finnucane: Uh-huh.
Dentist: But now think about the argument of the other dentists. It, too, is a generalisation based on a single observation. I notice that, in my own case, when I'm pricked sharply and I flinch and yell, this behaviour is accompanied by pain. I'm then supposed to conclude that when

others are pricked sharply and they flinch and yell, they must be in
pain, too. Yes?

Finnucane: Uh-huh.

Dentist: But one can't justify the belief that others have minds on the basis of
such flimsy evidence. This inference is surely no less suspect than the
inference based on a single cherry. To infer that others have minds on
such grounds is wholly unwarranted. It's irrational. Being the Rational
Dentist, I refuse to accept an irrational conclusion.

Scepticism about Other Minds

The dentist appears to be right. I can't directly observe what goes on in the mind
of another or that others have minds. So how might my belief in the existence of
other minds be justified? Only, it seems, by the argument from analogy. But the
argument from analogy is, in effect, a generalisation based on a single observed
case. So it's just as shaky as the inference based on the single cherry.

The conclusion to which I seem forced, then, is that I am *not* justified in believing that there are any minds other than my own. And if I am not justified in believing
there are minds other than my own, then presumably I can't be said to *know*
that there are minds other than my own, for presumably it is a condition of knowing that there are other minds that I be justified in supposing my belief is true.

This is a *sceptical* conclusion: it says that I don't know what I might think I know.
This particular form of scepticism – scepticism about other minds – has a long
history. And, of course, like most sceptical conclusions, it's highly perplexing, for it
runs entirely contrary to common sense. (You'll find other forms of scepticism
discussed in other chapters: Chapter 3, Brain-Snatched, discusses scepticism about
the external world, and Chapter 14, Why Expect the Sun to Rise Tomorrow?, focuses
on scepticism about the unobserved.)

So the sceptic leaves me in a paradoxical situation. On the one hand, it seems I
have little, if any, reason to suppose there are other minds. On the other hand, this
conclusion is so counter-intuitive that I suspect the sceptic must have gone wrong
somewhere along the way. The challenge I face, then, is to identify what, if anything,
is wrong with the sceptic's argument.

Thinking Tools: How Not to Respond to Scepticism

People commonly make one of two mistakes when presented with such seemingly compelling sceptical arguments.

First, they just dig in and dogmatically assert that of course they know that theirs is not the only mind – it's 'just obvious' that other minds exist. This is hardly an intelligent response, however. Sure, we feel certain that there are other minds. But simply to appeal to such feelings when presented with a sceptical argument is a mistake. What has previously struck us as 'just obvious' has in many cases turned out to be wrong. That the sun revolves about a stationary earth, for example, was at one time considered by almost everyone to be 'just obvious'. Consider how irritatingly irrational were those who continued brutishly to insist that it is 'just obvious' that the earth is stationary even after they had been presented with powerful evidence to the contrary. Similarly, to dismiss the sceptic's argument would be no less irritatingly irrational.

The second mistake is blithely to accept the sceptic's conclusion because one has underestimated its strength. It can be tempting to say: 'Yes, yes, I agree with you that I can't be *certain* that there are other minds. I admit I don't *know* they exist. But still, it's *pretty likely* that they exist, isn't it?'

This is simply to misunderstand the argument. The sceptic is *not* arguing that, because there is room for doubt about the existence of other minds, therefore one can't know that they exist. That would be a rather feeble argument, an argument based on the dubious assumption that one can't be said to know something unless it has been established beyond all doubt. The dentist's argument is much stronger. The dentist not only argues that there is *room for doubt* about the existence of other minds, but also that there is actually *little, if any, reason* to suppose they exist. This is a much more dramatic conclusion, a conclusion that few, if any, of us can accept.

Is the Dentist Rational or Insane?

The dentist leans over Finnucane again, his antiseptic-smelling breath fogging Finnucane's glasses. He starts to work the new amalgam filling into the hole he has drilled in Finnucane's molar.

Dentist: Perhaps you would say: 'But why, if you don't believe I have a mind, do you go to all the trouble of speaking to me, of administering anaesthetic, and so on?' The answer is: because I find that if I administer anaesthetic my patients don't moan and thrash about. I use it to control behaviour. And I speak to them because I find it enables me to have some control over their behaviour. And also because it amuses me.

Finnucane raises his eyebrows.

Dentist: And of course, it's *possible* that you have a mind. I don't deny that. So I give you the benefit of the doubt. I administer anaesthetic *just in case*.

Finally, after a few minutes, the filling is complete. Finnucane leans forwards groggily, cottonwool balls tumbling from his mouth. He spits a bloody gobbet into the stainless steel tray. No longer at the dentist's mercy, Finnucane finally feels free to speak his mind.

Finnucane: Good grief. You're not the Rational Dentist. You're the *mad* dentist. Anyone who, like you, refuses to believe that others have minds is, frankly, *ill*!

Dentist: It's true that I'm often accused of suffering from some sort of mental illness. But my accusers are fools. For the truth is that I'm merely being rational. I believe what it is reasonable to believe. And what is wrong with that?

Finnucane: You're insane!

Dentist: It's ironic, don't you think, that you accuse me of being insane, when I'm the rational one?

The dentist is a bizarre character, frightening even.* We would find profoundly disturbing anyone who genuinely refused to believe that others have minds. In fact, scepticism about other minds is, for anyone not in the grip of some sort of mental illness, surely impossible to believe. The kind of disengagement from others required permanently to maintain the view that, for all you know, they are merely mindless automata is surely the hallmark of a kind of insanity.

And yet, for all that, the dentist's seemingly 'insane' sceptical position may be the rational position to adopt. Perhaps he is right that we're the 'irrational' ones. The onus is clearly on us to explain why belief in the existence of other minds is justified.

Let's now take a look at two well-known attempts to solve this puzzle. The first involves defending the argument from analogy; the second involves an appeal to *logical behaviourism*.

1. Defending the Argument from Analogy

In response to the sceptical argument, you might point out that sometimes we *are* justified in generalising on the basis of a single observed instance.

Suppose I decide to take my Kawazuki K1000 stereo apart to find out how it works. I investigate its inner mechanism and establish how everything functions. Wouldn't I then be justified in concluding that *all* stereos of that make and model have the same sort of internal mechanism? Surely I would. *Yet this would be a generalisation based on a single observed instance*: my own stereo. And if we are sometimes justified in generalising on the basis of a single observed case, then perhaps we are also justified in doing so when it comes to other minds – in which case, the argument from analogy is sound after all.

This is an interesting suggestion. But there are problems with it. True, it seems I am justified in believing that all Kawazuki K1000 stereos have such-and-such an internal mechanism on the basis of having opened up just one. But I am only justified because I am in possession of considerable *background information* about such devices and their inner workings. For example, I know that my Kawazuki K1000 stereo is a piece of machinery mass-produced for profit. I know that it takes a considerable investment in time and money to develop an inner mechanism of this sort. So I know that the Kawazuki Corporation is hardly likely to have bothered developing lots of different internal mechanisms to do the very same job. It's because

---

* In fact, I've made the dentist slightly scarier than a sceptic need be, but I've tried not to overdo it. I didn't want the dentist to appear deliberately cruel and sadistic. After all, if the dentist clearly got some sort of perverse pleasure out of inflicting pain on Finnucane, that would suggest he did, after all, believe that Finnucane had a mind worth torturing.

I possess this sort of background information that I am justified in believing that all the other Kawazuki K1000 stereos have the same sort of inner mechanism.

However, *I am not warranted in generalising on the basis of a single observed case where such background information is missing.* For example, if, for all I knew, each Kawazuki K1000 stereo might just as easily have been made, not by a single manufacturer, but by one of thousands of entrants in a competition to come up with internal machinery that would make these boxes marked 'Kawazuki K1000' behave in the way they do – raising the volume when this knob is turned, changing the radio station when that button is pressed, and so on – then, of course, I am no longer warranted in supposing that the other boxes will contain the same internal machinery.*

So the question is: do I possess the kind of background information necessary to justify my inference about the existence of other minds?

It seems not. In the stereo example, my inference depends on my background knowledge about mass-produced machines and their internal mechanisms. But in the case of other minds, I don't appear to possess this sort of background knowledge. *For my mind is radically unlike anything else I have ever experienced.* For me to conclude that, as I have a mind, so, too, must other humans is akin to my entering a strange land, discovering that the first flower I examine contains a fairy, and then concluding that so, too, must all the other flowers. What I discover inside the first flower is so strange and unusual that no such inference is warranted.

It seems, then, that I'm still not justified in believing that there are minds other than my own.

2. The Logical Behaviourist Approach

Here is a different kind of solution to the puzzle of other minds, the solution offered by the *logical behaviourist.*

Consider the solubility of a sugar cube. Solubility is what is known as a *dispositional* property – its possession by a sugar cube consists of the fact that *if* the cube were placed in water under the right circumstances, *then* it would dissolve. Indeed, it's *true by definition* that something is soluble when it is disposed to dissolve in water, in just the same way that it's true by definition that all stallions are male or that all triangles have three sides.

Now, some philosophers have suggested that mental properties are also dispositional properties. Indeed, some suggest that all talk about minds and what

---

* My example is loosely based on one provided by Peter Carruthers in *Introducing Persons* (London: Routledge, 1986), p. 20.

goes on in them can be translated, without residue, into talk about behavioural dispositions. This is the position of the logical behaviourist.

Take pain, for example. To say that someone is in pain *just is*, according to the logical behaviourist, to say that they are physically disposed to behave in certain ways – to flinch, yell out, and so on. It's true by definition that those in pain are disposed to behave like that. This is not something we need to *discover*.

Logical behaviourism, if true, would neatly solve two classical philosophical problems concerning the mind. First of all, it would explain how material objects, such as our bodies, can possess minds. For an object to have a mind is for it to possess the right sort of behavioural dispositions. That's all there is to it. So we no longer have to make room for mysterious and ghostly extra 'somethings' – minds – in the world, *in addition to* physical objects and their various physical dispositions. The 'ghost in the machine', to borrow the behaviourist Gilbert Ryle's (1900–76) memorable phrase, disappears.

The other classical conundrum that would be solved is, of course, the one we have been discussing here: the problem of explaining how we come by knowledge of the existence of other minds. According to logical behaviourism, what makes the problem of other minds seem so intractable is a certain mistaken conception of what minds are like. If we think of the mind as the elusive 'ghost in the machine', then we are immediately struck by the problem of explaining how we establish the existence of this 'ghost' in others, for all we can observe of other human beings is their outward behaviour. But if Ryle is right, the mind is not a peculiar ghostly 'something' *hidden behind* the outward behaviour. Rather, the mind *just is* a highly complex set of behavioural dispositions.

Just as there is nothing particularly difficult about establishing what dispositional properties – such as solubility – a sugar cube has, so, if Ryle is right, there is nothing particularly difficult about establishing that human beings have minds. You need only establish how they are disposed to behave, and that can be done quite easily. Just as you can have good grounds for supposing that sugar cubes are soluble, so you can have good grounds for supposing that others feel pain.

Attack of the Zombies

Has the logical behaviourist solved the problem of other minds? No. Unfortunately, logical behaviourism is not a particularly plausible theory of the mind. Perhaps the most serious difficulty with it is raised by the *conceptual possibility of zombies*.

In the movies, zombies drool and stumble about. The kind of zombies I have in mind are rather different: their behaviour is exactly the same as that of a minded person. Philosophical zombies, as I shall call them, behave perfectly normally. However, like movie zombies, philosophical zombies have no minds: they are mere meat machines.

Imagine a world physically exactly like this one but populated by philosophical zombies. This imaginary world even contains a zombie version of you: just like you physically, but all is dark within. Of course, it's not remotely likely that this zombie world actually exists. But (and this is the key point) we can at least *make sense* of the possibility of such a world.

Contrast the suggestion that there might be a world that contains non-male stallions or a world that contains triangles with four sides. These worlds don't make sense. For, of course, it is a definitional truth that stallions are male and that triangles have only three sides. A zombie world makes sense in the way that a four-sided triangle world and a non-male stallion world don't.

But here's the problem for logical behaviourism. If logical behaviourism is true, then it should no more make sense to suggest that a zombie world might exist than it does to suggest that a four-sided triangle world might exist. Just as it's true by definition that a triangle has three sides, so it is supposed by the logical behaviourist to be true by definition that any creature that has such-and-such behavioural dispositions has a mind. Zombies, being creatures that lack minds but have the same behavioural dispositions as ourselves, should be ruled out by definition.

But we have just seen that zombies are *not* ruled out by definition. Then it follows that logical behaviourism is false. And if logical behaviourism is false, then it can't be used to solve the puzzle of other minds. The puzzle remains.

Conclusion

Most of us would say that Finnucane's dentist is irrational, insane even. But perhaps it is we who are irrational, not the dentist. Can I rationally defend my belief that there are minds other than my own?

I don't yet see how.

What to read next

Chapter 3, Brain-Snatched, and Chapter 14, Why Expect the Sun to Rise Tomorrow?, discuss other varieties of scepticism: scepticism about the external world and scepticism about the unobserved.

Further reading

Anita Avramides, *Other Minds* (London: Routledge, 2001).

K. T. Maslin, *An Introduction to the Philosophy of Mind* (Cambridge: Polity, 2001), Chapter 8.

9

BUT IS IT ART?

'I mean, they'd gone and fucking installed the work without me even being here. That's just not on. This is my bed. If someone else installs it, it's just dirty linen. If I do it, it's art!'

Tracey Emin (artist), quoted in *Evening Standard*, 12 September 2000

Today it seems that almost anything can be classified as a work of art: Damien Hirst's pickled shark or Tracey Emin's unmade bed, for example. But what is art, exactly? What is it that *Macbeth*, a piece of tribal sculpture, *The Nutcracker*, the ceiling of the Sistine Chapel and Emin's bed all have in common? What is the common denominator that makes each one of these things art? This is an extremely difficult question to answer. Here I explain one of the leading theories, taking in one of Ludwig Wittgenstein's (1889–1951) most important insights along the way.

What Is a Work of Art?

The scene: an art gallery. Fox, an artist, is peering intently at a Rothko. O'Corky tries to engage him in conversation.

O'Corky: You know, I'm just not sure it's art.
Fox: Of course it's art. It's hanging in an art gallery, isn't it?
O'Corky: So *you* know art when you see it, do you?
Fox: I'm an artist myself. I have exhibits in the next gallery.
O'Corky: Well, if you're an artist yourself, you if anyone should know what art is.
Fox: I suppose so.
O'Corky: So tell me, *what is art?*

This deceptively simple-looking question can quickly tie you up in knots. We ordinarily *think* we know what art is. But *do* we? In fact, we can easily construct counterexamples to most of the more obvious definitions of art. Take Fox's first attempt, for instance:

Fox: It seems to me that what qualifies something as a work of art is the fact that it is designed to be pleasing to our senses, to be *beautiful*.

O'Corky: That won't do. Much traditional art is pretty. But there are works of art that are not and were not even intended to be at all beautiful. Take Tracey Emin's unmade bed over there, for example. It's not particularly attractive, is it?

Fox: Well, I suppose not.

O'Corky: Yet you say it's art, don't you?

Fox: Er, yes.

O'Corky: So there you are: it's not necessary for a work of art to be beautiful.

In order to try to deal with O'Corky's objection, Fox might insist that Emin's bed *is* in its own way beautiful. But then pretty much every artefact ends up qualifying as 'beautiful' in this weak sense, even my socks. Yet my socks are not a work of art.

Alternatively, Fox might insist that Emin's bed is not *really* art, and so doesn't provide a counterexample to Fox's definition after all. Certainly, many believe there is something of the emperor's new clothes about the suggestion that an unmade bed might be a work of art. But we probably ought to be a little wary of such sceptical attitudes. Look back at the history of art and you will find that almost every new development met the reactionary claim that 'it's not really art'. That was exactly the attitude of many towards Impressionism, for example.

Thinking Tools: The Search for Necessary and Sufficient Conditions

In pursuing the question 'what is art?' we are seeking a certain sort of *definition*. Here are three examples of the kind of definition I have in mind:

- Necessarily: something is a vixen if and only if it's a female fox.
- Necessarily: someone is a brother if and only if he's a male sibling.
- Necessarily: something is a triangle if and only if it's a three-straight-sided plane figure.

These are very unusual definitions. Each picks out a feature (or combination of features) *that all and only* the so-and-sos have, not just in the *actual* situation, but *in any possible* situation. For example, in any possible situation all and only the vixens are going to be both female and foxes.

We are pursuing a similar definition of art. We want the following filled out:

- Necessarily: something is a work of art if and only if . . .

It won't satisfy us, therefore, to explain what a work of art is simply by pointing out a few examples. Nor will it do to pick out some feature or features that works of art happen, merely as a matter of fact, to possess.

We want to know what is *essential*. We want to know what *in any possible situation* is true of all and only works of art. To adopt the jargon: we want to identify that feature, possession of which is *both necessary and sufficient* to qualify something as a work of art. I call such definitions *philosophical definitions*.

The Method of Counterexamples

Fox's definition of art clearly fails to meet O'Corky's exacting standards. While it might be true of many works of art that they are beautiful, being beautiful is clearly not a *necessary* requirement. O'Corky demonstrates this by coming up with a *counterexample*.

A counterexample to a philosophical definition of *X* is some actual or possible thing that either: (i) is an example of *X* but fails to fit the definition, or (ii) fits the definition but is not an example of *X*. O'Corky criticises Fox's definition by coming up with a counterexample of the first sort: Tracey Emin's bed is a piece of art but it's not beautiful.

Fox has another attempt at producing a philosophical definition of art.

Fox: I think I can do better. Art need not be beautiful. It's enough that it *engage* us. A work of art is simply that which is made to *entertain* us.

O'Corky: You're wrong, I'm afraid. Much that's designed to entertain is not art. The game of hangman is not art but it engages and entertains. Toys,

card games – there are innumerable things that entertain that
aren't art.

O'Corky has again come up with counterexamples. Notice that, this time, his
counterexamples are all of the *second* sort: though they do fit the suggested
definition, they aren't art. Being engaging and entertaining are not *sufficient* to
qualify something as a work of art.

And so the conversation continues. Fox comes up with various definitions of art,
including the suggestions that art is, in essence, that which is designed to
communicate some emotion, or that which has no purpose. But in each case O'Corky
manages to devise a counterexample (you might wish to work out your own
counterexamples to these suggestions).

O'Corky: You see. You thought you knew what art is. But you don't. Not one of
              your definitions has been correct. In fact, neither of us knows what
              art is!

Fox: I must admit that it's harder to define 'art' than I thought. Still, I'm
              not sure it follows that we don't know what art is. After all, we both
              recognise that these counterexamples to my definitions are good
              counterexamples. How could we do that if we didn't know what
              art is?

This is a good question. On the one hand, our inability to give a philosophical
definition of art seems to indicate that we don't know what art is. Yet, on the other
hand, we are able to recognise the failings of the definitions that have been offered.
So it seems that, at *some* level, we *do* know what art is.

Socrates and the Method of Counterexamples

O'Corky and Fox are having a discussion of a fairly common sort. You hear similar
conversations at dinner parties and in cafés. Some of the earliest examples are found
in the dialogues of the ancient Greek philosopher Plato (c. 428–347 BC). In Plato's
dialogues, a character called Socrates, a real person about whom comparatively
little is known and from whom Plato developed many of his own ideas, asks of
various individuals, 'What is beauty?', 'What is justice?', 'What is courage?', 'What
is knowledge?', and so on. Socrates was also after philosophical definitions of these

things. In each case, despite the fact that those of whom Socrates asks such questions are often supposed to exhibit the quality in question (for example, he asks a soldier what *courage* is), Socrates always manages to come up with a counterexample to their suggested definition.

In Plato's dialogues, Socrates concludes that while we might *think* that we know what beauty, justice and courage are, in fact we *don't* know. O'Corky, after constructing counterexamples to the definitions that Fox offers him, similarly concludes that neither he nor O'Corky know what art is, despite the fact that Fox is himself an artist.

The history of Western philosophy is in large part constituted by similar dialogues between philosophers pursuing philosophical definitions. A what-is-X? question is asked. A philosopher comes up with a suggestion. A counterexample is produced. Another definition is offered. Another counterexample produced. And so on. In most cases we have still not succeeded in pinning down what's essential. The essence of art, beauty, justice, and so on is, it seems, highly mysterious, the quest to reveal it producing a kind of mental cramp.

Wittgenstein on Family Resemblance

In his *Philosophical Investigations*, Wittgenstein tries to provide therapy for this cramp. Wittgenstein suggests that the philosophical quest to reveal these hidden essences is actually a wild-goose chase.

Take a look at the following faces.

You will notice a 'family resemblance'. All the faces resemble each other to a certain extent. *Some* have the same pointy chin. *Some* have wavy eyebrows. *Some*

have big ears. However, there is no *one* feature that all the faces have in common. Rather, there's an overlapping series of similarities that links them together.

Wittgenstein suggests that very many of our concepts are similarly 'family resemblance' concepts. He illustrates his suggestion with the example of a game.

> Consider for example the proceedings that we call 'games'. I mean board-games, card-games, ball-games, Olympic games, and so on. What is common to them all? – Don't say: 'There must be something common, or they would not be called "games", – For if you look at them you will not see something that is common to all, but similarities, relationships, and a whole series of them at that. To repeat: don't think, but look! – Look for example at board-games, with their multifarious relationships. Now pass to card-games; here you find many correspondences with the first group, but many common features drop out, and others appear. When we pass next to ball-games, much that is common is retained, but much is lost. – Are they all 'amusing'? Compare chess with noughts and crosses. Or is there always winning and losing, or competition between players? Think of patience. In ball-games there is winning and losing; but when a child throws his ball at the wall and catches it again, this feature has disappeared . . . [T]he result of this examination is: we see a complicated network of similarities overlapping and criss-crossing: sometimes overall similarities, sometimes similarities of detail. I can think of no better expression to characterise these similarities than 'family resemblances'; for the various resemblances between members of a family: build, features, colour of eyes, gait, temperament, etc. etc. overlap and criss-cross in the same way. – And I shall say: 'games' form a family.*

O'Corky and Fox both assume that there *must* be one feature that all works of art have in common – that feature that makes them works of art. Many philosophers of art make the same assumption. Here is Clive Bell, for example:

> For either all works of visual art have some common quality, or when we speak of 'works of art' we gibber . . . There must be some one quality without which a work of art cannot exist . . . What is this quality?[†]

But why assume there must be one such feature? Why assume that, unless there is such a feature, when we speak of 'works of art' we must gibber? Perhaps art

---

* Ludwig Wittgenstein, *Philosophical Investigations*, Part I, Sections 66–7.
† Clive Bell, 'Significant Form', in Nigel Warburton (ed.), *Philosophy: Basic Readings* (London: Routledge, 1999), p. 373.

is also a family resemblance concept. Perhaps there is merely an overlapping pattern of resemblances between works of art, just as in the case of games. Perhaps our inability to pin down the elusive, hidden essence of art is due, not to ignorance on our part, but to the mistaken assumption with which we begin – that there *is* such an essence. In Wittgenstein's view, the feeling that we have failed to capture what is essential is produced in part by the assumption that our ordinary everyday explanations of what we mean by 'art' are somehow inadequate, that they fail to penetrate to the essence of the phenomenon. In Wittgenstein's view, art's hidden essence is a philosophical illusion.

Of course, it's not just the common nouns 'game' and 'art' to which Wittgenstein's notion of family resemblance applies. We have seen that a similar sort of intellectual cramp can be produced by asking the questions: 'What is knowledge?', 'What is courage?' and 'What is justice?'. It's even possible to produce the cramp by asking the question about ordinary household objects.

Try, for example, to provide a philosophical definition of the noun 'chair'. You will find that it's not as easy as you might have thought. There are four-legged chairs, three-legged chairs, even one-legged chairs. There are chairs with backs and chairs without. There are chairs with and without armrests. Some chairs are designed to be sat on, but not all (something might be used as and even properly described as a chair even though it was never designed for that purpose: for example, we can imagine a cave dweller pointing to a chair-shaped rock and saying, quite correctly, 'That's my chair'). And not everything that's regularly used for sitting on is a chair (a conveniently situated log might be used that way, for example). So what *is* a chair? What's the essential 'something' that, necessarily, all and only chairs have? The answer, perhaps, is that there is no such 'something'. 'Chair' is also a family resemblance concept.

Can Art Be Defined by a Formula?

Someone might insist that, even if there is no one feature common and peculiar to all works of art, nevertheless we should in principle be able to construct a *formula* that captures some more complex set of rules determining what is and isn't art.

Here's an example of such a formula. Suppose I introduce the term 'fubbyloofer' like so:

Necessarily: something is a fubbyloofer if and only if it has at least three of the following six characteristics: wheels, steering wheel, engine, lights, suspension, seats.

Notice there is no feature that all fubbyloofers need have in common.

Some fubbyloofers

Still, the conditions under which something qualifies as a fubbyloofer are neatly captured by my formula. Similarly, even if there's no one feature that all works of art need have in common, shouldn't we at least be able to construct a formula that neatly sets out precisely what is meant by 'art'? Indeed, until we are able to produce such a formula, don't we somehow remain ignorant about what art is?

Not according to Wittgenstein, who again draws our attention back to games.

What does it mean to know what a game is? What does it mean, to know it and not be able to say it? Is this knowledge somehow equivalent to an unformulated definition? So that if it were formulated I should be able to recognise it as the expression of my knowledge? Isn't my knowledge, my concept of a game, completely expressed in the explanations that I could give? That is, in my describing examples of various kinds of game; showing how all sorts of other games can be constructed on the analogy of these; saying that I should scarcely include this or this among games; and so on.[*]

According to Wittgenstein, our ordinary explanations of what we mean by 'game' – explanations that involve giving examples, drawing attention to similarities and differences, and so on – already capture precisely what we mean by the term. The illusion of hidden depths to our language, depths that we must dig down to and formalise if we are truly to understand what 'game' means, is generated by a failure to notice how our language actually functions. We don't usually set up clear rules or boundaries fixing exactly what does and does not fall under a given concept. The practice of using a term like 'game' is much more spontaneous and fluid than that. And there can be nothing more to the meaning of a term than is revealed in our ordinary practices of using and explaining its meaning to each other (otherwise how could we succeed in *learning* this meaning or *teaching* it to others?).

In short, we already know perfectly well what 'game' means. Nothing is hidden. In Wittgenstein's view, any formula that attempts to capture with more precision what we mean by 'game' can only succeed in introducing *new* boundaries around what we mean, not reveal existing ones.

And the same, you might argue, is true of 'art', as well as a great many other terms.

The Institutional Theory

Some philosophers impressed by Wittgenstein's comments about family resemblance still insist that a philosophical definition of art is possible. They admit that, were one to line up all and only those items that we call art and examine them one by one, one wouldn't discover a common feature that everything else lacks. But still, art *can* be defined. According to the *institutional theory*, just two things are required if something is to qualify as a work of art.

First, it must be an artefact, an artefact being something that has been worked on. The expression 'worked on' is used quite loosely here – merely placing something in an art gallery counts as 'working on' it. So a pebble deliberately positioned in an art gallery qualifies as an artefact.

* Ludwig Wittgenstein, *Philosophical Investigations*, Part I, Section 75.

Secondly, the artefact in question must have had the status of a work of art bestowed on it by some member of the 'art world', such as an author, gallery owner, publisher, collector or artist.

The institutional theory has the advantage of explaining why O'Corky and Fox are having difficulty in finding that feature which is shared by all and only works of art. What qualifies an artefact as a work of art is not an intrinsic, *exhibited* feature of the object, but rather the attitude of members of a certain community towards it. What makes all and only *these* things works of art is not a feature one might discover by closely observing them.

According to the institutional theory, members of the art world have the uncanny ability to make something a work of art just by deeming it to be one. A few years ago a cleaner left her bucket and mop in a modern art gallery. Passers-by took the bucket and mop to be a work of art. They were wrong, of course. But according to the institutional theory, if Tracey Emin had left the bucket and mop there as an exhibit, the passers-by would have been right: those cleaning materials *would* have constituted a work of art. The institutional theory explains why this is so. It explains what is otherwise very difficult to explain: namely, why, despite the fact that while two mass-produced buckets with mops may be absolutely indistinguishable in every observable respect, one is a work of art but not the other.

Criticism of the Institutional Theory

Some philosophers criticise the institutional theory on the grounds that, while it might tell us that members of the art community bestow on objects the status of art, it doesn't explain *why* they do so. Clearly, there are *reasons* why the status of art is bestowed on some objects but not others, reasons that the artist and other members of the art world can and often do give. The institutional theory fails to mention these reasons. It's therefore inadequate as a definition of art (one might also add that, if these reasons determine what is and isn't art, then shouldn't we aim clearly to specify these reasons – wouldn't that be philosophically far more informative than simply saying, 'Art is whatever members of the art world decide to call art'?).

Someone might also object that merely placing an object in a gallery does *not* make it a work of art, no matter who places it there. Even if Tracey Emin did place a bucket and mop in a gallery, these objects would *not* thereby come to be a work of art.

A defender of the institutional theory may insist that these objections muddle up two quite distinct issues. They may suggest that we need to distinguish art in the 'classificatory' sense from art in the 'evaluative' sense. Sometimes, by calling something a 'work of art', we don't just classify it as such, but we *evaluate* it: we are recommending it for appreciation. This evaluative sense is not what the institutional theory is concerned with, however. The first objection is therefore confused: it's asking for the reasons why we consider this or that worthy of appreciation, but these reasons don't determine what art is in the classificatory sense.

Arguably, the second objection also involves a muddle: that between art and good art. Perhaps an Emin-exhibited mop would not be *good* art. That doesn't entail that it wouldn't *be* art.

Another counterexample to the institutional theory is provided by the paintings of Alfred Wallis. Wallis painted seascapes in a primitive and haunting style. Wallis did not himself believe that what he was producing was art. But neither did any member of the art world at the time his earliest work was produced. The early pieces were recognised as art only later. But this entails that *at the time Wallis produced his first paintings, they weren't art*. They only became art later. But this is counter-intuitive. Surely it's true to say that what Wallis first produced was art, great art, even at the time he produced it. It simply wasn't recognised as such.

It seems, then, that even the institutional theory won't do.

The 'Definition Game'

In this chapter we have been playing a famous kind of philosophical 'game' – what one might call *the definition game*. We've been hunting for that feature (or combination of features), possession of which is both necessary and sufficient to qualify something as a work of art. Even the institutional theory claims that there is such a feature (it merely denies that it's an *exhibited* feature). But perhaps there really is no such feature. Perhaps we have been hunting for what doesn't exist. One of Wittgenstein's great contributions to philosophy was to question the assumption that lies behind this millennia-old game.

When next you hear a dinner-party guest playing the definition game with 'art' (or any other common noun, for that matter), try a Wittgensteinian approach. Ask him or her why they assume that there *must be* something that all and only works of art have in common.

What to read next

For another example of how the definition game is played, try Chapter 19, What Is Knowledge?. You'll find the method of counterexamples is also used repeatedly. Might Wittgenstein's comments about family resemblance be relevant there, too?

In Chapter 16, The Meaning Mystery, I explain more of Wittgenstein's views on meaning.

Further reading

Clive Bell, 'Significant Form', which appears as Chapter 40 of Nigel Warburton (ed.), *Philosophy: Basic Readings* (London: Routledge, 1999).

Nigel Warburton, *The Art Question* (London: Routledge, 2002).

1 0

CAN WE HAVE MORALITY WITHOUT GOD AND RELIGION?

It's widely held that morality requires both God and religion. Without God to lay down moral rules, talk of 'right' and 'wrong' can reflect nothing more than our own subjective preferences. Without religion to provide us with moral guidance, we are set adrift, morally rudderless, with moral chaos the inevitable result.

Daniel P. Moloney, writing in *American Prospect*, provides an example of this popular belief:

> Religious people are the first to admit that many religious people sin often and boldly, and that atheists often act justly. They explain these ethical atheists by noting that when atheists reject the religion in which they have been raised, they tend to keep the morality while discarding its theological foundation. Their ethical behavior is then derivative and parasitic, borrowing its conscience from a culture permeated by religion; it cannot survive if the surrounding religious culture is not sustained. In short, morality as we know it cannot be maintained without Judeo-Christian religion.*

Is the view that morality as we know it is ultimately dependent on God and religion actually correct? This chapter introduces some of the key philosophical arguments.

An Argument

The scene: Mr and Mrs Schnapper are arguing about whether to send their son Tom to a religious school. Mrs Schnapper believes they should. Mr Schnapper, an atheist, disagrees.

Mrs S: Tom should go to a religious school. All children should. Without religion to provide us with a firm foundation, morality collapses.

Mr S: Why?

---

* Quoted at www.prospect.org/controversy/lieberman/moloney-d-1.html

Mrs S: If there's no God to lay down what is right and what is wrong, then *things are right or wrong only because we say so*. But that makes morality unacceptably *relative* and *arbitrary*.

Mr Schnapper scratches his head.

Mr S: Why *relative*?
Mrs S: If things are right or wrong only because *we* say so, then for those who say killing is wrong, it is, and for those who say it's right, it is.
Mr S: I guess that's true.
Mrs S: But morality *isn't* relative, is it? Even if we said that killing is right, it would *still* be wrong. The fact is that killing is wrong *anyway*, whatever we might have to say about it. Right?

Mr Schnapper nods.

Mr S: Yes. Though I still don't see why the view that things are right or wrong only because we say so makes morality *arbitrary.*
Mrs S: If things are right or wrong only because *we* say so, then *before* we say so, nothing is right or wrong. Right?
Mr S: Yes.
Mrs S: But then our decision about what to call 'right' and what to call 'wrong' must be, from a *moral* perspective, entirely arbitrary.

An Argument for the Existence of God

Mr Schnapper is happy to agree that morality certainly isn't a matter of personal preference.

Mr S: OK, I'm happy to agree that killing *really is* wrong. It's not wrong simply because *we* say it is.
Mrs S: But then you must admit that the only reason killing *really is* wrong is that *God* says it is.
Mr S: So you argue like this: things aren't right or wrong simply because *we* say so; they are right or wrong *anyway*. But that can only be because there exists a God to say what is right and what is wrong. So, as

I agree that things aren't right or wrong simply because we say so, I
must accept that God exists. In effect, you're giving me *an argument
for the existence of God.*

Mrs S: Exactly.

Plato's Refutation of the Popular Argument

Mrs Schnapper's conclusion that morality is dependent on God is not new.
Fyodor Dostoevsky (1821–81) is supposed to have claimed that 'If there is no God,
then all things are permitted'. Even many atheists, including Jean-Paul Sartre
(1905–80), have been prepared to accept the same conclusion.

Mrs Schnapper's argument is certainly popular. But is it cogent?

Let's agree, for the sake of argument, that Mr and Mrs Schnapper are correct
when they suppose that things aren't right or wrong simply because we say so. Does
it follow that morality must come from God?

No, it doesn't follow. Mrs Schnapper believes that in the absence of God
morality becomes relative and arbitrary. But, as we're about to discover, the view
that morality is laid down not by us but by God actually makes it no less relative
and arbitrary.

The flaw in Mrs Schnapper's argument was first pointed out by Plato
(c. 428–347 BC) in his dialogue the *Euthyphro.* The difficulty becomes apparent once
we press the following question:

Are things wrong because God says so, or does God say that they are wrong
because they are?

This question raises a dilemma for Mrs Schnapper, for she can give neither answer.

Let's consider the second answer first: God says that things are wrong because
they are. God, being infinitely knowledgeable and wise, *recognises* the wrongness
of certain courses of action and tells us about it.

From Mrs Schnapper's point of view, the difficulty with this answer is that it
undermines her argument. If Mrs Schnapper concedes that God isn't required to
make things wrong – there is a standard of right or wrong that exists independently
of God's will – then her case against atheism collapses. For an atheist can then help
him or herself to this same independent moral standard.

Now let's turn to the first answer: things are wrong *because* God says so. That is to say, God actually *makes* certain courses of action wrong by decreeing them to be so. Had God decreed that killing is a good thing to go in for, then it would have been.

Unfortunately for Mrs Schnapper, this answer also undermines her argument. Mrs Schnapper argued that killing cannot be wrong merely because *we* say so: that would make right and wrong relative and arbitrary. But, as Mr Schnapper now points out, the suggestion that things are wrong only because God says so makes morality no less relative and arbitrary.

Mr S: In your view, morality is *relative* to whatever God says, correct?

Mrs S: Yes.

Mr S: If God had said that killing is right, then it would have been. True?

Mrs S: I suppose so.

Mr S: But a minute ago you said that killing is wrong *anyway*, whatever *we* might have to say about it. Well, surely the same is true of God: killing is wrong *anyway*, whatever God might have to say about it. So you see, in your view, morality is no less unacceptably relative.

Mr S: Also your view that things are right or wrong only because God says so makes morality *arbitrary*.

Mrs S: Why do you say that?

Mr S: You believe that killing is wrong not because *we* say so, but because *God* says so.

Mrs S:	That's right.
Mr S:	But then you must believe that, *prior* to God decreeing that killing is wrong, it *wasn't* wrong.
Mrs S:	Yes, I suppose I do.
Mr S:	But then, from a *moral* perspective, God's choice was *entirely arbitrary.* Morally speaking, He might just as well have flipped a coin. So you see, the very same problems that you had with the view that things are right or wrong only because *we* say so are also problems for the theory that things are right or wrong only because *God* says so.

Surely Mr Schnapper is right: if Mrs Schnapper's objections to the view that morality is ultimately laid down by us are good objections, then they are just as effective against her own view that morality is laid down by God.

Mr S:	So, *by your own reasoning*, we should agree that morality is ultimately independent of both our own will *and God's too.*

The view that things are right or wrong simply because God says so is called the *divine command theory*. Those who believe in God are certainly not obliged to accept the divine command theory. In fact, many important theists, including St Thomas Aquinas (1225–74) and Gottfried Leibniz (1646–1716), reject the divine command theory precisely because they recognise that it falls foul of Plato's dilemma.

The 'But God Is Good' Reply

In defence of the divine command theory, Mrs Schnapper might claim that while killing is wrong only because God says so, God never would have said otherwise. This is because God is good. A good God would never instruct us to go round murdering each other.

One difficulty with this reply is that by describing God as 'good', we presumably mean *morally* good. But on the divine command theory, to say that God is morally good is to say no more than that He says He is. But then that is something that even a God who instructs us to murder each other can say.

The Commands-Need-a-Commander Argument

Mrs Schnapper's first argument for morality being dependent on God fails. But she's not disheartened. She has another argument up her sleeve.

Mrs S: Look, moral principles take the form of *commands*, don't they? They say, 'Do not kill', 'Do not steal', and so on.

Mr S: Yes, they do.

Mrs S: Now, these commands are not simply *our* commands, are they?

Mr S: I've already agreed that things aren't wrong simply because we say so.

Mrs S: Well, where there is a command, there must be someone who has issued that command. If the command-issuer is not us, then who is it?

Mr S: God, you will no doubt say.

Mrs S: Precisely. So the existence of moral commands requires the existence of God.

Again, this is a well-worn line of argument. Unfortunately for Mrs Schnapper, it's also flawed.

Refutation of the Commands-Need-a-Commander Argument

One of the flaws in Mrs Schnapper's second argument becomes apparent once we ask why we ought to obey God's commands.

Mr S: But why ought I to obey God? The mere fact that someone issues commands does not entail that anyone ought to obey them. If I command you to do the washing-up, that does not put you under any moral obligation to do it, does it?

Mrs S: Definitely not.

Mr S: So why ought we to obey God's commands? You want to ground all moral obligations in God's commands. But commands, by themselves, do not generate moral obligations.

Mrs S: *Your* commands do not create moral obligations. But God's commands do.

Mr S: Why?

This is a question that those who wish to ground morality in God's commands need to answer. Mrs Schnapper makes the following suggestion.

Mrs S: Because we are already under a *general* moral obligation to obey God, that's why.

Mr S: But why, in turn, does this *general* obligation exist?

Mrs S: H'm. Good question.

Mr S: The problem you face is this. You want to ground *all* moral obligations in God's commands. But that raises the question of why we are morally obliged to obey God's commands. So there is still an obligation that you have yet to account for.

Mrs S: Perhaps this general obligation exists because God commands us to obey all His commands.

Mr S: I'm afraid that won't do. After all, *I* can command you to obey all *my* commands, but that *still* doesn't put you under any moral obligation to do the washing-up, does it?

Mrs S: No, I guess not.

The attempt to ground moral obligation in God's commands is doomed to fail. For commands can generate moral obligations only where there already exists a moral obligation to obey them. So the divine command theory of moral obligation actually ends up presupposing what it is supposed to account for: the existence of moral obligations.

We have just looked at two arguments for the conclusion that only a theist can allow for genuine moral value. We have also seen that neither argument is cogent.

Will We Be Good without God?

Let's turn to a slightly different sort of argument. Mrs Schnapper now suggests, not that there *cannot* be good without God, but that we *will not* be good without God.

Mrs S: Perhaps you're right. Perhaps atheists need be no more or less committed to morality being relative and arbitrary than theists. Still, without God we no longer have any real *motivation* to behave morally, have we? We're unlikely to bother with being good unless we believe that God exists.

Mr S: Why not?

Mrs S: Because it's our fear of divine disapproval and punishment that keeps
           us in line. Unless we believe that there is a God, any reason we might
           have for behaving well evaporates. *That's* why we should send Tom to
           a religious school.

Many agree with Mrs Schnapper that unless people believe in God they are unlikely
to act morally. Voltaire (1694–1778), for example, refused to allow his friends to discuss
atheism in front of his servants, saying: 'I want my lawyer, tailor, valets, even my wife
to believe in God. I think that if they do I shall be robbed less and cheated less.'

But is it true that unless we believe in God we are unlikely to behave morally?
Many now happily admit to being atheists. Yet these atheists do, for the most part,
behave pretty morally.

Indeed, as Mr Schnapper now argues, it's difficult to defend even the view that
theists are *more* likely to be moral than atheists.[*]

Mr S: While there have been many selfless and noble believers, there have
           also been a great many self-serving and ignoble ones. There are
           innumerable examples of disgustingly brutal and immoral things
           being done in God's name, from the Crusades to the Spanish
           Inquisition to the destruction of the World Trade Center. In fact, it
           seems to me that religious belief is just as likely to promote
           immorality as it is morality.

Mrs S: Perhaps.

As Mr Schnapper also points out, those who do the right thing primarily out of fear
are not generally considered particularly morally worthy.

Mr S: Someone who does the right thing, not out of fear of punishment, but
           out of respect and concern for other human beings, is surely far more
           moral than is someone who acts solely out of fear of punishment. So
           it seems to me that if, as you suggest, the religious do the right thing
           mainly out of fear, then they are actually *less* moral than are atheists
           who do it out of respect and concern for others.

---

[*] Incidentally, statistics indicate that, among US citizens, those who believe in God are over forty times
more likely to end up in prison than are atheists. See, for example, www.freethought.freeservers.com/
reason/crimestats.html Of course, these statistics do not establish that religion is actually a *cause* of
unlawful behaviour. Belief in God is more prevalent among the less well-off, who are also much more
likely to end up in prison.

Mrs Schnapper is prepared to admit that someone who acts simply out of fear is not particularly moral.

Mrs S: You may be right. But not *all* religious people do the right thing out of fear, do they? It's only those who do who fall foul of your criticism.

Mr S: That's true.

Mrs S: And suppose I concede that most atheists *do* seem to behave morally, perhaps even as morally as those who believe in God? Still, that may only be because they have been brought up within a culture that has or, until recently, had a strong religious tradition. Whether or not they realise it, the atheist's ethical commitments derive from that religious tradition. But if religion continues to wane, moral chaos must be the inevitable result. First-generation atheists may not be particularly immoral. Second- or third-generation atheists will be.

Mr S: An intriguing suggestion. But you haven't given me the slightest reason to suppose it's *true*, have you?

Mrs S: Well, not yet, no.

Mr S: In fact, not only have you not given me any reason to suppose it's true, but it's very obviously *not* true.

Mrs S: How do you know?

Mr S: Because there have been cultures that have had a highly developed morality, but that have either not had religion, or else have not had a religion that's much concerned with laying down morality.

Mrs S: For example?

Mr S: The ancient Greeks. They weren't perfect, of course. They had slavery. But then so did the highly religious southern states of America. The ancient Greeks were morally sophisticated. Their moral code was very similar to our own. They, too, thought it wrong to murder, steal, and so on. Ancient Greece was a civilised place to live in. Yet their religion was not particularly concerned with laying down right and wrong in the way ours is. You don't find Zeus and the other Greek gods handing down moral commandments.

Mrs S: Interesting.

Mr S: In ancient Greece, religion and morality were largely separate domains. So there have been entire civilisations – morally highly

> developed civilisations – that have done very well indeed without a
> religiously based morality.
>
> Mrs S: Perhaps that's true.
> Mr S: So then why send Tom to a religious school? Your claim that, without
>   a religiously based morality, civilisation must inevitably collapse just
>   doesn't hold water.

As most societies that we would call civilised also have (or, until recently, had) a moralizing religion, many infer that a moralising religion must be a necessary condition of both morality and civilisation. Take away the moralising religion and morality and civilisation will inevitably collapse.

But of course, the mere fact that civilisations tend to have moralising religions doesn't establish that such religions are a necessary condition of civilisation. After all, most successful civilisations tend to have swimming pools, yet no one would suggest that without swimming pools civilisation will collapse, would they?

True, there is no obvious link between swimming pools and morality, as there is between religion and morality. But, as Mr Schnapper points out, the religions of several successful civilisations – including those found in ancient Rome and Greece – have been largely unconcerned with laying down right and wrong. Still more interestingly, when religions do go in for moralising, it turns out to be roughly the same moral code they lay down every time, even when the religions involved otherwise differ greatly. All this tends to suggest, not that morality and civilisation cannot flourish without a moralising religion, but that moralising religions reflect a morality that exists and is inclined to flourish in any case. There seems to be a more or less universal moral code – a code that includes prohibitions on murder and stealing, for example – to which human beings are drawn anyway. Where religion exists, it tends not to challenge this basic code but merely to formalise it and add a few refinements of its own (such as prohibitions on eating certain foodstuffs).

Daniel P. Moloney, quoted at the beginning of this chapter, boldly asserts that the atheist's morality is parasitic upon religious morality (and Judeo-Christian morality at that). In fact, Moloney appears to have things back to front: it seems that *religious morality is ultimately parasitic upon non-religious morality.*

Is Moral Knowledge Dependent on Religion?

Many believe that, without religion, moral knowledge is impossible. Only a religious text and tradition can provide us with the kind of objective yardstick we need if we are to be able to distinguish what *is* right from what merely *seems* right to us. Or so Mrs Schnapper now argues.

Mrs S: There's still a huge problem facing atheists like yourself, a problem we believers do not face. The problem is to explain how we come by moral *knowledge*.

Mr S: What's the problem?

Mrs S: Morality is rooted in religious texts such as the Bible. There's the authority of a text and a tradition to which believers can appeal. If I want to know whether something is wrong, I look to the Bible. There's something firm and immovable to which I can turn for guidance.

Mr S: Like a lighthouse in a storm?

Mrs S: Exactly. But atheists are cast adrift without any means of distinguishing right from wrong except how they feel. Atheists lack the lighthouse of an external authority to which they can turn for help. Morally speaking, there's no way for atheists to distinguish how things *seem* to them from how things *really* are.

Mr S: I see.

Mrs S: But if you cannot distinguish appearance from reality, then you cannot be said to *know*, can you?

Mr S: I suppose not.

Mrs S: But then atheists can't really to be said to *know* right from wrong, can they? So you see, for moral knowledge you need religion.

Again, this is a prevalent line of argument. But Mr Schnapper is not persuaded.

Mr S: I don't see that the religious have any less of a problem with moral knowledge.

Mrs S: Why not?

Mr S: Well, as I've already pointed out, it's not true that morality is inseparable from and rooted in religion. The ancient Greeks were

	morally pretty sophisticated and aware. Yet their religion didn't lay down moral commandments.
Mrs S:	True.
Mr S:	So it seems that humans have an in-built sense of right and wrong that operates *anyway*, independently of their exposure to religion. Indeed, even those who believe in God need to rely on this prior moral sense in deciding whether or not to continue to accept the religion in which they were brought up. They also need to rely on it when deciding how to interpret that religion's commandments.
Mrs S:	How do you mean?
Mr S:	Well, Leviticus says that it is sinful to lend money for interest, to eat shellfish and to wear jackets made from a linen/wool mix. The New Testament also suggests that the rich should give away their money. Yet you, a Christian, ignore all these biblical instructions.
Mrs S:	Yes, I suppose I do.
Mr S:	The Bible also says that it is wrong to kill. Yet plenty of Christians favour the death penalty. So these Christians have a particular *interpretation* of that commandment, don't they?
Mrs S:	Yes. They interpret it to mean something like: 'Don't kill the innocent.'
Mr S:	Right. So Christians pick and choose from what it says in the Bible, and then go on to interpret those passages they are prepared to accept in sometimes highly idiosyncratic ways. Now, how do they do this without relying on some *prior* moral sense?
Mrs S:	I'm not sure.
Mr S:	You see? How to tell right from wrong is no less a problem for the religious than it is for the atheist. I admit there *is* a difficulty about explaining how we come by moral knowledge. But religion doesn't solve that problem.

Certainly, we are usually prepared to accept a religion only to the extent that its moral code coheres with our existing moral point of view. Those parts that clash with the dominant moral perspective tend either to be ignored (like the Old Testament prohibition on eating shellfish or the New Testament's insistence that a rich man is no more likely to enter the kingdom of heaven than a camel is likely to pass through the eye of a needle) or reinterpreted.

Conclusion

My conclusion is not that we shouldn't attempt morally to educate our children. In fact, I can't think of anything more important. Nor am I suggesting that this should never be done in religious schools. My aim has simply been to question the increasingly popular assumptions that morality is dependent on God and religion, that there cannot be moral value without God, and that we will not be good unless religion is there to show us the way.

What to read next

Chapters 7, Does God Exist?, and Chapter 1, Where Did the Universe Come From?, also discuss arguments for and against the existence of God.

Further reading

James Rachels, *The Elements of Moral Philosophy* (Singapore: McGraw-Hill, 1999), Chapter 4.

11

IS CREATIONISM SCIENTIFIC?

What makes for a good scientific theory? The answer to this question isn't as obvious as you might think. Even scientists struggle with it. This chapter examines the claims and methods of creationists in order to bring out some of the difficulties in pinning down precisely what good science really is.

Creationism *v.* Orthodox Science

Creationists believe that the biblical account of the creation of the universe is literally true. God brought into existence the earth and all its life forms in just six days. According to creationists, this event took place less than 10,000 years ago (they base their calculation of the age of the universe on the number of generations listed in the Bible). They also believe that the biblical account is at least as well supported by the available scientific evidence as its rival.

The overwhelming majority of contemporary scientists, however, hold that the universe is much, much older. The universe, they say, started between ten and twenty billion years ago with the Big Bang, an unimaginably violent explosion in which matter, space and time itself came into being. The earth, according to the orthodox theory, is approximately four and a half billion years old. The first embryonic life forms emerged some three and a half billion years ago. Evolution, via the process of natural selection, then produced more complex life forms, including the first mammals about 200 million years ago and modern man – *Homo sapiens* – some 120,000 years ago.

Creationism has its own institute – The Institute of Creation Science – as well as its own conferences, publications and PhD-qualified researchers. For many of these people, creationism isn't just a scientific crusade, it's a moral crusade. According to H. M. Morris, a leading creationist:

Evolution is the root of atheism, of communism, nazism, behaviourism, economic imperialism, militarism, libertinism, anarchism, and all manner of anti-Christian systems of belief and practice.[*]

---

[*] H. M. Morris, *The Remarkable Birth of Planet Earth* (San Diego: Creation-Life Publishers, 1972), p. 75.

In the United States, creationists have fought hard to get creationism taught in schools. Two states, Arkansas and Louisiana, have now passed 'balanced treatment' laws, requiring that creationism be taught alongside evolution as equally respectable science. Even President George W. Bush believes creationism and evolution should be taught alongside each other; a spokesman said: 'He believes it is a question for states and local school boards to decide but believes both ought to be taught.'

Creationists have succeeded in persuading large swaths of the general public that their theory is at least as scientifically respectable as the Big Bang/evolution alternative. Recent Gallup polls indicate that about forty-five per cent of US citizens believe that God created human beings 'pretty much in [their] present form at one time or another within the last 10,000 years'.* Even college graduates are drawn to creationism: about a third of college-educated Americans believe that the biblical account is literally true. A Tennessee academic who recently surveyed his own students writes that scientists like himself are 'having to fight the battles of the Enlightenment all over again. Medieval ideas that were killed stone dead by the rise of science 300 to 400 years ago are not merely twitching; they are alive and well in . . . schools, colleges and universities.'†

Yet there seems, on the face of it, to be overwhelming empirical evidence against creationism.

Take, for example, the *fossil record*. Examination of the rock beneath our feet reveals strata that have been laid down apparently over many millions of years. Fossils can be found embedded in these strata. And one finds different life forms fossilised in different levels. At the lowest levels, only very simple creatures are found. Higher up, one discovers more complex forms, including the dinosaurs. Higher still, one finds mammals. Only most recently deposited layers reveal traces of man.

This layering of the fossil record tallies well with the theory of evolution but seems to contradict the biblical account, in which all life forms were produced more or less simultaneously less than 10,000 years ago. If the biblical account were correct, one would presumably expect to find examples of the entire range of life forms fairly randomly distributed throughout the strata (assuming, that is, that the few thousand years that have elapsed since creation would suffice to allow such rock strata even to form).

---

* *Guardian*, p. 14 of 'The Editor' section, 17 November 2001.
† Ibid.

According to creationism, for example, man and all the other mammals walked the earth at the same time as the dinosaurs. So surely one should expect to find fossils of both man and these other mammals muddled up in the same layers as dinosaur fossils. Yet mammals only ever appear in the higher strata. This seems to count fairly decisively against creationism.

Another piece of evidence that appears to weigh heavily against the claim that the universe is only a few thousand years old is provided by the light we see coming from long-dead stars. A light year is the distance travelled by light in one year. Many of the visible stars are many millions of light years away. It seems, then, that the light coming from these stars must have left them many millions of years ago. But if the universe is only a few thousand years old, how is this possible? It seems that God must have created the light *on its way* to the earth. But this entails that many of the astronomical events that we are now witnessing never happened. For example, suppose we seem to observe a supernova explosion 30,000 light years away. No such explosion took place. Rather, God created the illusion that it happened by sending these patterns of light and other radiation from a point less than 10,000 light years away. But this requires that God is a deceiver – He has deliberately produced the illusion of a much older universe, presumably in order to fool us. This is a conclusion few creationists are willing to accept.

Further evidence of a very old universe is supplied by, for example, plate tectonics. The observed rate at which the continental plates move across the surface of the earth, combined with the ample evidence of the plates having journeyed many thousands of miles, points to the earth being many millions of years old, not a few thousand.

How Creationists Defend Their Theory

The empirical evidence against creationism might seem overwhelming. But creationists argue that the situation is not so simple. Indeed, they have shown considerable ingenuity in trying to show how their theory also fits the available data.

Take the fossil record, for example. Creationists maintain that the layering in the fossil record can be explained by reference to the biblical Flood. The rains that caused the Flood were responsible for producing huge mud deposits that then metamorphosed into the rock strata we find beneath our feet. Creationists insist that the ordering of the life forms within these layers can also be accounted for in their theory. For example, some have suggested that the reason one finds dinosaurs below mammals is that dinosaurs were slow, cumbersome and relatively unintelligent creatures that were likely to have been buried before the faster and more intelligent mammals that would have run to higher ground. As www.christiananswers.net attempts here to explain, nor should one expect to find fossils of humans in the lower sedimentary layers.

> The layering we find in the fossil record can be more reasonably explained by Flood geologists as due to the order of burial of the different ecological zones of organisms by the Flood waters. For example, shallow marine organisms/ecological zones would be first destroyed by the fountains of the great deep breaking open, with the erosional runoff from the land due to torrential rainfall concurrently burying them. On this basis we would probably not expect to find human remains in the early Flood strata, which would contain only shallow marine organisms. The fossil record as we understand it at the moment certainly fits with this.*

Defenders of creationism have also shown imagination in accounting for the light we see coming from distant stars. For example, some have suggested that the impression of great age is due to a 'time dilation' caused by the rapid expansion of the universe out from the centre point at which the earth is located. Technical papers filled with equations have been published in support of this rival theory.

So creationists have been busy constructing a theory of increasing complexity to account for what we observe of the universe around us. They also believe that their theory 'fits' the evidence at least as well as the orthodox alternative. What creationist scientists practise certainly *looks* to many like solid, respectable science. As I say, some hundred million American citizens, many of whom are intelligent, college-educated people, believe that the earth is less than 10,000 years old. Have all these people been duped? Or is creationist science good science after all?

Falsificationism

One of the most intriguing theories of how science develops is offered by Karl Popper (1902–94). Popper actually accepts David Hume's (1711–76) extraordinary conclusion (explained in Chapter 14, Why Expect the Sun to Rise Tomorrow?) that scientific theories are never confirmed (we need not bother ourselves with Hume's argument here). However, in Popper's view, this is not a problem, as science does not proceed by means of theories being confirmed, but by means of theories being *falsified*.

---

* www.christiananswers.net/q-aig/aig-c014.html

Take, for example, the hypothesis that all swans are white. An observation of a single non-white swan is enough to falsify this hypothesis. Similarly, an observation of an action unaccompanied by an equal and opposite reaction is enough to falsify the hypothesis that all actions are accompanied by equal and opposite reactions.

That's not to say that all scientific hypotheses yet to be falsified are equally scientifically respectable. Popper points out that some theories are more falsifiable than others.

A vaguely formulated theory, for example, can be extremely difficult to falsify. Whatever happens, it may be possible for a defender of the theory to sidestep an apparent falsification by saying: 'Ah, but that is not quite what I meant.' A theory that's precisely formulated using clearly defined terms can be more easily falsified than one that is woolly.

In Popper's view, the more easily a theory can be falsified, the better. Wide-ranging and precisely stated theories are to be preferred to theories that have only a narrow focus or are vaguely formulated. Science progresses by means of the construction and testing of bold, highly falsifiable hypotheses.

Indeed, in Popper's view, a theory that is unfalsifiable – because whatever happens will be consistent with it – cannot properly be considered 'scientific' at all. Any *genuinely* scientific theory must have empirically testable consequences.

A Falsificationist Criticism of Creationism

Some falsificationists have attacked creationism on the grounds that it's unfalsifiable, and so not really science. Is this criticism fair?

Note, first of all, that creationism is not particularly precisely stated: it's difficult to say exactly what we should expect to observe given that creationism is true. This, by itself, makes creationism hard to falsify.

Secondly, the method adopted by creationists is not to test their theory by trying to falsify it. Rather, almost all their energies are expended on trying to protect their theory from being falsified. New bits are constantly being added to the basic creationist theory in order to account for what would otherwise be anomalous empirical data.

For example, when *still* no human fossils are found in the same layers as dinosaur fossils, creationists invoke an extra bit of theory to explain this, stating that the reason no human fossils are found is that God did not just drown these human beings, but He obliterated all sign of them: '[s]uch is God's abhorrence of sin that its penalty must be seen for what it is – utter destruction and removal of all trace."*

In short, whatever is discovered that might at first sight seem to falsify creationism is always, with some ingenuity, shown by the creationists to be consistent with their theory after all. Either the basic creationist theory is amended or added to in some way, as with the addition of the God-destroyed-all-the-human-remains hypothesis to explain the absence of human fossils below a certain point, or else the veracity of the contrary 'evidence' is challenged.

So there is, according to the falsificationist, a fundamental difference between the creationists' method and the scientific method. The creationists' energies are expended almost entirely on devising ways of protecting their theory from being falsified. Whether or not one is prepared to accept falsificationism as a general theory of how science proceeds, the fact that the creationists' method takes this form does appear quite damning.

A Creationist Reply

But hang on a moment. Is this really a fair criticism of creationism? Perhaps the situation isn't quite as simple as this simple falsificationist criticism of creationism makes out. Surely the strategy of 'adding on' a bit to a theory in order to protect it from being falsified is actually perfectly respectable. Mainstream scientists do it, too.

Here's an example. Newton's theory of universal gravitation predicted a particular path for the planet Uranus. However, Uranus's actual orbit deviated from the predicted path. The planet was seen to wobble in and out of its projected orbit as it travelled around the sun. This observation appeared to falsify Newton's theory.

So why wasn't Newton's theory abandoned? What happened was this. Some scientists supposed that there must be *another*, as yet undiscovered planet in the vicinity of Uranus, a planet near enough and massive enough to affect Uranus's orbit, thus explaining the wobble in a manner consistent with Newton's theory.

THERE MUST BE A PLANET HERE...

It subsequently turned out that there was such a planet: the planet Neptune. Indeed, it was those wobbles in Uranus's orbit that led to Neptune's discovery.

So here, too, we find an extra bit of theory being bolted on to the original in order to protect it from falsification. The 'mystery planet' hypothesis was added to Newton's theory in order to save it from being falsified. And the addition of this hypothesis was considered scientifically respectable even before any mystery planet was discovered. So why shouldn't creationists make similar moves?

Ad Hoc Moves

A falsificationist may point out that there's at least one important difference between the creationist's God-destroyed-all-the-human-remains hypothesis and the Newtonian mystery planet hypothesis. For the mystery planet hypothesis introduces all sorts of *additional, independently testable consequences* to Newton's original theory, thereby making it *even more falsifiable than it was before*. The destructive God hypothesis, on the other hand, does not.

To illustrate this, note that the mystery planet hypothesis is highly falsifiable. For one can look and see if there really is a planet at the position at which one would expect to see one if Newton's theory is correct. This becomes a further, independently testable consequence of the original theory. And, of course, a planet *was* discovered at the predicted position. On the other hand, the addition of the God-destroyed-all-the-human-remains hypothesis to the original creationist theory adds nothing to that theory in terms of independently testable consequences. This, according to many falsificationists, makes it an ad hoc manoeuvre, and so scientifically disreputable. While you can legitimately protect your core theory from being falsified by 'adding on' a hypothesis to protect it, such an addition must not be ad hoc.

Are Ad Hoc Moves Always Disreputable?

In their defence, creationists may point out, again correctly, that even this sort of ad hoc move is sometimes made by mainstream scientists.

Consider, for example, the heliocentric model of the universe on which the earth revolves about the sun. Soon after the heliocentric model was formulated by Copernicus, it was criticised by defenders of the old Aristotelian earth-centred model on the grounds that there was no observable *parallax*.

To illustrate: imagine that you walk around a lamppost while continuing to look exactly due north towards the houses across the street. As you rotate around the lamppost, your viewing position moves from side to side, making the houses in front of you wobble back and forth across your field of vision.

To begin with, number 93 is directly in front of you. Then it is number 91. Then it is number 93 again. Now if the earth goes round the sun, one would similarly expect the fixed stars to 'wobble' back and forth across our astronomical field of vision. But no such wobble could be detected. This appeared to falsify the new heliocentric theory. Indeed, it seemed strongly to confirm the old Aristotelian model on which the earth is fixed, with the sun rotating about it. However, some defenders of the heliocentric model suggested that the reason there is no observable 'wobble' is that the stars are *too far away for the effect to be discernible*. The effect of parallax diminishes the further the relevant bodies are away from the observer. Just as one should not expect to discern any wobble if the houses viewed from one's lamppost vantage point are across the other side of town rather than just across the street, so one should not expect to discern any wobble in the stars' position if they, too, are at some relatively vast distance from us.

But by adding to the heliocentric theory the hypothesis that the stars are at some much greater distance than previously thought, weren't those defenders of the heliocentric model making an ad hoc manoeuvre? Yes, they were. For the addition of that hypothesis added little, if anything, to the original theory in terms of independently testable consequences. Yet the addition of the distant stars hypothesis did not and does not now strike us as being particularly scientifically disreputable.

The question, then, is: why shouldn't creationists indulge in similarly ad hoc moves?

Are Cats Martian Secret Agents?

Perhaps the best answer to this question is to point out that while scientists may occasionally make such ad hoc moves in defence of a theory, they ought not to make a habit of it. If more or less all their energies are expended on defending their core theory by ad hoc means, then they're no longer doing science. Their core theory has become an item of faith, to be defended come what may.

In fact, *any* theory, no matter how absurd, can continuously be defended against falsification by constantly adding to the core theory in order to make it 'fit' the data.

Suppose, for example, that I were to suggest that cats are really Martian secret agents. The fact that cats have fairly small brains, do not appear to possess any linguistic ability, do not appear to possess a method of transmitting their secret reports back to Mars, and so on might seem straightforwardly to falsify my hypothesis. But in each case more or less ad hoc moves can be made to salvage my theory. Perhaps cats do possess language – they just hide this ability from us. Perhaps their brains, while small, are particularly efficient, thus accounting for their superior intelligence. Perhaps their transmitters are located in their brains, which explains why we don't find them secreted about the house. By constantly adding to my basic theory in this way, I can continue to make it 'fit' all the available empirical evidence.

However, the mere fact that my theory can, given sufficient ingenuity, be made consistent with all the available evidence clearly does not establish that my theory is as scientifically respectable as the orthodox theory that cats are comparatively unintelligent and benign creatures. For almost all my energies are being expended on protecting my theory from being falsified. *That*, surely, explains why the activity I'm engaged in is not really science. My method may *resemble* the scientific method in certain respects, but differs essentially from it. Indeed, were I to continue to defend my cats-are-Martian-secret-agents theory in this manner, not only would I start to infuriate my audience, but I would quite properly be suspected of suffering from some sort of mental illness.

Yet the approach of creationist 'scientists' is essentially similar. Orthodox scientists who attempt to dismiss creationism quickly by wheeling out evidence that seems straightforwardly to falsify it often find themselves tied up in knots by opponents, who, armed with an array of more or less ad hoc moves developed by the Institute of Creation Science, are able to show how creationism really does 'fit' the evidence after all. We aren't talking about one or two ad hoc moves being used to save a theory: we're talking about a theory made up of almost nothing else.

Confirmation

I have pointed out that the fact that creationists expend almost all their energy on 'adding on' ad hoc hypotheses to protect their core theory from being falsified tends to undermine its claim to scientific respectability. I am not suggesting, however, that the theory of falsificationism – which states that science progresses only through theories being falsified – is correct. There are well-known problems with falsificationism. Perhaps the most obvious is that falsificationists actually *accept* Hume's conclusion (explained in Chapter 14) that we never possess *any* grounds for supposing that a scientific theory is true. This is highly counter-intuitive. Surely, there *are* grounds for supposing that certain scientific theories are true. Theories aren't just falsified; they are also confirmed. So let's set aside Hume's worries about confirmation in order to consider the following question. Assuming, for the sake of argument, that scientific theories *can* be empirically confirmed, under what circumstances are they *best* confirmed?

It seems that in order for a theory to be strongly confirmed it needs to make predictions that are both surprising and true. That's to say, the theory should predict things that are likely if the theory being tested is true but *unlikely* otherwise. And these otherwise-unlikely-to-be-true predictions should turn out to be correct.

Consider, for example, the discovery of Neptune. In order to account for the wobbles in the orbit of Uranus, Newton's theory of gravitation required that there be an as yet undiscovered planet at a specific location. Now the probability of finding a planet at that location by chance was, of course, extremely small: space is mostly empty. So when it was discovered that there really was a planet at the predicted spot, that very strongly confirmed Newton's original theory. This is because the appearance of a planet at exactly that spot would otherwise be very surprising – a huge coincidence, in fact.

When a prediction derived from a new theory and subsequently confirmed is, on the other hand, what one would have *expected anyway*, given the old theory, this provides little, if anything, in the way of support for the new theory. Consider, for example, Einstein's theory of relativity. This theory predicts the tidal effect of the moon on the earth's oceans. To what extent does the existence of tides support

Einstein's theory over Newton's earlier theory? Not at all. For Newton's theory also predicts tides. The prediction about tides didn't come as much of a surprise.

Notice that the theory that life on earth has evolved is also strongly confirmed, for it also makes predictions that are both surprising and true.

Here's just one example. The theory of evolution predicts that, where fossils are discovered, they will be found in a particular order within rock strata. It predicts that there will be no *reversals* – one will never find, for example, even a single example of a mammal that was fossilised at the same time as and within the same rock layer as some very early, primitive life form. Evolutionary progression will be exhibited up through the strata. If, on the other hand, creationism is true and no process of evolution took place, then, prima facie, such reversals should be the rule rather than the exception. For example, mammals should appear more or less uniformly throughout the rock strata. Certainly, there should be a substantial percentage of such reversals (notice that, even if the creationists' Flood theory were correct, one should still expect a *reasonable percentage* of reversals: for example, at least *one or two* mammals among the millions of fossils excavated from the lower layers). The fact that, even today, after millions and millions of fossils have been excavated, not one single creditable and well-substantiated example of such a reversal has ever been recorded very strongly confirms the theory of evolution.

Is Creationism Strongly Confirmed?

This point about confirmation – that, in order to be strongly confirmed, theories need to make predictions that are both surprising and true – indicates another way in which creationism fails the test of scientific respectability. For it seems creationism is never strongly confirmed.

Evolutionists take risks, in the sense that they make predictions that, if their theory were false, would almost certainly be false. In predicting no reversals in the fossil record, for example, evolutionists take a huge risk. For, as I've explained, such reversals should otherwise be pretty common: if evolution were false, one would expect to find the fossils jumbled up across the rock layers. Were numerous, well-substantiated examples of such reversals suddenly to show up, that would spell disaster for the theory of evolution. But they don't show up, so the theory of evolution is strongly confirmed.

Creationism, on the other hand, generates few, if any, unexpected predictions, and still fewer predictions that are strongly confirmed. If, for example, we ask creationists what we should expect to observe in the fossil record given their theory is true, they hedge. Were any species reversals found, they would, of course, be quick to claim that this confirmed their theory. But when no reversals are found, they deny this disconfirms their theory. Indeed, they claim that the absence of such reversals is what one should expect, given that the biblical account of the Flood is true. Because creationists are careful to take no risks with their predictions, their theory is never strongly confirmed.

Conclusion

It's tempting, when faced with creationist claims, simply to wheel out contrary evidence: the fossil record, for example. The problem with this strategy is that creationists soon tie their opponents up in knots. Just like a defender of my cats-are-Martian-secret-agents theory, they confound and infuriate their critics by constantly amending or adding to their core theory in order to protect it from being falsified.

In order to deal more effectively with creationists' claims and arguments, one needs to take a step back and look at their *method*. Sure, the approach adopted by creationists does in certain respects strongly resemble the scientific method. For in each case a theory of increasing complexity is developed, often with considerable ingenuity, to 'fit' the available empirical evidence.

However, despite the obvious resemblance to the scientific method, the strategy adopted by creationists is essentially unscientific. Almost all the creationists' energies are expended on devising ways of dealing with apparent falsifications. And, because they take great care not to make surprising predictions, their theory is never strongly confirmed.

In short, what creationists practise isn't good science – it's bunk.

What to read next

Chapter 14, Why Expect the Sun to Rise Tomorrow?, discusses Hume's famous argument, briefly alluded to above, that science is an essentially irrational activity.

Further reading

A thorough examination of the claims of creationism is provided by:

Philip Kitcher, *Abusing Science* (Cambridge, Mass.: MIT Press, 1982).

Popper's position on what distinguishes science from non-science is explained clearly and succinctly in:

Karl Popper, 'The Problem of Demarcation', in Nigel Warburton (ed.), *Philosophy: Basic Readings* (London: Routledge, 1999).

A short but penetrating discussion of creationism is also to be found in the excellent:

Theodore Schick Jr and Lewis Vaughn, *How to Think about Weird Things*, second edition (California: Mayfield, 1999), pp. 171–9.

For a useful Internet resource, see: http://books.nap.edu/html/creationism

1 2

DESIGNER BABIES

PHILOSOPHY GYM CATEGORY
WARM-UP
MODERATE
MORE CHALLENGING

Whenever genetic modification or selection are discussed, two bogeymen always threaten to pop up and stifle rational debate: Hitler and Frankenstein. We're all familiar with the link between genetics, eugenics and the Nazi pursuit of racial purity. And most of us are at least a little afraid that geneticists, by meddling in things they do not fully comprehend, will unleash some sort of Frankenstein's monster – the original 'designer baby'. So compelling are these nightmarish visions of where fiddling with the stuff of life might lead that almost every development in the field is met with near panic.

Is this sort of response merely a product of ignorance and hysteria? Or are such anxieties well founded? In this chapter we get to grips with some of the key questions involved by looking at the issue of *designer babies.*

Selection of Sex

The scene: a laboratory at some unspecified time in the future. Professor Susan Clone is seated at her desk, surrounded by test tubes, electronic devices and other scientific-looking clutter. There's a knock at the door. A young woman enters.

Prof Clone: How can I help?
Mrs McDadd: My husband and I wish to have a baby. It's important to us that it's a girl. Could you arrange it?
Prof Clone: Perhaps. Can I ask why you want a girl?
Mrs McDadd: We would just *prefer* a girl.

The choice the McDadds wish to make is already technologically possible. In vitro fertilisation (IVF), where one or more fertilised eggs are implanted in the womb, is now commonplace. It's comparatively easy to screen the eggs before implantation to ensure that only male or only female eggs are used. Precisely this is already done for couples who run the risk of passing on a hereditary disorder affecting one sex only, such as haemophilia.

So sex selection for *therapeutic* purposes is already carried out. Why not also allow parents to choose their child's sex merely to satisfy a preference? Couples already use contraceptives and other technological devices to determine both whether and when they have children. Why not let them use IVF to determine sex?

The Human Fertilisation and Embryology Authority, which regulates IVF in the UK, does *not* permit parents to select for sex merely as a matter of preference. Why not? The most often given reason is that it's likely to produce an imbalance in the sexes. Many cultures have a strong preference for boys. If many more boys than girls are born, many heterosexual males will end up unable to find a life-partner. In his report on reproductive technologies to the European Commission, the philosopher Professor Jonathan Glover argues that to allow free choice is generally laudable, but not where it can impact badly on the lives of others:

> One alarming consequence [of allowing sex selection] is a serious imbalance in the next generation. Perhaps those who will be members of that generation have an interest in averting this. And, in the nature of things, their voice will not be heard at the time the decision is taken.[*]

We might also question the *motives* behind the preference. Clearly, some parents will select because they feel one sex is 'superior' to the other. Shouldn't we be dealing with such sexist attitudes rather than pandering to them by allowing choice based on prejudice?

Even if the parents' motive isn't sexist, the fact remains that the choice they are exercising is essentially egocentric, made for their own benefit rather than that of their child.

> It is a simple point: there is no known general truth that girls are happier than boys, or vice versa. The preference is surely not for the sake of the child, but for the parents themselves. Many parents put their children first, and this other, more egocentric attitude is one that may be less beneficial to the children.[†]

Glover concludes that we shouldn't give parents the option of choosing their child's sex. However, not all philosophers agree. The philosopher Professor John Harris denies

---

[*] Jonathan Glover (and others), *Fertility and the Family* (London: Fourth Estate, 1989), p. 143.
[†] Ibid.

that the fact that some will select for the wrong reason justifies us in denying choice to all.

> Gender preference is not necessarily an expression of sexism, and the task of sifting the motives or the effects of particular selections would be impossible. It is better by far to champion freedom and to fight prejudice by other means.[*]

Harris also doubts whether a lasting sexual imbalance is necessarily inevitable. He points out that a shortage of one sex may be self-correcting as the affected generation is then likely to place a higher value on the scarcer sex. Harris indicates that there are also other, less brutal and coercive mechanisms available by which such imbalances might be avoided. The tax system, for example, might be used to provide incentives and disincentives, much as it is currently used to discourage pollution and encourage charitable donations. In Harris's view, an outright ban is probably unnecessary.

As I say, in the UK at this moment in time the use of IVF to satisfy the preference of parents for one particular sex is banned. At the time and place at which Professor Clone works, however, no such restrictions are in place.

Intelligence and Health

Back at the laboratory . . .

Prof Clone: No problem. A girl will be arranged. Do you have any other preferences?

Mrs McDadd: Other preferences?

Prof Clone: Yes. I can also offer a choice with regard to height, intelligence, hair and eye colour, build and health.

Mrs McDadd: Actually, there *are* some other choices we would like to make.

Prof Clone: Such as?

Mrs McDadd: Can you ensure that our baby has above-average intelligence?

Prof Clone: Yes, I think so. Of course, one's intelligence is a product of a number of factors, not just one's genes. Education, a stimulating environment and encouragement – all have their part to play. Nevertheless, genes play an important role in determining intelligence. Through genetic manipulation I can ensure that there is at least a *high probability* that your child will have above-average intelligence. Would you like that arranged?

---

[*] John Harris, *Clones, Genes and Immortality* (Oxford: Oxford University Press, 1992), p. 194.

There are two main methods by which genetically enhanced intelligence might be achieved. The first is through *screening*. Suppose that certain genetic indicators or markers for intelligence could be identified. Then Mrs McDadd's fertilised eggs could be screened and an egg or eggs possessing just those markers implanted.

The second method would be by operating directly on the genetic code, perhaps by inserting sequences that tend to produce high intelligence. If, for example, Einstein's high intelligence was largely a result of a particular sequence in his DNA, then that sequence could be spliced into the DNA of other children, thereby giving them a good chance of higher intelligence, too.

Of course, both these techniques require what may not be true: that there are isolatable genes or markers for high intelligence. But let's suppose, for the sake of argument, that such genes can be identified. Then either of these two methods might be used to produce babies with enhanced intelligence.

In fact, it is the second of these techniques that Professor Clone proposes to use.

Prof Clone: Above-average intelligence. Fine. I'll arrange it. I'll splice in the relevant sequence from a Nobel Prize-winning friend of mine.

Mrs McDadd: Fantastic! And what about health and physique?

Prof Clone: Well, I could weed out any genes that have been shown substantially to increase the probability of disability or susceptibility to disease. I could also splice in genes for vitality, a good physique, and so on. In fact, I can even build in immunities to all sorts of common ailments and diseases, from the common cold to cancer. Would you like me to do so?

Mrs McDadd: Definitely.

Is such manipulation ethical? Assuming that it's possible, should we allow parents to have their children genetically modified for intelligence and health?

We are more than happy for parents to try to enhance intelligence and health through *education*. If a school were to develop a programme that resulted in pupils gaining dramatically in both, it would no doubt be applauded. Parents would rightly seek to get their children admitted. They would demand to know why similar techniques weren't being used at other schools. We surely have a duty to try to pass on the benefits of such educational developments to as many children as possible.

But now consider a slightly different situation. Suppose it's discovered that such increases in health and intelligence can be safely and effectively achieved by genetic engineering. John Harris puts the question succinctly:

> If we could engineer enhanced intelligence and health into the embryo should we not do so? If these are legitimate aims of education could they be illegitimate as the aims of medical, as opposed to educational, science?*

In fact, as Harris indicates, despite the gut feeling of many that the genetic alternative would be unethical, it's not easy to see precisely *why* there is anything wrong with using genetic as opposed to educational techniques to achieve the same end result.

Are the Risks Too Great?

One possible objection to the use of such techniques is that they are too risky. In fact, there are two ways in which one might operate on genes in order to produce the desired results, as Professor Clone now explains.

Prof Clone: The genetic changes you require can be achieved in two ways. I can change *just* your child, or I can make changes that can be passed on from generation to generation, to your child's child and your child's child's child. The first type of modification is to the *somatic* cells; the second is to what are known as the *germ* cells.

Mrs McDadd: Well, if you can make improvements, I would like them to be inheritable. That would seem much better value.

Prof Clone: Germ line modification it is, then.

As Professor Clone explains, germ line changes to the human genome are changes that will potentially be with us *forever*. Now, some see germ line modification of human beings as being particularly risky.

> While genetic manipulation of human somatic cells may lie in the realm of personal choice, tinkering with human germ cells does not. Germ cell therapy, without the consent of all members of society, ought to be explicitly forbidden.†

---

* Ibid., p. 173.
† Suzuki and Knudtsen, quoted in Harris, p. 198.

An obvious potential problem with germ line manipulation is that, if anything goes wrong, we may have to live with our mistake for eternity. The blunder is likely to be passed on, spreading out into the human race as a whole. So while we take a risk when we make changes to somatic cells, we take a much greater risk if our mistakes will affect the germ line.

In fact, it can be extremely difficult to predict exactly what might be the long-term consequences of adding a gene here or deleting a gene there. The result of increasing intelligence by altering a particular gene might also be, say, a marked decrease in social skills. Yet it may take years, even decades, for such harmful side-effects to be detected.

Also, given the extraordinary power of genetic engineering, when things do go wrong, they are much more likely to go *very wrong indeed*. Any error may be potentially catastrophic. You might argue, then, that it's better that all forms of genetic modification be outlawed.

Still, this may be to err too much on the side of caution. Imagine, for the sake of argument, that there's ample evidence that by simply deleting a specific gene we can remove an extremely debilitating, painful and life-shortening condition that affects millions. And suppose that, even after decades of intensive research by impartial scientists, there's still no evidence of any harmful side-effects. Shouldn't we then go ahead and delete the gene? Wouldn't a refusal to delete the gene in these circumstances be criminally overcautious?

Let's get back to Mrs McDadd. Suppose, for the sake of argument, that we do know that the genetic changes Mrs McDadd wants to make are safe. Is there then any good reason why Professor Clone should not go ahead?

Designer Baby Syndrome

Mrs McDadd: What about looks? I'm a huge fan of Anita Sopwith Camel, the film actress and singer. Is there any chance you might be able to make my daughter look like Anita?

Prof Clone: Look like her? I can do better than that. I know for a fact that Ms Sopwith Camel is allowing couples to make *clones* of her. Expensive but – for you, perhaps – worth it.

Mrs McDadd: I can have my own Anita?

Prof Clone: Not quite. Your daughter won't be Anita. But she'll be genetically identical to her. It will be as if your daughter is Anita's identical twin.

Mrs McDadd: And she will sing like Anita?

Prof Clone: I can't guarantee that. Anita Sopwith Camel is a product of both her genes and her environment. Your daughter will no doubt have a different upbringing and environment. So she will differ from Anita in various ways. You may find your daughter can't sing. She may not even want to sing. She's going to have a unique mind of her own.

Mrs McDadd: Still, just think! I can see myself now, walking down the shopping mall with my own little Anita. Imagine how envious all the other mothers will be!

Mrs McDadd's attitude might give us pause for thought. She seems to think of her future daughter as some sort of trophy, an expensive designer item to be shown off. This attitude is clearly abhorrent. But aren't such attitudes inevitable if the procedures Professor Clone is offering become widely available? Doesn't this give us reason enough to ban the use of such technologies outright?

The philosopher Hilary Putnam asks us to imagine the following scenario.

Imagine that one's children come to be viewed simply as parts of one's 'lifestyle'. Just as one has the right to choose one's furniture or express one's personality, or to suit one's personal predilections, or (even if one does not wish to admit it) 'to keep up with the Joneses', so, let us imagine that it becomes the accepted pattern of thought and behaviour to 'choose' one's children (by choosing whom one will 'clone' them from, from among available relatives, or friends, or, if one has lots of money, persons who are willing to be cloned for cash). In the Brave New World I am asking us to imagine, one can have, so to speak, 'designer children' as well as 'designer clothes'. Every narcissistic motive is allowed free rein.[*]

Putnam finds the thought of such a society thoroughly repellent, as do most of us. According to Putnam, this is because we would be using people – our own children – as *means*, not *ends*. Rather than being valued for their own sake, we would value our offspring only to the extent that they made us feel good about ourselves, and in a fairly superficial way at that.

On the other hand, perhaps such attitudes are far from inevitable. Personally, if a fairy godmother were to grant me a wish, it would be for my child – that she should grow up healthy, disease-free, bright, attractive and alert. Nothing wrong with that,

---

[*] Hilary Putnam, 'Cloning People', in J. Burley (ed.), *The Genetic Revolution and Human Rights* (Oxford: Oxford University Press, 1999), pp. 7–8.

you may say. I want these things, not for myself, not to enhance *my own* lifestyle, but *for her*. But suppose that technology is able safely to grant me my wish. Why shouldn't I be allowed to make use of it? Yes, some people might choose to guarantee themselves a bright, healthy, attractive baby for shallow, selfish reasons. But then many will choose for the right reasons. Again, does the mere fact that *some* may choose for the wrong reasons justify us in denying choice to all? I don't believe it does.

Eugenics and the Nazis

What of the Nazis and their use of genetics in pursuit of racial 'purity'? This, clearly, was morally unacceptable. So how does genetic engineering for health, intelligence and attractiveness differ, morally speaking? Indeed, *does* it differ?

Some have suggested that the use of genetic techniques to 'weed out' genes that might result in disability ought to be banned on the grounds that those who are in some way disabled are certainly not 'defective'. By weeding out such genes, are we not saying, in effect, that it would have been better had those with disabilities never been born? Are we not eliminating those who are perceived to be 'inferior'? Are we not doing what the Nazis did?

I don't believe so. The suggestion is not that it would be better if those people who now have disabilities were eliminated. Nor is it that it would be better had these people never been born. The suggestion is merely that it would have been better had they not been born with their disability.

The suggestion that it is *always* wrong to try to reduce the probability of a future child being born with a disability is clearly absurd, for it would follow that it's wrong of mothers to take folic acid at conception in order to reduce the risk of their having children with Down's syndrome.

Of course, we ought to remain on our guard against the politically and maliciously motivated use of genetic techniques. But just because there are people who would abuse the technology does not give us a reason to ban it. After all, *every* technology can be abused, from the sewing machine to the space rocket. We are not going to ban them all, are we?

Immortality

Professor Clone had a further surprise for Mrs McDadd.

Prof Clone: There is something else I can offer you, something special. I can make Anita *immortal*.

Mrs McDadd: You mean, like a Greek god?

Prof Clone: Sort of. Let me explain. Why do people get old? Why does their skin wrinkle and their hair go grey? Why do they become decrepit and die?

Mrs McDadd: Don't they just wear out, like a car?

Prof Clone: No. The main reason these things happen is that they are genetically determined to happen. Your genes have evolved to *kill you off* after a certain period of time.

Mrs McDadd: My goodness. Why?

Prof Clone: Well, natural selection, the process that produced us, requires that generations come and go. A generation that came and refused to go would be a problem. So each of us has a gene that functions like a ticking clock, ticking down to the time at which we are turned off. I can stop that clock.

Mrs McDadd: Really?

Prof Clone: Undoubtedly. In fact, with her ageing gene turned off, Anita will remain 'young'. Yes, the years will roll by, but she will be as sprightly at 200 as she was at 22.

Mrs McDadd: Fantastic!

Prof Clone: Of course, that doesn't mean that Anita will last for ever. She might be run over by a bus or catch some fatal disease. But she won't die of old age.

This kind of 'immortality' may perhaps become possible in the not too distant future. Should it be allowed?

One obvious problem raised by the widespread use of the technique would be *overpopulation*. If a large percentage of humans live for hundreds of years with reproduction continuing apace, resources will soon become disastrously overstretched.

But it's not obvious that the only way to prevent such a catastrophe is simply to ban the introduction of 'long-life' genes. For example, it might be made a condition of receiving such genes that the recipient be made infertile.

A New Class Divide

Many would argue that whether or not we want to regulate the use of these genetic techniques, they are going to be used anyway. The wealthy will certainly want the advantages that genetic engineering can provide. And money finds a way. Genetic engineers, realising the fortunes they can make, will set up clinics in poor countries unwilling to ban procedures that can provide a dramatic boost to their economies. So, like it or not, it's only a matter of time before we begin to see the emergence of a longer-living elite whose members are not just far wealthier than the rest of us, but also far healthier, far more intelligent and far more attractive. The human race is about to divide into two distinct classes: GM humans versus the rest.

Prof Clone: As you know, Mrs McDadd, this is a very exclusive club. Only the wealthy can afford to be genetically enhanced. And being genetically enhanced means they inevitably become wealthier still. Your lottery win has allowed you to buy your daughter entry to a world that would otherwise be beyond her wildest dreams.

Mrs McDadd: What other advantages are there?

Prof Clone: If you thought that a private education opened doors, wait until you see what membership of the GM club bestows. Its members form a very closed, privileged and tightly knit group. Indeed, you will find that the genetic enhancement of your child is an investment you will want to protect. My own son is heavily genetically enhanced. I don't want him mating with some commoner and undermining the investment I've made. Genetically modified humans quite sensibly stick to their own kind. Commoners will only dilute their superior genes.

Mrs McDadd: I see. But isn't this polarisation of the human race into two classes deeply unfair? I'm having a pang of guilt.

Prof Clone: Feel a little guilty, if you like, but it's the way of the world. Do really want your daughter to miss out on all these benefits?

Mrs McDadd: Would a cheque be OK?

Prof Clone: Fine.

What to read next

Chapter 2, What's Wrong with Gay Sex?, also discusses the principle that we should never use people as means rather than ends.

Further reading

Jonathan Glover (and others), *Fertility and the Family* (London: Fourth Estate, 1989).

John Harris, *Clones, Genes and Immortality* (Oxford: Oxford University Press, 1992).

THE CONSCIOUSNESS
CONUNDRUM

Scientists are grappling with 'the problem of consciousness': the problem of explaining how that walnut-shaped lump of grey matter between your ears is capable of producing a rich inner world of conscious experiences. Will they ever solve this mystery? Some think it's only a matter of time. Yet there are arguments that appear to show that consciousness is something that it is *in principle* impossible for science to explain.

The Private Realm of Consciousness

Take a look at something red: a ripe tomato, for example. As you look at this object, you are conscious of having a certain experience – a colour experience. As the philosopher Thomas Nagel explains,[*] there's *something it is like* to have this experience, something *for you*, the subject.

We spend our lives immersed in a vibrant flow of such experiences: the smell of a flower, the taste of an orange, the rough sensation of wood under one's fingertips, a zinging pain, a melancholic moment. We can focus our attention on the subjective quality of these experiences and savour them. An interesting feature of this rich inner life we lead is that it seems peculiarly hidden from others. Others can observe my body and outward behaviour, but my experiences are hidden inside. Indeed, they would appear to be 'hidden inside' in a very strong sense. For they are not *physically* hidden, as, say, my brain is physically hidden inside my skull. Things that are physically hidden can in principle be revealed. Surgeons might one day be able to open up my skull and observe what physically goes on inside me when I have a colour experience. But they can never enter my mind and observe what the experience is like *for me*, from my point of view.

---

[*] Thomas Nagel, 'What Is It Like to Be a Bat?', in Douglas R. Hofstadter and Daniel Dennett (eds), *The Mind's I* (London: Penguin, 1981).

What Is It Like to Be a Bat?

There are also conscious experiences no human being has ever enjoyed. Take bats, for example. Bats manage to find their way around in the dark by using echo-location. The bat emits a sound (inaudible to humans), and the loudness of the echoes and the direction from which they come allow the bat to build up a picture of its environment.

Echo-location allows bats to 'see' using sound. Now ask yourself: what must it be like to be a bat, to experience the world as the bat does? No doubt there is something it's like for the bat when it 'sees' using echo-location. It must be a very strange experience, radically unlike any of the experiences we humans enjoy. But, as Nagel points out, we can't know what the experience is like. We could discover everything there is to know about what happens in a bat's nervous system when it 'sees' using sound. But that still wouldn't allow us to know what the experience is like for the bat. Its subjective character would remain unknown to us. It seems the bat's experience, like yours and mine, is essentially private.

The realm of conscious experience is responsible for what continues to be one of the most profound and intractable of mysteries, a mystery with which both philosophers and scientists are currently very much engaged. The mystery concerns how our physical bodies and our conscious minds are related. The problem, as we shall see, is that, on the one hand, it seems your conscious mind must be physical, yet, on the other hand, it seems it cannot be.

Two Competing Theories of Consciousness

Scientists tell us that when you looked at that red object a minute or so ago, the following happened. Light of certain wavelengths was reflected off the object into your eye, where it was focused on to your retina to produce an image. Your retina is covered with millions of light-sensitive cells, some of which are sensitive to differences in wavelength. The light falling on to these cells caused them to emit electrical impulses which then flowed down the nerves linking your eye to the back of your brain. That caused something to happen in your brain.

But what about your experience? According to the philosopher René Descartes (1596–1650), your conscious mind is a distinct entity capable of existing on its own, independently of anything physical. So, in Descartes' view, after something happened in your brain, something else had to happen: your brain caused something to happen in your mind. Your mind and brain may *interact*. But they are not *identical*.

According to many contemporary scientists and philosophers, however, it's a mistake to think of conscious experience in this way. Professor Susan Greenfield, for example, in her BBC television series 'Brain Story', insists that 'you are your brain'. Your experience isn't something extra – something on top of what happens physically. Rather, the mental *just is* part of what's going on physically.

Certainly, scientists sometimes reveal that what might seem like two distinct things are actually one and the same thing. Take the morning star and the evening star, for example. For a long time we thought these heavenly bodies were distinct. Then astronomers discovered that they are one and the same object seen twice over (the planet Venus).

Scientists have also established that certain properties are identical. For example, they have discovered that heat is a molecular motion, electricity is a flow of electrons and water is H_2O.

So why shouldn't it also turn out that pain just is a certain state of the brain? Admittedly, pain doesn't seem like a brain state. But so what? After all, heat doesn't seem like molecular motion – yet that's just what it is.

Substances and Properties

We have been looking at two competing theories about consciousness. First, there are those who believe that your conscious experiences are nothing over and above what goes on in your brain. Secondly, there are those who, like Descartes, deny this. But before we get to the arguments for and against these two positions, it will be useful if we distinguish two rather different versions of the second position.

In Descartes' view, your mind and body are distinct *substances*: each is capable of existing independently of the other. Your conscious mind could, in principle, be detached from everything physical and exist on its own. This position is called *substance dualism*.

Hardly any scientists or philosophers are now prepared to accept substance dualism. But there are still plenty of philosophers (and at least some scientists) around who believe that there are two distinct and irreducible kinds of *property*: physical properties and mental properties. This position is called *property dualism*.

According to property dualism, there's only one kind of stuff – physical stuff. But objects made out of this physical stuff can have two quite different sorts of property. In the view of the property dualist, there are both mental properties and physical properties: the mental properties of a human being are extra properties that exist in addition to all of his or her physical properties.

An Argument Against Dualism

Let's now turn to one of the most popular arguments against all forms of dualism.

In effect, dualists want to introduce an extra layer of facts in addition to the physical facts. There are facts about physical substances and properties. But according to dualists, there are also non-physical substances and/or properties. The facts about these non-physical substances/properties are facts *in addition to* the physical facts. So there are two fundamentally different and irreducible sorts of fact.

Many scientists and philosophers consider the suggestion that there are such 'additional' facts thoroughly unscientific. Why is this?

Suppose that at a dinner party I am given the choice between a glass of wine and a glass of beer.

I like both, but decide on this occasion to have wine. I reach out and select a glass of white.

WINE OR BEER?

Scientists tell us that such physical movements have physical causes. The movement of my arm was caused by the action of muscles in my arm, which was itself brought about by electrical activity in the efferent nerves running from my brain.

This electrical activity was in turn caused by physical activity in my brain, which was brought about by further preceding physical causes, including the stimulation of my nervous system by light reflected off the glasses on the tray in front of me and the sound of someone speaking to me. These physical causes in turn had physical causes, which in turn had physical causes, and so on.

Indeed, it seems that if scientists were furnished with knowledge of the laws of nature, plus all the physical facts about my body and my environment as they were, say, a minute prior to my deciding to reach out and grasp that glass of wine, it would be possible *in principle* for them to figure out that my arm would do what it did. That movement of my arm was fixed in advance by how things stood physically.

But if this is correct – if what happens physically is fixed in advance by the preceding physical facts – then there is no possibility of any non-physical fact affecting how things turn out. The non-physical must be causally irrelevant to what goes on physically.

But if dualism is true, then my conscious mind is non-physical. But then it follows that my *mind can make no difference to what goes on physically*. Suppose, for example, that I had decided to pick up a glass of beer instead. Because of the physical facts, my arm would have been compelled to reach out and grasp that glass of wine anyway. Indeed, if dualism is true, you could take my mind away altogether and my body would *still* carry on in exactly the same way.

But this is absurd, surely? My mind can and does affect how my body behaves. But as it is only the *physical* facts that affect how things turn out physically, the only way in which the facts about what happens in my mind can have a physical effect *is if they are themselves physical facts*. But then it follows that dualism (both substance and property) is false.

Many scientists and philosophers are convinced by this and other arguments that the facts about what goes on in the conscious mind must ultimately be physical facts. However, the issue is far from settled. There are also powerful arguments that appear to show that these scientists and philosophers are mistaken. One of the best-known arguments is presented by the philosopher Frank Jackson. Jackson's argument runs as follows.

Mary and the Black and White Room

A girl called Mary is born. Before she has any visual experiences, Mary is placed in a black and white room by scientists who wish to study her. The scientists arrange that Mary never has a colour experience (they hide Mary's pink hands from her by using white gloves, and so on). Mary experiences only black, white and shades of grey.

Mary grows up in her black and white environment. She develops a fascination with science. Indeed, Mary eventually becomes the world's greatest brain expert. She finds out everything there is to know about what goes on inside a human's brain when they describe what they are seeing as 'red'. She discovers all the physical facts about the brains of colour perceivers: how their neurons are firing, how the brain chemistry is balanced, and so on.

Then, one day, one of the scientists studying her brings a ripe tomato into her black and white world.

Mary is stunned. She now has an experience that she's never had before. She finds out what it is like to have a colour experience. Mary discovers a new fact: the fact that the experience of red is *like this* (I'm looking at that red object again). But Mary previously knew all the physical facts. So the fact that the experience is *like this* is not a physical fact. Facts about the qualitative character of our conscious experiences – about what it is like to have them – are not physical facts.

The Explanatory Gap

Jackson seems to have shown that there are more facts than just the physical facts. But there's a further conclusion you might wish to draw. Jackson's story also appears to show that *not everything can be explained or understood by science.* We can't explain or understand why red things look *like this* by appealing only to the physical facts about us. We come up against what contemporary philosophers call an *explanatory gap* at this point.

Contrast the case of heat. Identifying heat with vigorous molecular motion allows us to deduce the various properties of heat. Discovering what's going on at the molecular level allows us to understand why objects that are heated char and blacken, why they tend to make nearby objects hot, and so on.

But a full understanding of the goings-on in the human brain will not allow us to understand why pain feels the way it does or explain why ripe tomatoes produce *this* sort of visual experience. Mary knows everything there is to know about what goes on in the brains of colour perceivers, but this knowledge does not allow her to understand what an experience of red is actually like. Indeed, none of the physical facts she discovers go any way towards explaining why such physiological states should be accompanied by conscious states *at all*.

The Analogy with Life

Jackson's argument appears to show both that

1. there are more facts than the physical facts, and
2. it is *in principle* impossible for the physical sciences to account for consciousness.

But many scientists are dismissive of such conclusions. They often suggest that the current situation with respect to consciousness is similar to the situation 200 years ago with respect to life. Life at that time constituted a great mystery. We simply had no idea how mere physical matter could be organised in such a way as to produce an animate, living thing. Many thought that something extra – a mysterious and supernatural 'vital force' – had to be added to a physical object in order to imbue it with life.

Today, of course, the explanation of life is mostly within our grasp. Darwin's theory of natural selection, advances in genetics, and so on, have allowed us to explain many of the properties of life. Even where a scientific explanation of some particular feature of life currently eludes us, we can at least now see how such an explanation might in principle be constructed just by appealing to physical facts.

Many scientists argue that, similarly, just because a scientific explanation of consciousness *now* eludes us doesn't mean that no such explanation is possible. There's no need to suppose that consciousness must be something mysterious and supernatural that exists *in addition to* what we find within the natural, physical world. These are early days in the scientific investigation of consciousness. Our current inability to imagine how consciousness might be explained by appealing only to physical facts may simply be due to our lack of an adequate theory, just as in the case of life.

Conclusion: A Mystery

We have been grappling with the mystery of how to accommodate consciousness within the physical universe. Many scientists believe that consciousness must ultimately be reducible to and explicable in terms of the physical. Indeed, given that the conscious mind is able causally to affect what goes on physically, it seems it must itself be physical.

But there are powerful objections to this belief. Jackson's story about Mary and the black and white room seems to show that it is in principle impossible for the facts about the character of our conscious experience to be reduced to and explained in terms of physical facts. It seems there must be more facts than just the physical.

Many scientists reject all forms of dualism out of hand. But unless they can show what is wrong with Jackson's argument (and, indeed, the other very convincing-looking arguments that are around), their dismissive attitude towards dualism looks hasty. Blindly to reject such arguments looks more like prejudice than a rationally held position.

Of course, it may be that there's something wrong with Jackson's argument (see the box below). But the onus is on those who reject all forms of dualism to show precisely *what* is wrong with it. And, of course, showing what's wrong with such arguments is the job not of empirical science, but of logic and philosophy.

So can science ever solve the mystery of consciousness? The answer is: perhaps, but not by itself. Science will need the help of philosophy.

Thinking Tools: The Masked Man Fallacy

This section explains what may be wrong with Jackson's argument. There is a popular form of argument often used to establish that two things are not identical. You search for a property that one of the two things has that the other lacks. If you can find such a property, it follows that the items in question are non-identical.

For example, if you want to establish that K2 and Everest are distinct mountains, all you need to do is to find a property one mountain possesses that the other lacks. You might argue like this:

- Everest has the property of being over 29,000 feet high.
- K2 doesn't have the property of being over 29,000 feet high.
- Therefore Everest is not identical to K2.

This is a sound argument: each of the two premises is true, and the logic is impeccable. The argument really does establish that Everest and K2 are distinct.

Those who argue that mind and body are non-identical often appeal to the same form of argument. Here, for example, is an argument (often attributed to Descartes) called *the argument from doubt*:

- I don't doubt that I exist. After all, by trying to doubt that I exist, I demonstrate that I do exist, so my attempt at doubting that I exist must inevitably be self-defeating.
- I do doubt that my body exists. It seems to me that I might be a disembodied mind, with all my experiences being generated by some sort of malevolent demon (for more on this sort of doubt, see Chapter 3, Brain-Snatched).
- But then it seems that my body has a property that I lack: my body has the property of being *something the existence of which I doubt*. I lack this property. So it surely follows – by an argument analogous to that about Everest and K2 – that I'm not identical with my body.

Here's the argument laid out more formally:

- My body possesses the property of *being something the existence of which I doubt*.
- I don't possess the property of *being something the existence of which I doubt*.
- Therefore I am not identical with my body.

This sort of argument has convinced many that mind and body are non-identical. But despite the similarity to the Everest/K2 argument, this is a bad argument. What we have here is an example of the *masked man fallacy*. Here's another example of the fallacy. Suppose I witness a bank being robbed. This leads me to believe that the masked man robbed the bank. Later, detectives inform me that their lead suspect is my father. Horrified, I try to prove that my father cannot be the masked man. I point out that the masked man has a property my father lacks: he's someone I believe to have robbed the bank. I argue like this:

- The masked man has the property of *being someone I believe robbed the bank*.
- My father lacks the property of *being someone I believe robbed the bank*.
- Therefore my father is not identical with the masked man.

This is obviously a bad argument, despite sharing the same form as the sound Everest/K2 argument. It could yet turn out that my father *is* the masked man, despite the fact that both premises are true. Why is this?

The problem is that this form of argument does not work for *all* kinds of property. It works for properties such as being more than 29,000 feet high. It does not work with properties such as being someone I believe to have robbed the bank. More generally, this form of argument is invalid whenever the property in question involves *someone's psychological attitude towards a thing*.

For example, in the masked man case, I try to show that my father and the masked man are distinct by pointing out that I have an attitude towards one that I don't have towards the other: I believe one robbed the bank but not the other. But such attitudes are incapable of revealing whether or not the items in question really are distinct. Here are a couple of other examples:

- John Wayne is someone Michael knows appeared in *True Grit*.
- Marion Morrison is not someone Michael knows appeared in *True Grit*.
- Therefore John Wayne isn't Marion Morrison.

- Heat is widely recognised as something with which to cook food.
- Molecular motion is not widely recognised as something with which to cook food.
- Therefore heat isn't molecular motion.

Both these arguments have true premises but false conclusions ('John Wayne' is the stage name of Marion Morrison). The problem, again, is that what someone may know or believe or recognise about one thing but not another is not the sort of property one can use to establish the non-identity of those things. The argument from doubt involves the same fallacy.

What of Jackson's argument about Mary? Does it also involve the masked man fallacy? I think that, as it stands, it does. But you should check for yourself. Of course, none of this is to say that I believe dualism is now defeated. There may be better arguments for dualism than Jackson's, arguments that don't involve the masked man fallacy.

What to read next

This chapter might usefully be read in conjunction with Chapter 6, Could a Machine Think? Look for where some of the arguments overlap.

In Chapter 15, Do We Ever Deserve to Be Punished?, I briefly discuss the discovery that the universe is not after all governed by strict and exceptionless laws, but merely by probabilistic laws. So it turns out that the most that someone furnished with full information about my physical body and environment could ever predict about my future behaviour is what I will *probably* do. After reading Chapter 15, you might wish to return to this chapter to consider the question: does this discovery undermine the argument against dualism presented above? Even if it does, might some version of that argument still be salvaged?

Further reading

Jackson's story about Mary and the black and white room appears in:

'Epiphenomenal Qualia', in W. Lycan (ed.), *Mind and Cognition* (Oxford: Blackwell, 1990).

For a breezy and yet quite thorough introduction to the problem of consciousness, see:

David Papineau and Howard Selina, *Introducing Consciousness* (Cambridge: Icon, 2000).

An interesting collection of pieces on the mind can be found in the now quite old but nevertheless still excellent:

Douglas R. Hofstadter and Daniel Dennett (eds), *The Mind's I* (London: Penguin, 1981).

The Mind's I includes Thomas Nagel's famous paper, 'What Is It Like to Be a Bat?', which is also included as Chapter 38 of Nigel Warburton (ed.), *Philosophy: Basic Readings* (London: Routledge, 1999).

WHY EXPECT THE SUN
TO RISE TOMORROW?

Every morning we expect the sun to appear over the horizon. But according to the philosopher David Hume (1711–76), our expectation is wholly irrational. This chapter gets to grips with Hume's extraordinary argument.

An Absurd Claim?

The scene: MacCruiskeen, a scientist, is watching the sunrise. She's accompanied by her close friend Pluck, a student of philosophy.

Pluck: Beautiful sunrise.

MacCruiskeen: Yes. And right on time, too.

Pluck: Yet there was no good reason to expect it to rise this morning.

MacCruiskeen: But the sun has risen every morning for millions of years. Of course it was going to rise this morning as well.

Pluck: There's no reason to suppose it will rise tomorrow, either. In fact, it's just as sensible to expect that a huge million-mile-wide bowl of tulips will appear over the horizon instead.

MacCruiskeen: I agree we can't be *certain* the sun will rise tomorrow. Some cataclysmic event might destroy the earth before then. But it's very *unlikely* that anything like that will happen. The *probability* is that the sun will rise, surely?

A TULIP SUNRISE

Pluck: You misunderstand me. I'm not just saying we can't be certain the sun will rise tomorrow. I'm saying *we have no more reason to suppose that it will rise than we have to suppose that it won't.*

MacCruiskeen: That's absurd. The evidence – such as the fact that the sun has risen every morning for millions of years – overwhelmingly supports my belief that the sun will rise tomorrow, too.

Pluck: You're mistaken.

Pluck's position might seem ridiculous. But Hume has an argument that appears to show that she's right. Not only is our belief that the sun will rise tomorrow wholly unjustified, but so, too, are all our scientific theories.

Before we look at Hume's argument, I need briefly to explain the difference between deductive and inductive reasoning.

Thinking Tools: Inductive and Deductive Reasoning

An *argument* consists of one or more claims or *premises* and a *conclusion* arranged in such a way that the premises are supposed to *support* the conclusion. Arguments come in one of two forms: *deductive* and *inductive*.

1. Deductive arguments
Here is an example of a deductive argument:

- All cats are mammals.
- My pet is a cat.
- Therefore my pet is a mammal.

Two things are required for a good deductive argument. First of all, the premises must be true. Secondly, the argument must be *valid*. The expression 'valid', in this context, means that the premises must *logically entail* the conclusion. In other words, to assert the premises but to deny the conclusion would be to involve oneself in a *logical contradiction*. The above argument is valid. A person who claims that all cats are mammals and that their pet is a cat but who also denies their pet is a mammal has contradicted him or herself.

2. Inductive arguments
Suppose you observe a thousand swans and discover them all to be white.

You don't come across any non-white swans. Then surely you have pretty good reason to conclude that all swans are white. You might reason like this:

- Swan 1 is white.
- Swan 2 is white.
- Swan 3 is white . . .
- Swan 1,000 is white.
- Therefore all swans are white.

This is an example of an inductive argument. Inductive arguments differ from deductive arguments in that their premises are supposed to *support*, but *not* logically entail, their conclusions. The above argument is not, and is not intended to be, deductively valid. To assert that the first thousand swans examined are white but that not *all* are white is not to contradict oneself (in fact, not all swans *are* white: there are black swans from New Zealand).

Nevertheless, we suppose that the fact that if all the swans we have observed so far are white, then that makes it *more likely* that all swans are white. The premises *support* the conclusion. We believe that an inductive argument can *justify* belief in its conclusion, despite not providing a logical guarantee that if the premises are true then the conclusion will be.

Why Is Induction Important?

We rely on inductive reasoning in arriving at beliefs about what we have not observed, including, most obviously, our beliefs about what will happen in the future.

Take, for example, my belief that the next time I sit in a chair it will support my weight. How is this belief justified? Well, I have sat in a great many chairs and they have always supported my weight before. That leads me to think it likely that the next chair I sit in will support my weight, too.

But notice that the statement that all the chairs I have ever sat in have supported my weight does not *logically entail* that the next chair will. There is no *contradiction* in supposing that even though I have never before experienced a chair collapse beneath me, that is what's about to happen.

But it then follows that I can't justify my belief that the next chair will not collapse by means of a *deductive* argument from what I have observed. So *if my belief is justified at all, it must be by means of an inductive argument.*

Science is heavily dependent on induction. Scientific theories are supposed to hold *for all times and places*, including those we have not observed. Again, the only evidence we have for their truth is what we have observed. So, again, we must rely on inductive reasoning to justify them.

The Unjustified Assumption

We have seen that inductive reasoning is important. Science depends on it. If it can be shown that inductive reasoning is wholly irrational, that would be a catastrophic result. Yet that's precisely what Hume believes he can show.

Let's return to Hume's argument. Hume believes it is no more rational to suppose the sun will rise tomorrow than it is to suppose that it won't. Hume's argument, in essence, is simple: it's that *induction rests on a wholly unjustified and unjustifiable assumption.* What is this assumption? Pluck proceeds to explain.

Pluck: Your belief that the sun will rise tomorrow is irrational. Hume explained why. Whenever you reason to a conclusion about what you haven't observed, you make an *assumption*.
MacCruiskeen: What assumption?
Pluck: You assume that *nature is uniform*.
MacCruiskeen: What do you mean?
Pluck: I mean you assume that those patterns that we have observed locally are likely to carry on into those portions of the universe that we haven't observed, including the future and the distant past.
MacCruiskeen: Why do I assume that?
Pluck: Well, put it this way: if you *didn't* believe that nature is uniform, then the fact that the sun has, in your experience, risen every day *wouldn't* lead you to expect it to continue to rise, would it?
MacCruiskeen: I guess not.
Pluck: So you see – *it's only because you assume nature is uniform that you conclude that the sun will continue to rise in the future.*

It appears that Pluck is right. Whenever we reason inductively, we make an assumption about the uniformity of nature. We assume that the universe is patterned throughout in just the same way.

Imagine an ant sitting in the middle of a bedspread. The ant can see that its bit of the bedspread is paisley-patterned. So the ant assumes the rest of the bedspread – the bits it can't see – are paisley-patterned, too. But why assume this? The bedspread could just as easily be a patchwork quilt. The bedspread could be paisley here, but plaid over there and polka-dotted over there. Or perhaps, just over the ant's horizon, the print on the bedspread turns to a chaotic mess, with blobs, lines and spots muddled up quite randomly.

We are in a similar position to the ant. The universe could also be a huge patchwork, with local regularities, such as the ones we have observed – the sun rising every day, trees growing leaves in the spring, objects falling when released, and so on – but no *overall* regularity. Perhaps the universe becomes a chaotic mess just over the horizon, with events happening entirely randomly. What reason have we to suppose this isn't the case? As Pluck is about to explain, it seems we have none.

Pluck: So the problem is this: unless you can *justify* your assumption that nature is uniform, your use of induction is itself unjustified. But then so, too, are all those conclusions based on inductive reasoning, including your belief that the sun will rise tomorrow.

MacCruiskeen: True.

Pluck: So how do we *justify* the assumption that nature is uniform?

We have just two options: we can either appeal to *experience* – to what you have observed – or you might try to justify the assumption *independently of experience*. MacCruiskeen is happy to admit that we cannot know that nature is uniform without observing nature.

MacCruiskeen: Obviously, we can't know independently of experience that nature is uniform.

Pluck: I agree. Our five senses – sight, touch, taste, hearing and smell – provide our only window on the world. Our knowledge of nature is dependent on their use.

MacCruiskeen: True.

Pluck: Which means that, if the assumption that nature is uniform is to be justified at all, it must be by appeal to what we have *experienced* of the world around us.

MacCruiskeen: Yes. But *isn't* the claim that nature is uniform justified by experience?

Pluck: No. To say that nature is uniform is to make a claim about what holds for *all* times and places.

MacCruiskeen: True.

Pluck: But you can't directly observe *all* of nature, can you? You can't observe the future. And you can't observe the distant past.

MacCruiskeen: Also true.

Pluck: But then your justification of the claim that nature is uniform must take the following form. You observe nature is uniform *around here* at the *present time*. Then you *infer* that nature is also like that at all those other times and places. Correct?

MacCruiskeen: I suppose so.

Pluck: But that is *itself* an inductive argument!

MacCruiskeen: Yes, it is.

Pluck: Your justification is, therefore, *circular*.

Here we reach the nub of Hume's argument. It seems that, if it can be confirmed at all, the assumption that nature is uniform can only be confirmed by observing that nature is uniform *around here* and then concluding that this is what it must be like *overall*.

But such a justification would itself be inductive. We would be using precisely the form of reasoning we're supposed to be justifying. Isn't there something unacceptably circular about such a justification?

The Circularity Problem

Pluck certainly thinks so.

MacCruiskeen: What is the problem with the justification being circular?

Pluck: Look, imagine that I think The Great Mystica, the psychic who works
              at the end of the pier, is a reliable source of information.

MacCruiskeen: That would be very foolish of you!

Pluck: But suppose my justification for trusting The Great Mystica is that she
              claims to be a reliable source of information. I trust her because she
              says she's trustworthy.

MacCruiskeen: That would be no justification at all! You need some reason to
              suppose that The Great Mystica is trustworthy *before* you trust her
              claim that she is.

Pluck: Exactly. Such a justification would be unacceptably circular because it
              would *presuppose* that The Great Mystica was reliable.

MacCruiskeen: I agree.

Pluck: But your attempt to justify induction is unacceptable for the very
              same reason. To justify induction you must first justify the claim that
              nature is uniform. But in attempting to justify the claim that nature is
              uniform you rely on induction. That won't do. You're just *presupposing*
              that induction is reliable.

We can now sum up Hume's extraordinary argument. All inductive reasoning, it
seems, relies on the assumption that nature is uniform. How, then, might this
assumption be justified? Only by experience, surely. But we cannot *directly observe*
that nature is uniform. So we must *infer* that it is uniform from what we have directly
observed: that is, from a *local* uniformity. But *such an inference would itself be
inductive*. Therefore we cannot justify the assumption. So our trust in induction is
unjustified.

'But Induction *Works*, Doesn't It?'

Perhaps you're not convinced. You might suggest that there is one very obvious
difference between, say, trusting induction and trusting The Great Mystica. For
induction *actually works*, doesn't it? It has produced countless true conclusions in
the past. It has allowed us successfully to build supercomputers, nuclear power-
stations and even to put a man on the moon. The Great Mystica, on the other hand,
may well have a very poor track record of making predictions. That's why we are
justified in believing that induction is a reliable mechanism for producing true beliefs,
whereas trusting The Great Mystica is not.

The problem, of course, is that this is itself an example of inductive reasoning. We are arguing, in effect, that induction has *worked until now*, and therefore induction will continue to work. Since the reliability of induction is what is in question here, it seems that this justification is, again, unacceptably circular. It is, after all, just like trying to justify trust in the claims of The Great Mystica by pointing out that she herself claims to be reliable.

An Astonishing Conclusion

The conclusion to which we have been driven is a sceptical one. Sceptics claim that we do not know what we might think we know. In this case the scepticism concerns *knowledge of the unobserved*. Hume and Pluck seem to have shown that we have no justification for our beliefs about the unobserved, and thus no *knowledge* of the unobserved.

Hume's conclusion is a fantastic one. It's a good test of whether someone has actually understood Hume's argument that they acknowledge its conclusion is fantastic (many students new to philosophy misinterpret Hume: they think his conclusion is merely that we cannot be *certain* what will happen tomorrow). In fact, so fantastic is Hume's conclusion that MacCruiskeen cannot believe that Pluck is really prepared to accept it.

MacCruiskeen: You're suggesting that what we've observed to happen so far gives us *no clue at all* as to what will happen in the future?

Pluck: Yes. Things *may* continue in the same manner. The sun may continue to rise. Chairs may continue to support our weight. But we have *no justification whatsoever* for believing any of these things.

MacCruiskeen: Let me get this straight. If someone were to believe that it's just as likely that a huge bunch of tulips will appear over the horizon tomorrow morning, that chairs will vanish when sat on, that in future water will be poisonous and objects will fall upwards when released, we would ordinarily think them *insane*. Correct?

Pluck: Yes, we would.

MacCruiskeen: But if you're right, these 'insane' beliefs about the future are actually just as well supported by the available evidence as is our 'sensible' belief that the sun will rise tomorrow. Rationally, we should accept that these 'insane' beliefs are actually just as likely to be true!

Pluck: That's correct.

MacCruiskeen: You *really* believe that? You really believe it's just as likely that a million-mile-wide bowl of tulips will appear over the horizon tomorrow morning?

Pluck: Well, actually, no, I don't.

MacCruiskeen: Oh?

Pluck: I do believe the sun will rise tomorrow. For some reason, I *just can't help myself*. I see that, *rationally*, I *shouldn't* believe. But while I realise that my belief is wholly irrational, I can't stop believing.

Hume's Explanation of Why We Believe

Like Pluck, Hume admitted that we *can't help* but believe that the sun will rise tomorrow, that chairs will continue to support our weight, and so on. In Hume's view, our minds are so constituted that when we are exposed to a regularity, we have no choice but to believe the regularity will continue. Belief is a sort of involuntary, knee-jerk response to the patterns we have experienced.

Thinking Tools: Reasons and Causes – Two Ways of Explaining *Why* People Believe What They Do

Hume's explanation of why we believe that the sun will rise tomorrow does not, of course, give us the slightest reason to suppose that this belief is actually *true*.

It is useful to distinguish two very different ways in which we can 'give the reason' why someone believes something. We may give the *grounds* or *evidence* that a person has for holding a belief. Or we may explain what has *caused* this person to believe what they do.

It's important to realise that *to offer a causal explanation of a belief is not necessarily to offer any sort of rational justification for holding it.* Consider these explanations:

- Tom believes he is a teapot because he was hypnotised during a stage act.
- Anne believes in fairies because she is mentally ill.
- Geoff believes in alien abduction because he was indoctrinated by the Blue Meanie cult.

These are purely causal explanations. To point out that someone believes they are a teapot because they were hypnotised into having that belief during the course of a hypnotist's routine is not to provide the slightest grounds for supposing that this belief is true.

The following explanation, on the other hand, gives the subject's grounds for belief (which is not yet to say they are good grounds):

- Tom believes in astrology because he finds that newspaper astrology predictions are quite often correct.

Interestingly, ask the hypnotised person why they believe they are a teapot and chances are they will be unable to answer. The correct *causal* explanation is unavailable to them (assuming they don't know they have been hypnotised). But nor will they be able to offer a convincing *justification* for their belief. They may simply find themselves 'stuck' with a belief that they may themselves recognise is irrational.

Hume admits that, similarly, his explanation of why we believe the sun will rise tomorrow does not supply the slightest grounds for supposing that this belief is true. Indeed, we have no such grounds. It is, again, a belief we simply find ourselves 'stuck' with.

Conclusion

If Hume is right, the belief that the sun will rise tomorrow is as unjustified as the belief that a million-mile-wide bowl of tulips will appear over the horizon instead. We suppose the second belief is insane. But if Hume is correct, the first belief is actually no more rational. This conclusion strikes us as absurd, of course. But Hume even explains *why* it strikes us as absurd: we are made in such a way that we *can't help* but reason inductively. We can't help having these irrational beliefs.

Hume's argument continues to perplex both philosophers and scientists. There's still no consensus about whether Hume is right. Some believe that we have no choice but to embrace Hume's sceptical conclusion about the unobserved. Others believe that the conclusion is clearly ridiculous. But then the onus is on these defenders of 'common sense' to show precisely *what* is wrong with Hume's argument. No one has yet succeeded in doing this (or at least no one has succeeded in convincing a majority of philosophers that they have done so).

What to read next

This chapter introduces scepticism about the unobserved. Chapter 8, The Strange Case of the Rational Dentist, and Chapter 3, Brain-Snatched, introduce other forms of scepticism: scepticism concerning other minds and scepticism about the external world.

In Chapter 19, What Is Knowledge?, I discuss the possibility that justification is not required for knowledge. Might this suggestion help us to defeat the sceptic?

Further reading

A good discussion of the problem of induction can be found in:

Chris Horner and Emrys Westacott, *Thinking through Philosophy* (Cambridge: Cambridge University Press, 2000), Chapter 4.

A simple but effective introduction to the problem of induction and to some of the philosophical issues surrounding science is provided by:

Nigel Warburton, *Philosophy: The Basics*, second edition (London: Routledge, 1995), Chapter 5.

DO WE EVER DESERVE
TO BE PUNISHED?

We think of ourselves as able to make free choices on which we can act. Surely I'm free to choose between working today or not working, having a cup of coffee or doing without, stealing from the supermarket or acting honestly? That's the 'common-sense' view.

We also suppose that, when a person acts nobly and generously, they deserve our praise, and that when they act badly they deserve condemnation and, in some cases, even punishment.

But is any of this true? As we discover in this chapter, the findings of science appear to suggest otherwise.

Divney's Defence

The scene: a courtroom. The case of Divney, a serial killer, has come before the jury. Divney is defending himself. We join him in mid-flow.

Divney: I admit killing these people.
Judge: And you have no remorse?
Divney: None.
Judge: That's all you have to say for yourself?
Divney: No. I shall prove I do not deserve to be punished.

The judge raises an incredulous eyebrow.

Judge: And how will you do that?
Divney: By proving that *I couldn't help it*.
Judge: What do you mean? You mean someone *forced* you to commit these crimes?
Divney: I don't mean that. No one put a gun to my head. Yet I had no option but to kill them.

Judge: I see. You're claiming to suffer from some sort of mental illness, then?
Divney: I'm quite sane. But I *didn't act freely*. So I don't deserve punishment.

Divney's claim might seem outrageous. Yet the findings of science appear to back him up, as Divney now explains.

Hard Determinism

Judge: I'm not sure I understand.
Divney: Allow me to call my expert witness, the world's leading physicist, Professor Hatchjaw.

Hatchjaw is ushered into court.

Prof Hatchjaw: Good afternoon.
Divney: Professor, could you explain *determinism* to the court?
Prof Hatchjaw: Certainly. Determinists claim that the universe is governed by strict and exceptionless laws – the laws of nature. They also believe that the state of the universe at any particular moment in time, plus the laws of nature, together *necessitate* what will happen in future.

Hatchjaw is right. Indeed, determinists believe that, given full knowledge of the state of the universe a million years ago, plus knowledge of the laws of nature, a physicist could, in principle, predict everything that has ever happened since, down to the movement of the very last atom.

Divney: I see. And determinism applies to *everything* that goes on in the universe? It applies even to my actions?
Prof Hatchjaw: Of course. The movements of your body fall under the same natural laws as everything else.
Judge: Stop for one moment. I don't understand. There are no *laws of human behaviour*, are there? For example, there's no law that says that if someone is hungry, they will eat. Yes, hungry people tend to eat. But some choose not to. Occasionally, they even starve themselves to death. Doesn't this show that human behaviour is *not* under the control of laws?

Prof Hatchjaw: Perhaps there are no laws of human behaviour. I don't claim there are. But a human being is a storm of tiny particles: electrons, protons, neutrons, and so on, all whirling and whizzing about in a very complex way.

Now, according to determinism, each and every one of these particles is in the vice-like grip of rigid and inexorable natural laws. The particles out of which a human being is made cannot do anything other than what they in fact do. So you see, humans are *not* free. They *do* fall under the same physical laws as everything else.

'.. human being is a storm of tiny particles'

Divney: So it's true, isn't it, that according to determinism, I couldn't do anything other than what I did? I wasn't free to do otherwise?

Prof Hatchjaw: Yes, that does appear to follow.

The position just sketched out by Hatchjaw is that of *hard determinism*. In Hatchjaw's view, you are a cog in the great universe-machine, no more able to do your own thing than is, say, one of the little cogs in my wristwatch. Determinists take the view thateverything you have ever done or will ever do is preordained by nature. Hard determinists also believe that *the truth of determinism entails that we lack free will.*

Moral Responsibility

If we lack free will then, as Divney now explains, it seems we can't be held morally responsible for what we do.

Divney: Now, I can only be held responsible for events over which I have some control. That's the view of the law, isn't it?

Judge: It is.

Divney: But, as you've just heard the world's leading physicist explain, *I couldn't have done anything other than what I did.* If I was unable to do otherwise, then surely I can be held neither legally nor morally responsible for killing those people.

This part of Divney's defence also appears to be sound. We wouldn't hold someone pushed out of a window responsible for killing the person on top of whom they happened to land. But then how can we legitimately hold Divney responsible for what he did? He was no more able not to kill those people than a cloud is able to drift against the wind or a river to run uphill.

Judge: If what you say is true, then no one *ever* deserves to be punished.
Divney: That's right. We're *all* helpless puppets dancing on nature's strings.

Divney's defence might *seem* compelling. But is it watertight?

The Feeling of Freedom

The judge was unconvinced.

Judge: It's obvious we *are* free. We're inwardly aware of our own freedom to do otherwise. Here's an example. Right now, I'm completely free either to raise my arm or not raise my arm.

The judge raises his arm.

Judge: There, I raised my arm. But I could just as easily have chosen not to. I was aware, at the moment I made the decision, that I was able to do either.

The judge is certainly correct that we *feel* ourselves to be free. In fact, this feeling of freedom is often at its most acute when we are tempted to do wrong. It's precisely because one believes that one is free either to steal that cake or not steal it that one agonises over which course of action to take.

Divney: It may *feel* to you as if you are able to make a free choice, but appearances are deceptive. As we've just seen, science shows you to be in the iron grip of the same exceptionless laws that govern tides, rock falls, planetary motions and all other natural phenomena. What leads you astray is the fact that you know that sometimes you raise your arm and sometimes don't. That leads you to suppose you could do either now. But the fact that you sometimes raise your arm and sometimes don't doesn't entail that what happens on each occasion is not *made* to happen by laws lying entirely beyond your control.

The philosopher Arthur Schopenhauer (1788–1860) makes much the same point as that just made by Divney in his book *On the Freedom of the Will.*[*] Schopenhauer points out that water behaves in many different ways. Sometimes it runs quickly downhill; at other times it lies quietly in a lake. It can also form a rough and turbulent sea. Water can behave in all these ways. But that doesn't show that the water in my glass is now free to behave in any of these ways independently of what the laws of nature dictate.

Is Divney's defence sound?

Compatibilism

Many philosophers insist that, while determinism may be true, it's compatible with free will. This is the position of the *compatibilist*. The key compatibilist idea is that what we ordinarily mean when we claim that someone 'acted freely' is actually consistent with the truth of determinism. According to a compatibilist, even if determinism is true, Divney may nevertheless have 'acted freely' and so may still deserve punishment for what he did.

It is a compatibilist that the prosecution now calls to the witness box.

Prosecution: May I call my own expert witness, the philosopher Professor Siddery.
Prof Siddery: Good afternoon.
Prosecution: Professor Siddery, you believe, as have a number of philosophers
            down through the centuries, that determinism and free will are
            actually *compatible*, do you not?
Prof Siddery: That's correct. It seems to me that Professor Hatchjaw is confused.
Prosecution: In what way?
Prof Siddery: Hatchjaw has muddled up two quite different ways in which we
            use the word 'free'.

---

[*] Arthur Schopenhauer, *On the Freedom of the Will* (Oxford: Blackwell, 1985), p. 43.

Prosecution: In what way?

Prof Siddery: I admit that Divney did not 'act freely' if by this you mean simply that he *could have done otherwise*. However, when we *usually* describe people as 'acting freely', that is not what we mean.

Prosecution: What *do* we mean?

Prof Siddery: We mean only that they would have done otherwise *if they had so chosen*.

This move is made by the philosopher G. E. Moore (1873–1958). According to Moore, even if determinism is true, we can still act freely. For an act to be free is for it to be true that we could have acted differently had we so chosen. Even if determinism is true, it can still be correct to say that we would have acted differently had we so chosen. So determinism is compatible with free will after all.

Prosecution: Your view is that Divney did act 'freely', as that word is usually used? He does have free will?

Prof Siddery: Yes, he does.

Prosecution: So, whether or not determinism is true, Divney can still be held responsible for what he did?

Prof Siddery: Again, yes. Divney acted *voluntarily*, in the sense that he *did as he wanted*. For that reason, he can be held responsible and does deserve punishment.

A Problem for Compatibilism

The compatibilist position is attractive because it allows us to hold people responsible for their *voluntary* actions, for doing what they *want* to do, whether or not determinism is true.

But is compatibilism plausible? Not according to the hard determinist, who typically accuses the compatibilist of verbal trickery, of redefining 'freely' to suit their own ends.

Divney: Professor Siddery, you say that I acted freely simply because I would have acted differently *had I so chosen*? And you suggest this means that I can be held responsible for what I did?

Prof Siddery: Correct.

Divney: I see. It seems to me that you are overlooking a key fact. Yes, I would have acted differently if I had chosen otherwise. But of course *I couldn't have chosen otherwise.* Everything that goes on in my mind – including the choices I make – is fixed by what is going on inside my brain. And what goes on in my brain falls under the same natural laws as everything else. So I *couldn't* have chosen otherwise, could I?

Prof Siddery: No. But is that relevant to the question of whether or not you are blameworthy?

Divney: Yes, it is! Here's an analogous case. Without him knowing, I hypnotise someone into always choosing orange juice rather than lemonade. He is then offered a glass of each and, because of the hypnotism, he chooses orange juice. Now, this person's action is, on your rather peculiar definition of 'free', free. For it's true that *he would have acted differently had he so chosen.* Correct?

Prof Siddery: Yes.

Divney: He even 'feels' free.

Prof Siddery: I suppose so.

Divney: Yet this hypnotised person didn't make a free choice, did he? For his mind is in the grip of forces beyond his control. His *choice* was *itself* determined – in this case, by me and my hypnotic powers.

Prof Siddery: True.

Divney: Now, this is *not* what we would ordinarily consider to be an example of a 'free action', is it?

Prof Siddery: I guess not.

Divney: But if this hypnotised person does not act freely, despite its being true that he would have acted differently had he so chosen, *then your definition of freedom is unacceptable.*

The judge asks for clarification.

Judge: And you think this shows that *you* cannot be held responsible?

Divney: Of course. Someone whose mind is entirely in the grip of forces beyond his control cannot be held responsible for what he does, even if it is true that, as Professor Siddery puts it, 'they would have done otherwise if they had so chosen'. The hypnotised person *isn't* responsible for his action. Now, Hatchjaw explained that *my* mind is in the grip of forces beyond *my* control – it's wholly in the grip of the laws of nature – so *I* cannot be held responsible.

Libertarianism: Supernatural Souls

This is a powerful criticism of compatibilism. Perhaps the position can be modified to take account of it. But perhaps it can't. Perhaps the only way to allow for freedom and moral responsibility is to reject determinism. Those who take this route are called *libertarians.*

It is a libertarian that the prosecution now calls to the witness box.

Prosecution: I call my second expert witness: the Reverend O'Feersa.
Revd O'Feersa: Hello.
Prosecution: Reverend, I believe you also take the view that each of us is free?
Revd O'Feersa: Yes. But I reject compatibilism. I also reject determinism. In my view, each of us is a *soul*. It's this soul that makes choices and decisions. Now, in my view the soul *stands outside the natural order of things.* It's something non-physical. It's *supernatural*.
Prosecution: The soul is not in the grip of natural law?
Revd O'Feersa: Precisely. The soul is *free.*
Prosecution: Which means that Divney's choice was free, and that he can be held morally responsible?
Revd O'Feersa: Yes.

Divney cross-examines.

Divney: Personally, I don't believe in the existence of such peculiar things as souls. The onus must be on you to justify your view that they exist. Surely it would be wrong to send me to prison on the grounds that this happens to be your *opinion*. You need to back your view with *grounds*.
Revd O'Feersa: I think I can supply such grounds. Each of us is internally aware of his or her own freedom not to do what nature commands.

But, as both Divney and Schopenhauer have already pointed out, this feeling of freedom seems to count for very little: it does not establish that one is not in the grip of natural law.

Divney thought the Reverend O'Feersa's conclusion patently absurd.

Divney: What you suggest is ridiculous. Can you explain to me *how* the soul controls the body?

Revd O'Feersa: The soul controls the body by affecting what happens in the brain. That in turn affects how one's body behaves.

Divney: But, as Professor Hatchjaw has already testified, everything that happens in the universe, including what happens in the brain, is determined by natural law. What happens in the brain is fixed in advance by nature and can't be altered.

Revd O'Feersa: Professor Hatchjaw is wrong about that.

Divney: Really?

Revd O'Feersa: Yes. While the universe is, generally speaking, governed by laws, these laws do not always apply to the brain. The soul – something spiritual rather than material – can come in and *override* natural law from outside the system, as it were, and make something happen that wouldn't otherwise happen.

Divney: That's your opinion? That the laws of nature apply throughout the entire universe *except this one spot*? You believe that the human brain functions as a sort of aerial to pick up transmissions from a soul-thing that lies outside the natural order?

Revd O'Feersa: That is my view.

Divney: But this is scientifically absurd!

The suggestion that the laws of nature apply everywhere except in our brains is certainly a lot to swallow. One would need very good grounds for supposing this claim to be true.

Do we have such grounds? We have already seen that the mere fact that we *feel* free is hardly compelling evidence.

A Different Libertarian Position

The prosecution has one last stab at undermining Divney's defence. They appeal to a rather different sort of libertarian position, one that does not require that one buy into the supernatural soul theory favoured by the Reverend O'Feersa.

Prosecution: May I call Professor Hatchjaw back to the witness box? Professor Hatchjaw, you have spoken about determinism. But is determinism true?

Prof Hatchjaw: Well, *strictly speaking*, no. I've been simplifying a bit. The truth is that we scientists have known for some time that there is a certain amount of indeterminacy in the universe. The subatomic particles are not in the vice-like grip of *strict and exceptionless* laws. To a certain extent, what will happen is left open by the laws of nature. Einstein refused to accept this: he famously insisted that 'God does not play dice'. But it seems that Einstein was wrong. Quantum mechanics rejects determinism. It says that, up to a point, what happens in the universe is random, a matter of pure chance.

Prosecution: Now, this means, I take it, that there are likely to be certain events that took place in Divney's brain on the day he committed the murders that *weren't* determined, that were random?

Prof Hatchjaw: True.

Prosecution: In which case Divney's choices and actions need *not* have been determined?

Prof Hatchjaw: Yes, I suppose that's true, too.

Has the prosecution established that Divney may be culpable after all?

In fact, while quantum indeterminacy may entail that some of Divney's choices and actions were not determined, it seems that this is not enough to allow Divney free will, as Divney now explains.

Divney: An ingenious suggestion. But it won't work. You see, free will is no more compatible with the suggestion that our actions are a product of random events than it is with the suggestion that they are a result of determined ones.

Judge: Why so?

Divney: Suppose that, due to some random event in my brain – a neuron
            spontaneously firing all by itself, say – my arm suddenly shoots out
            and hits you on the nose. Surely I am morally blameless. The fact that
            a bit of my behaviour issued from some chance event suffices to show
            that it was *not* within my control and that I should *not* be held
            responsible for it.

It seems that Divney is right. What we need, for moral responsibility, is for *Divney
himself* to be in control of his actions. Unfortunately, the suggestion that his actions
are a result of random events gives him no more control over them than does the
suggestion that they are determined by natural law.

The Verdict

Judge: I must say that I've been very impressed by your defence. I think
            you've succeeded in showing that there is, as you say, very reasonable
            doubt about your culpability. Science appears to be on your side.
Divney: So I'm to be released?
Judge: No. I agree that you're morally blameless. Yet I'm still justified in
            locking you away. One can still make a good case for locking people
            up, even if it's true that they lack free will and do not *deserve* to be
            punished.
Divney: What case?
Judge: Even though you don't deserve punishment, punishment is still
            appropriate. For it will *deter others* from committing similar crimes.
Divney: That's true, I suppose.
Judge: I could also send you somewhere where you might be *rehabilitated*.
            You could be given therapy, perhaps, to prevent you from committing
            such crimes again.
Divney: Also true, I guess.
Judge: Most important, if I thought it likely that you would re-offend . . .
Divney: Oh, I would, I would.
Judge: . . . then I'm justified in locking you up to *prevent* you from re-
            offending.

Divney is led off to the cells.

Conclusion

While we ordinarily believe that people often deserve punishment, the findings of modern science throw this 'common-sense' view into serious doubt. It seems that whatever we do, we cannot be blamed for doing it. There may still be a role for prison and other forms of punishment. But it seems we're going to have to revise our attitudes about punishment radically. Either that or we must identify the flaw in Divney's argument.

What to read next

In this chapter, a 'common-sense' view is challenged by philosophical argument. We are presented with an argument that seems to show that, appearances to the contrary, we are not free. For other examples where philosophical argument produces highly counter-intuitive consequences, see Chapter 3, Brain-Snatched, Chapter 8, The Strange Case of the Rational Dentist, Chapter 14, Why Expect the Sun to Rise Tomorrow?, and the paradoxes of Chapter 25, Seven Paradoxes.

Further reading

A clear overview of the arguments of this chapter is provided by:

Chris Horner and Emrys Westacott, *Thinking through Philosophy* (Cambridge: Cambridge University Press, 2000), pp. 1–16.

THE MEANING
MYSTERY

Language is an extraordinarily powerful tool – the most important tool we possess. How do our sounds, squiggles and other signs come by their astonishing power to mean something? Indeed, what *is* meaning, exactly? This chapter introduces some of the key ideas of two philosophers: John Locke (1632–1704) and Ludwig Wittgenstein (1889–1951).

Where Does Meaning Originate?

Take a look at the following sequence of straight and curved lines.

I AM HAPPY

In English these lines mean *I am happy*. But there could be other languages in which this same combination of lines conveys quite a different thought. There might be an alien civilisation for which they mean *my trousers are in tatters* (I don't say this is likely, of course, but it's possible). The lines are in themselves devoid of any particular meaning.

The same is true of other forms of representation, including diagrams, illustrations and samples. They don't have any *intrinsic* representational power or meaning.

You might wonder about this. Here's a well-known example from the philosopher Wittgenstein.

You might think that this simple combination of lines just *has* to represent a person climbing a hill. But as Wittgenstein points out, this same image could also be used to represent a man sliding down a hill backwards.

Indeed, we can imagine one-eyed aliens for whom this combination of lines is used to represent a face

or a map-maker for whom this image represents where the treasure is buried ('O' marks the spot).

There's nothing intrinsic to the lines themselves that makes them mean one of these things rather than another.

What of a simple patch of red? Surely that can mean only one thing: red.

Not so. A red patch might have all sorts of meanings. If the patch is square, for example, then it might mean *red square*. Or it might simply mean *square* (the sample just happens to be red). If the patch is scarlet, then it might be used to represent just *that* shade of red. Or it could also be used to represent a much wider section of the colour spectrum, such as red, purple and blue. A red patch might be used to symbolise blood or to warn of danger. I could use a red blob to record in my diary those days on which I ate a chocolate biscuit. In fact, a red patch might be used to mean pretty much anything.

The moral is that nothing is intrinsically meaningful. Anything can be used to represent or mean more or less anything under the right conditions.

Meaning as an 'Inner' Process

But if nothing *intrinsically* means or represents anything, then how do our words and other symbols come by their representational powers? What gives them meaning? The answer, of course, is that *we* do. But how?

Here's one traditionally popular suggestion.

Suppose that a parrot starts to mimic the expression 'I am happy'. Of course, the parrot doesn't mean anything by these words. It's probably unaware even that the words have a meaning. On the other hand, when I say 'I am happy', I don't just *say* something: I *mean* something.

So, although we say the same words, only one of us means something by them. Why is this? Why do I mean something but the parrot doesn't? After all, both the parrot and I engage in *the same outward, observable process.* We both say, 'I am happy'.

It seems, then, that the essential difference between us must be *hidden*. In meaning something, I must be engaged in an additional process, a process that accompanies the outward process of saying the words, a process that the parrot doesn't engage in. When I say 'I am happy', the outward physical process of saying is accompanied by *an inner mental process of meaning*. It is the inner mental process that breathes life into our words and transforms them from mere sounds into significant utterances.

Locke's Theory of Meaning

An example of the view that meaning is essentially 'inner' is provided by the seventeenth-century philosopher John Locke.

In Locke's view, the mind is like a container. At birth, the container is empty. Gradually, our senses begin to furnish this inner space with objects. Locke calls these mental objects 'Ideas'. We have simple Ideas, such as the Idea of the colour red. Locke seems to think of the Idea of red as being a mental image of some sort. We also have complex Ideas that are built out of simple Ideas. For example, my Idea of a snowball is made up of simpler Ideas, including those of white, cold, hard and round.

In Locke's view, Ideas form the building blocks of thought. Our thoughts are made up of sequences of Ideas. And words obtain their meaning by standing for these Ideas:

Words in their primary or immediate Signification, stand for nothing, but the Idea in the Mind of him that uses them . . .*

The difference between me and the parrot, in Locke's view – the difference that explains why I mean something by and understand what I say and the parrot

---

* John Locke, *An Essay Concerning Human Understanding* (Oxford, Clarendon Press, 1975), Book III, Part ii, Section 1.

doesn't – is that, unlike the parrot, I have correlated the outward string of words 'I am happy' with a sequence of mental objects. The outward process of saying the words is accompanied by an inner parade of Ideas. No such mental parade takes place inside the mind of the parrot.

This is called the *Ideational theory of meaning.*

How to Pick Out a 'Red' Object

The Ideational theory provides an explanation of how we are able to understand and apply a word correctly. For example, suppose I ask you to pick out something red from your environment. No doubt you did so effortlessly. Yet all I gave you were some squiggly lines: 'red'. How did you know what to do with them?

It seems that in the Ideational theory, something like the following must have happened. You engaged in a sort of internal 'looking-up' process. On receiving the word 'red', you looked up in your memory – which functions, in effect, as a storehouse of Ideas – the Idea with which you have previously learned to correlate that word. This Idea, a sort of memory image of the colour red, provides you with a template or sample with which other things can be compared. You then compared this Idea with the objects around you until you got a match. You then picked that object.

You may not be conscious of having engaged in such an inner 'looking-up' process. But perhaps that is because, for a mature language user like yourself, the process is so quick and habitual that you no longer need to pay it any attention.

A Popular Picture

Down through the centuries, many thinkers have been drawn to the 'inner process' model of meaning and understanding sketched out above. Indeed, the inner process model might well strike you as being 'just obviously' true. How else, you might wonder, are we to think of meaning and understanding, if not in terms of such processes taking place in the mind? Almost everyone finds themselves drawn to the inner process model when first they start to think about meaning and understanding.

It may surprise you, then, to discover that the inner process model is now rejected by the vast majority of philosophers. One of the main reasons for this is the influence of the later work of Wittgenstein. Wittgenstein constructed powerful arguments that show that the inner process model doesn't explain what it's supposed to.

Here are two of Wittgenstein's best-known criticisms of the inner process model.

Argument 1: How to Pick the Right Inner Object?

Let's return to the suggestion that to understand a word is to engage in an inner looking-up process. Think about the following scenario:

> Pedro runs a paint shop. Pedro receives lots of orders for paint written in English. Unfortunately, Pedro cannot read English. So John, who can, set up a little filing cabinet in Pedro's office. In the cabinet are cards. On each card is a blob of paint. The cards also have labels taped to them. On each label is printed the English word for the colour that appears on the card. When Pedro gets an order, he simply checks the English colour word on the order form against the labels in his file. When he finds the right card, he pulls it out and compares the colour on the card with the tins of paint in his shop. Pedro then dispatches a tin of that colour.

It was suggested a moment ago that a similar looking-up process must explain your ability to apply the term 'red' correctly. Only we supposed that the looking-up process must take place *in your mind.* You have a *mental* filing cabinet, if you like – a storehouse of Ideas – in which you have previously filed memory images of colours correlated with their English names. When you received the word 'red', you went to your mental filing cabinet and pulled out the right sample. You then compared the objects around you with this memory image until you found a match.

But does this inner looking-up process really explain your ability to pick out those things to which the word 'red' applies? Not according to Wittgenstein, who points out that the process actually presupposes what it's supposed to explain. To see why, ask yourself the following question: how did you pick out the right memory image?

'I don't see the problem,' you might say. 'Why can't I just go to my mental filing cabinet and look up the right mental image, the one I previously correlated with the word "red"?'

The difficulty is that a mental image is not objective. It's not the sort of thing you might attach a label to and put in a drawer for future reference. Once you're no longer aware of a mental image, it's gone. So when next you want to conjure up a mental image of 'red', how do you know what sort of image you are supposed to be imagining? You need *already* to know what 'red' means in order to know that. Yet it was your knowledge of what 'red' means that the mental image was supposed to explain.

So the 'inner process' explanation of how you are able to apply 'red' correctly is circular. It's suggested that you are able to pick out the right external object by comparing it with an inner object. But this takes for granted your ability to pick out the right *inner* object. We've taken for granted precisely the ability we're supposed to be explaining.

The situation is quite different when it comes to an *objective* sample, like a piece of coloured card. Pedro doesn't need to know what 'red' means in order to find the right coloured sample in his filing cabinet. This is because the word 'red' is physically, objectively taped to the right piece of card.

Argument 2: How Does the Inner Object Come by Its Meaning?

Even if you can somehow manage to call up the right memory image without already knowing what 'red' means, there remains a problem. The suggestion that words and other signs ultimately come by their meaning by being correlated with inner objects – Ideas – seems satisfactory only while one forgets to ask: and how in turn do these *inner* objects come by *their* meaning?

Suppose that you correlate the word 'red' with a mental image of a red square. Do you thereby give 'red' a meaning?

No. We have already seen that public samples – a red square painted on a piece of card, for example – can be interpreted in innumerable ways. But exactly the same difficulty arises with respect to mental samples. They are no more *intrinsically* meaningful than are public samples.

Let's suppose, for example, that your mental image is of a scarlet square. Should you then apply 'red' only to scarlet objects? Or would an orange object do? Or perhaps your sample just happens to be red, and it really represents squareness. So should you pick out only square objects? And so on. Your mental image fails to provide the answers to any of these questions.

It's clear that we have again gone round in a circle. This time we have explained how words and other signs come by their meaning only by presupposing that certain signs – the mental ones – *already* have a meaning. So the mystery of how meaning ultimately originates remains.

Round and Round in Circles . . .

Wittgenstein points out that the explanations provided by the inner process model are circular. The model tries to explain how public words and signs have meaning by appealing to private, inner objects, but then takes the meaning of these inner objects for granted. It also tries to explain how you are able to identify which external objects are 'red', but only by presupposing that you already possess the ability to identify which internal objects are 'red'.

Here are two more examples of circular explanations. We once tried to explain how the earth is held up by supposing that it sits on the back of a great animal: an elephant. Of course, this explanation didn't really remove the mystery with which we were grappling, for we then needed to explain what held the elephant up. So we introduced another animal – a turtle – for the elephant to sit on.

But then what did the turtle sit on? Should we have introduced yet another animal to support the turtle, and another animal to support that animal, and so on without end?

The problem is that our explanation really just took for granted what it was supposed to explain: why *anything at all* gets held up.

A similar circularity plagues the suggestion that the behaviour of a person can be explained as the result of the behaviour of lots of little people running around inside controlling the full-size person much as if they were controlling a ship.

The explanation is circular because we now need to explain the behaviour of these little people. Do we suppose that they have still smaller people running around inside their heads? If so, do these still smaller people have people running round in *their* heads?

Of course, to point out that these explanations are circular is not to prove that there is no elephant or that there are no little people running around inside our heads. But if the only reason for introducing the elephant and those little people in the first place was to explain certain things which, it turns out, they don't explain but just take for granted, then whatever justification we thought we had for introducing them is entirely demolished.

The same, of course, goes for the inner, mental 'looking-up' machinery introduced by the inner process model. By showing that this machinery takes for granted what it's supposed to explain, Wittgenstein demolishes the justification we thought we had for introducing it.

Meaning and Use

The temptation against which Wittgenstein warns us is that of thinking of meaning and understanding as mysterious inner activities or processes.

We are tempted to think that the action of language consists of two parts: an inorganic part – the handling of signs – and an organic part, which we may call understanding these signs, meaning them, interpreting them, thinking them. These latter activities seem to take place in a queer kind of medium, the mind. And the mechanism of the mind – the nature of which, it seems, we don't quite understand – can bring about effects that no material mechanism could.*

So in what does the difference between myself and the parrot essentially consist, in Wittgenstein's view, if not in something inner? Broadly speaking, it consists in what we are able to do. I possess a whole range of abilities that manifest my grasp of what is meant by 'I am happy'. For example, if asked, I can explain what the expression 'happy' means. I can point to examples. I can use the expression appropriately. I can also use these words to construct many other different sentences. Parrots, on the other hand, can do none of these things.

The revolution in thinking about meaning brought about by Wittgenstein's later work lies in this shift in focus from what goes on 'inside' to our publicly observable abilities. Meaning isn't 'hidden'. It lies on the surface, in the use to which we put our words and other signs. In Wittgenstein's view, to grasp the meaning of a word is not to have correlated it with some mysterious inner object, but, roughly speaking, *to know how it's used.*†

What to read next

In Chapter 6, Could a Machine Think?, I look at an argument – Searle's Chinese Room Thought-Experiment – that appears to show that more is required for understanding than simply being able perfectly to replicate the outward behaviour and abilities of beings like ourselves. Searle believes that even a mindless automaton could do that. But we have just seen that in Wittgenstein's view your understanding resides entirely in what is publicly observable. Who is right: Wittgenstein or Searle?

Further reading

An excellent and detailed discussion of the issues raised in this chapter can be found in:

Simon Blackburn, *Spreading the Word* (Oxford: Clarendon Press, 1982), Chapter 2.

---

* Ludwig Wittgenstein, *The Blue and Brown Books* (Oxford: Blackwell, 1972), p. 3.
† Some readers might feel a little short-changed. And perhaps rightly so. Wittgenstein has pointed out why one particular explanation of how I am able to identify that *that* is red (I am looking at a red object as I write) fails. But how *am* I able to do this, then? Wittgenstein doesn't offer an alternative theory. In fact, Wittgenstein's view is that we don't need a theory. But that's another story.

KILLING MARY TO SAVE JODIE

One of the Ten Commandments handed down to Moses was 'Thou shall not kill'. But is it *always* wrong to kill? Most of us believe that there are exceptions to the rule. We believe, for example, that it would be morally acceptable to shoot dead a maniac about to embark on an orgy of killing in a school playground if that was the only way to stop him. Here I discuss another possible exception – that of killing one *innocent* person in order to save another. Is that ever morally acceptable?

The Case of Jodie and Mary

Not very long ago, two girls were born connected at the lower abdomen. The parents, from the island of Gozo in the Mediterranean, travelled to Britain so that their daughters could receive specialist medical treatment. British doctors found that one of the two girls – Mary – had only a rudimentary brain. She also depended for her blood supply on the heart and lungs of Jodie, her twin sister, who, according to evidence given in court, was a 'bright and alert baby, sparkling and sucking on her dummy'. The prognosis was bad. Leave the girls attached and both would die within months. Separate them and Jodie had a good chance of surviving, if with some physical handicaps. The immediate result of such an operation, however, would be the death of Mary. The doctors wanted to operate. The parents, devout Catholics, objected, insisting that, as it is wrong to kill, and as the operation would clearly result in the killing of Mary, 'God's will' must be that the doctors allow both girls to die. The parents took the case to court. The doctors won the case, and the operation went ahead. Mary died. But Jodie has survived.

A Utilitarian Approach

Should the operation that saved Jodie by killing Mary have taken place? Is this the kind of situation in which we ought to kill to save a life? The Manchester doctors involved in caring for Jodie and Mary judged that it is. Interestingly, these doctors have been accused of adopting a well-known philosophical position: that of the *utilitarian*.

Utilitarianism has been developed and refined in various ways. Two early practitioners were Jeremy Bentham (1748–1832) and John Stuart Mill (1806–73), but it continues to have many followers. In its simplest form, utilitarianism is the view that the right thing to do when faced with a moral decision is always to *maximise happiness*.

For example, ought I to steal that small child's sweets? That may give me the pleasure of eating the sweets, but it will deny that same pleasure to the child and cause her considerable unhappiness to boot. Therefore, according to the utilitarian, I ought not to steal the sweets.

In the case of Jodie and Mary, performance of the utilitarian calculation might seem a fairly straightforward matter. We are presented with two courses of action. We can operate and save Jodie by killing Mary, or we can refuse to operate, with the inevitable result that both children will die. From a utilitarian perspective, it might seem clear that we should operate, for that will at least produce one happy individual rather than none.

How plausible is such a utilitarian justification for killing Mary to save Jodie?

The Transplant Case

Notoriously, utilitarianism faces a very powerful sort of counterexample. Here's one example.

You are the doctor in charge of two seriously ill patients. One has terminal cancer, and will die shortly. The other has a heart condition that will soon become fatal if a replacement heart is not found quickly. You discover that the heart of the cancer patient would actually make a perfect donor organ for the heart patient. So you can save one of these two lives by killing one patient by giving his heart to the other. Or you can do nothing, with the result that both lives will soon come to an end. What should you do?

From a utilitarian perspective, the morally proper course of action seems clear. If you operate, one happy individual will return to his family, where he can live out a long and contented life. Fail to operate, and both lives are lost, resulting in not one but two sets of grieving relatives. The right thing to do, therefore, must be to kill the cancer patient in order to save the heart patient.

Of course, most of us are aghast at the suggestion that the right thing to do in this situation would be to kill one patient in order to save the other. We feel strongly that the cancer patient would be the victim of a grave injustice were he to be killed so that his heart might be taken. To take this life, even if the result would be another life saved, would surely be morally very wrong indeed.

It seems to follow, then, that the utilitarian view that what is morally right is equivalent to whatever produces the most happiness cannot be correct. And if we reject utilitarianism, then we can't use it to justify the killing of Mary to save Jodie.

Thinking Tools: Rule Utilitarianism

To digress for a moment, there's a version of utilitarianism that may be able to deal with the transplant case. *Rule utilitarians*, rather than calculating the consequences of each action individually, believe that we should adopt those *rules* that, if followed, will result in the greatest happiness.

A rule utilitarian might well argue that the rule 'Do not kill' should always be obeyed, even though obeying it may occasionally, as in both the transplant case and Jodie's and Mary's case, result in less happiness, because following this rule will *in general* produce greater happiness.

But there are also problems with rule utilitarianism. One of the most serious difficulties becomes apparent when one considers why I should follow the rule even in a situation where the result is less happiness. It seems ridiculous to insist that I should tell the truth to the serial killer who demands to know where my children are hiding, even if telling the truth does *in general* lead to increased happiness. Indeed, it would surely be wrong for me to tell the truth under such circumstances. But that is not something the rule utilitarian can allow.

Conclusions One Might Draw . . .

To sum up: the transplant case provides a powerful counterexample to those forms of utilitarianism that might be used to justify the killing of Mary to save Jodie. But there are at least two further conclusions some might wish to draw.

First, some may conclude that what the transplant case shows is that we ought to abide by God's commandment 'Thou shall not kill' even in those situations where by killing we can save a life. This appears to be the position of the priest at the village from where Jodie and Mary came. In fact, the priest appealed to such a similar transplant case to back up his position.

> It is the same principle as organ donation. Transplants are valid and moral when the donor is dead, but Mary is not dead. She is alive, she is a human being. It is wrong to kill her, no matter how good the intention.[*]

In the priest's view, killing is wrong, *period*. It remains wrong even in a situation where the outcome is an innocent life saved. Keith Male, spokesperson for the pro-life charity Life, takes a similar view. About the decision to allow the operation on Jodie and Mary to take place, he said:

> This decision is deplorable. It transgresses a fundamental principle of our law that it is never permissible to kill, or commit a deliberate lethal assault on an innocent person, whatever good may come of the action.[†]

Secondly, one may argue that what the transplant case reminds us of – or ought to remind us of – is that human beings have moral *rights*, the most fundamental of which is the right to life. In the transplant case the utilitarian calculation requires that the cancer patient's right to life should be infringed. But that would clearly be wrong. It was similarly wrong to kill Mary to save Jodie, for by so doing we infringed Mary's right to life. As Dr Richard Nicholson, editor of the Royal Society of Medicine's *Bulletin of Medical Ethics*, argues:

> The issue of what rights accrue to each part of Siamese twins has never been addressed in law. Given the existence of two recognisably human beings, one cannot argue coherently that they do not both have rights. If both have rights, the two most fundamental rights – to life and to justice – must be respected. So both Jodie and Mary have a right to life and a right to justice, or in other words to be treated equitably. Surgical separation would deny Mary both rights.[‡]

---

* *Guardian*, 22 September 2000, p. 2.
† *Daily Express*, 23 September 2000, p. 4.
‡ Richard Nicholson, *Independent on Sunday*, 10 September 2000, p. 30.

At this point you might be forgiven for supposing that an overwhelming case has been made for the immorality of killing Mary to save Jodie. But I don't believe that is the right conclusion to draw. Like both the priest and Dr Nicholson, I reject utilitarianism – certainly those varieties that require that we murder the cancer patient in order to save the heart patient. I am also sympathetic to the view that human beings have moral rights, rights that – generally speaking – ought not to be infringed. However, I am not convinced that the right thing to do in Jodie's and Mary's case was to allow both children to die.

The Astronaut Case

Think about the following case.

You have been sent into space on a rescue mission. Two astronauts are trapped in different sections of a spaceship, their air running out. You reach the ship with minutes to spare, but the oxygen supplies to the two parts of the ship are connected in such a way that it is possible to rescue only one of the astronauts by shutting off the air supply to – and thereby killing – the other. Do you allow both astronauts to die? Or do you save one of the two astronauts?

Surely *the right thing to do is to save one of the two astronauts*, even though you can do so only by killing the other. Here is a case in which it seems very clear to most of us that the right course of action *is* to kill an innocent person so that a life might be saved.

The Submarine Case

We saw above that Dr Nicholson argues that we ought not to save Jodie by killing Mary because this would involve denying Mary her right to life. While I'm happy to acknowledge that human beings have moral rights, including the right to life, there are clearly circumstances in which such rights should be infringed. Rights ought, generally, to be respected. But not at any cost.

Consider, for example, the following situation.

You're the President of the United States of America. You know that a US submarine crew is, due to an equipment malfunction, unwittingly about to launch a nuclear strike that will result in the deaths of millions of innocent people. The only way of averting disaster is to send a missile to annihilate the submarine and its crew. What should you do?

Surely the right thing to do in this situation is to destroy the submarine, despite the fact that this would involve denying those on board their right to life.

That the right to life can in some circumstances justifiably be overridden also seems clear in the astronaut case. Would Dr Nicholson insist that, because we should respect these astronauts' right to life, we should stand back and watch both of them suffocate?

Exceptions to 'Thou Shall Not Kill'

The village priest argued that it is always wrong to kill, no matter what good may come of it. He also used a transplant case to back up his position.

But what would the priest say about the astronaut and submarine cases? Would he insist that we ought to allow millions to die rather than destroy the submarine? Would he say that the two astronauts should be left to suffocate? For these are the only courses of action left open to one who insists on following God's commandment 'Thou shall not kill' without exception.

Yet to take this extreme view is perverse, isn't it? Is it really 'God's will' that we should stand back and let *both* astronauts die?

Of course, if it's allowed that the astronaut case is one in which it's morally acceptable to kill to save a life, then it's no longer clear why Jodie's and Mary's case should be considered any different. Indeed, to my moral eye, the case of the conjoined twins looks essentially similar to that of the astronauts.

Those who believe that we should follow God's commandment without exception may bite the bullet and insist that it is wrong to kill even in a situation in which the result would be millions of lives saved. They might try to make their position appear more palatable by maintaining that death is not the end. The same view has been expressed by some commentators on the twins' case. They have suggested that it only seems heartless to follow God's commandment and allow both girls to die while we forget that both children can look forward to eternal life with God.

This defence of the judgement that both girls ought to be left to die may appeal to some. But in order for it to be a *rational* defence, we need to provide good grounds for supposing that such an afterlife really does await us. It won't do simply to assert that it awaits. It is, to say the least, unclear whether any such grounds exist.

Why the Manchester Doctors Need Not Be Utilitarians

We have seen that it is sometimes wrong to kill the innocent to save life. But we have also seen that the astronaut and submarine cases appear to show that it's sometimes wrong *not* to kill the innocent to save life. To accept that there are situations in which it's right to kill the innocent to save life does *not* require that one adopt the principle that one should *always* do so. Nor does it require that one embrace utilitarianism. Dr Nicholson suggests otherwise. He supposes that the Manchester doctors who thought it right to operate must be utilitarians.

> What has so far held sway among the professionals . . . is a crude utilitarian approach. Any life is better than no life, goes the argument, so separation must be the right answer.*

But as should now be clear, the doctors who believed it right to save Jodie by killing Mary need not be utilitarians. Indeed, they may reject utilitarianism precisely because they recognise that, as the priest points out, it is obviously and intuitively wrong to murder a cancer patient to save a heart patient.

Respecting Both Sets of Moral Intuitions

The priest introduces a live transplant case in order to appeal to a certain moral intuition. We feel, intuitively, that it would be wrong to murder, say, a cancer patient in order to save a heart patient.

---

* Ibid.

Our intuition about this sort of case is then used to justify the conclusion that it's *always* wrong to take an innocent life, no matter how good the intention. It then follows that it was wrong to take Mary's life to save Jodie's.

But the intuition to which the priest appeals – that it's wrong to kill in the transplant case – does *not* entail that it's *always* wrong to take an innocent life. And, in fact, there are equally strong intuitions that the priest overlooks. There is the intuition that it *is* right to take innocent life in both the submarine and astronaut cases.

Once one starts appealing to such moral intuitions, one cannot arbitrarily pick and choose among them. If we are expected to respect the intuition regarding the transplant case, then surely we ought also to respect the intuition concerning the submarine and astronaut cases. But then the priest's justification for not killing Mary to save Jodie collapses.

In fact, as I say, the Jodie and Mary case seems, intuitively, to be morally much more like the astronaut case than it does the transplant case (or, at least, that's how it strikes me). So this sort of appeal to intuition seems in the end actually to *support* the killing of Mary to save Jodie.

A Difficult Challenge

The challenge facing those who, like me, wish to respect both sets of moral intuitions lies in explaining *why* it is acceptable to kill one astronaut to save the other, but not acceptable to kill the cancer patient to save the heart patient. We recognise intuitively that it is sometimes right to take an innocent life in order that life might be saved, and sometimes not. What's not so easy is to *justify* drawing the line where we do. What's the essential difference between the astronaut and transplant cases? I'm not sure I can answer that question adequately. You may have ideas of your own.

Appendix: Should the Parents' Decision Have Been Overruled?

It's one thing to take the view that the right thing to do was to save Jodie by killing Mary. It's quite another to claim that it was right this judgement was enforced despite the parents' wishes. Some might take the view that, while it was, on balance, right to operate, it was wrong to impose this decision on the parents. After all, it is the parents, not we, who will have to live with the consequences of the operation.

They face having to care over many years for a physically handicapped child, a child who will constantly remind them that, as they see it, 'God's will' has been denied.

It was also reported that the parents believed both that their own community might stigmatise Jodie because of her handicaps and that it lacks the economic and medical resources necessary to give Jodie a good quality of life.

I sympathised with the parents' predicament. But I also believe it right that their views were overridden. We do not ordinarily allow those whose religious beliefs require that a life be lost that might otherwise be saved to have their way. We do not, for example, allow Jehovah's Witnesses to deny their children life-saving blood transfusions, despite the fact that this is what their faith demands.

What of the other objections: that Jodie will have to live with physical handicaps within a family and community that may be both unsympathetic towards her and ill-equipped to cope?

It seems to me that these factors are largely irrelevant. We would not accept them as reasons for allowing an unconjoined child to die who could otherwise be saved. So why were they relevant in this case? Jodie is a bright, alert and otherwise healthy girl with perhaps a hundred years of life ahead of her. To suggest that we should have let her die because her handicaps might make her something of a burden and because she may end up stigmatised by ignorant people cannot be right. It would be odd for anyone who believes in an exceptionless 'right to life' to claim otherwise.

What to read next

This chapter provides an example of how philosophical thinking can be applied to life: in this case, to the issue of what is morally the right course of action to follow. For other examples of how philosophical thinking can be applied to ethical issues, see Chapter 2, What's Wrong with Gay Sex?, Chapter 21, Should You Be Eating That?, and Chapter 12, Designer Babies.

Further reading

You might try John Stuart Mill, 'Higher and Lower Pleasures', and Bernard Williams, 'A Critique of Utilitarianism', which feature as Chapters 13 and 14 of:

Nigel Warburton (ed.), *Philosophy: Basic Readings* (London: Routledge, 1999).

A good introduction to utilitarianism can be found in:

Chris Horner and Emrys Westacott, *Thinking through Philosophy* (Cambridge: Cambridge University Press, 2000), Chapter 5.

THE STRANGE REALM

OF NUMBERS

Mathematics is woven inextricably into the fabric of modern life. Whether you're tiling the bathroom, working out how long it will take to travel to Glasgow, designing a toaster or trying to put a person on the moon, maths is essential. Without it, our lives would be almost unimaginably different. But what *is* maths, exactly? In performing a mathematical calculation, are we, as some mathematicians and philosophers believe, exploring a strange realm of numbers that's 'out there' independently of us? Or are mathematics and its truths ultimately made by us?

Tiling the Bathroom

The scene: Kraus is studying maths and Bridie science. They are about to tile their bathroom floor with one-foot-square tiles. Bridie previously measured the floor to be 12 feet by 12 feet. Kraus calculated that $12 \times 12 = 144$, and bought 144 tiles. He has just laid the tiles out over the floor and found that they fit exactly.

Kraus: Perfect. It's astonishing how maths can do that.

Bridie: Do what?

Kraus: The floor measured 12 feet by 12 feet. I then used a mathematical rule – the rule of multiplication – to calculate that precisely 144 tiles would be required to cover it. And when I lay out the tiles, it turns out that 144 tiles *do* cover the floor exactly.

Bridie: You find that surprising?

Kraus: I do. Whether we're tiling a bathroom floor, calculating the height of a mountain or working out how much fuel to put in a rocket, maths always gives us the right answer. As long as we put accurate data in, maths cannot fail to produce the correct result. How does maths come to be so reliable and informative?

Conventionalism

Bridie remains unimpressed.

Bridie: Actually, maths isn't informative *at all*. To say there are '144' tiles and to say there are '12 × 12' tiles are *just two different ways of saying the very same thing*.

Bridie points out of the window into the field next door.

Bridie: Suppose you tell me that the creature I see over there in the far distance is a stallion. I then predict that the same creature is both male and a horse. Would you be impressed if my prediction turned out to be true?

Kraus: Obviously not.

Bridie: Why?

Kraus: Because there's a *linguistic rule* or *convention* that says that the expressions 'male horse' and 'stallion' are interchangeable. That's stipulated. So your 'prediction' is hardly shocking, is it? By saying it's a male horse you haven't given me any more information than I gave you by saying it's a stallion.

Bridie: I agree. But *isn't exactly the same true of the 'prediction' that 12 × 12 tiles is 144 tiles?*

Kraus: Why do you believe that?

Bridie: Because the rules by which we calculate are also stipulations or conventions that we happen to have laid down. These rules entail that the expressions '12 × 12' and '144' are similarly interchangeable. So to say that there are '12 × 12 tiles' and to say that there are '144' tiles is, again, *to give the same piece of information twice over.*

The theory that mathematical truths are 'true by convention', because they either are or are more or less remote consequences of conventions that we have laid down, is known as *conventionalism*. No doubt the rules involved in performing mathematical calculations are far more complex than the single, simple rule that says that 'stallion' and 'male horse' are interchangeable. But in Bridie's view the principle remains the same.

Mathematical Facts

Kraus has quite a different theory about mathematics.

Kraus: Mathematical truths aren't true by convention.
Bridie: Why are they true, then?
Kraus: They're made true by *facts*.
Bridie: What sort of facts?
Kraus: *Mathematical* facts, of course. Suppose I say that all stallions are male. As you say, *that's* trivially true, true by convention. But now suppose I claim *that all stallions have ears*. That's *not* true by convention, is it?
Bridie: No. There might be one or two earless stallions somewhere in the world.
Kraus: Yes, there might be. So if my claim that all stallions have ears is true, it's made true by a *fact*. There's a fact 'out there' in the world that *makes* my claim true. All the stallions *really do* have ears. Correct?
Bridie: Yes.
Kraus: I believe *the same is also true of our mathematical beliefs.* Reality doesn't contain just astronomical, geographical, physical and chemical facts. It also contains mathematical facts, such as the fact that $12 \times 12 = 144$. It's these external *mathematical* facts that make our *mathematical* beliefs true.

Two Kinds of Truth

Kraus and Bridie agree that there are, in effect, *two kinds of truth*. Some truths, such as the truth that all stallions are male, are 'trivially' true: they are *true by convention*. Other truths, such as the truth (if it is one) that all stallions have ears, are *made true by facts*.

If it's true by convention that all stallions are male, then that would explain why we don't need to go and examine any stallions in order to know that they're all male. How things might happen to stand in the world is irrelevant. It doesn't matter what the facts 'out there' might happen to be: a truth that is true by convention will be true in any case. It's 'trivially' true.

A claim made true by a fact, on the other hand, is not 'trivially' true. In fact, the claim risks being false precisely because the world may not be as it's claimed to be. As Kraus points out, it might turn out that not all stallions have ears. In order to know whether a non-trivial claim is true, *we have to investigate whether the facts really are as they are claimed to be*: we have to go out and observe those stallions.

Bridie believes that the truths of mathematics are true by convention. They are, like the truth that all stallions have ears, *truths of our own invention*. Kraus, on the other hand, believes that the truths of mathematics are made true by independent mathematical facts. This is the view of the mathematical *realist*.

Which, if either, position is correct?

The Strange Realm of Numbers

Let's begin by getting a little clearer about what sort of fact it is that Kraus believes makes a mathematical judgement true. We know where to look if we want to find out what the astronomical, geographical, physical or chemical facts are. Where should we look if we want the mathematical facts? Kraus explains as follows.

Kraus: We mathematicians often think of ourselves as playing a role similar to that of astronomers. Just as astronomers investigate the heavens by using their telescopes to reveal strange new objects and facts – such as pulsars, quasars and the occurrence of the Big Bang – so mathematicians investigate a still higher and more sublime realm, *the realm of numbers.*

Bridie: Of numbers?

Kraus: Yes. And it's an extraordinary realm. Numbers, it seems, are things even more peculiar than pulsars and quasars, for they are not *physical* things at all.

Bridie: I agree the number 2 certainly isn't the sort of thing you might trip over.

Kraus: That's true. It isn't *physically* located anywhere. And yet *it exists.*

Bridie: If numbers aren't physical and have no physical location, then I'm not sure I can make much sense of the suggestion that they exist. Surely it's only the physical universe, with its physical objects, forces and properties, that really exists?

Kraus: No. There's more to reality than just the physical.

Bridie:	What's this strange realm like?
Kraus:	The realm of numbers is eternal. The physical universe had a beginning in time – the Big Bang – and will eventually come to an end. But the realm of numbers is without beginning or end. $2 + 2 = 4$ is a timeless truth: it would still be true even if the physical universe and everything in it were destroyed.
Bridie:	I see.
Kraus:	The stars up there are in a permanent state of flux. But the realm of numbers never alters. It's the facts about these strange objects – numbers – that make our mathematical judgements true or false. My belief that $12 \times 12 = 144$ is true because it accurately pictures how things stand in the realm of numbers.

Of course, being a conventionalist, Bridie believes that this strange realm that Kraus believes is 'out there' is an illusion.

Bridie:	It seems to me that this 'realm of numbers' that mathematicians investigate is *actually a theme park entirely of their own devising*. All mathematicians are *really* doing when they calculate is working out what the consequences are of certain conventions that they themselves have laid down for manipulating symbols (and sometimes they add new conventions, too). Mathematics and its truths are entirely our own invention.

Is Kraus right? Does mathematics describe some sort of sublime independent reality? Or is mathematics ultimately a theme park of our own making?

Why Our Senses Can't Confirm Mathematical Claims

Bridie thinks she can prove that realism is false. The first part of her argument involves showing that mathematical knowledge is not based on experience.

Bridie:	I can prove that mathematics doesn't describe a reality 'out there'.
Kraus:	How?
Bridie:	To begin with, notice that our knowledge of mathematical truths is *not based on experience*.

Kraus: I don't believe that. Surely experience *does* confirm that 12 × 12 = 144. If I count out 12 lots of 12 tiles, and then I count them altogether and find I have 144, that confirms that 12 × 12 = 144, doesn't it?

Kraus might appear to be correct, but the situation is not so simple, as Bridie now explains.

Bridie: No, it doesn't. Suppose you count 12 lots of 12 rabbits into an empty pen. Will you then have just 144 rabbits in the pen? Not necessarily. When you count them again you may find they have reproduced, giving 150 rabbits. Correct?

Kraus: Yes.

Bridie: Maths doesn't say you won't get 150 rabbits when you count them a second time. What maths says is simply that if you counted 12 lots of 12 rabbits into the pen, then you counted 144 rabbits into the pen. Maths makes no prediction about how many rabbits you will have the next time you count them.

It seems that Bridie is correct. Maths doesn't say what will happen when you physically combine things. Bringing two rabbits together can produce more than two rabbits. When we talk about 'adding' in mathematics, we're not talking about *physically* combining things, as in a recipe. For example, physically 'adding' 20 two–pound lumps of enriched uranium 235 together can produce not a 40-pound lump of uranium but a nuclear explosion. Indeed, we can mathematically 'add' things together that remain physically light years apart – stars, for example.

Bridie: But then neither does maths have anything to say about how many tiles you will get when you count them a second time. Extra tiles might appear. Some might disappear. They could all vanish in a puff of smoke. Maths doesn't claim otherwise. So the fact that when you count the tiles again you happen to get 144 doesn't confirm that 12 × 12 = 144, because *maths doesn't say you will get, or even that you're likely to get, 144 the second time around.*

Again, Bridie appears to be correct. You can't and don't need to appeal to experience in order to justify a mathematical claim. Admittedly, you need experience to learn what the various mathematical symbols mean – you need experience to learn how the mathematical language is used. But once you've grasped that, in principle you need no *further* experience to see that what's expressed by '12 × 12 = 144' is true. That 12 × 12 = 144 can be confirmed by *reason alone*. It's something that can be worked out 'in the head'. This sort of knowledge – knowledge that is not dependent on experience – is called *a priori knowledge*.

Why Maths Can't Be 'Out There'

Bridie continues with the next step in her argument.

Bridie: When a truth is merely true by convention, you can know it's true simply by grasping the relevant conventions. For example, we saw before that you don't need to go out and examine any stallions in order to know that all stallions are male. It's enough that you understand what 'stallion' means.

Kraus: True.

Bridie: But when a claim is made true not by convention but by a fact, then you obviously need to *check up on that fact* in order to establish whether or not the claim is true. So, for example, you need to examine reality to find out whether it's true that all stallions have ears.

Kraus: Again, true.

Bridie: But mathematical realists like yourself believe that mathematical truths are made true not by convention but by mathematical facts, facts that exist 'out there' independently of us in what you called the 'realm of numbers'. And this raises the question: *if you're correct, then how do we come by our knowledge of these facts?*

Kraus: I'm not sure I follow.

Bridie: If you believe that in performing mathematical calculations we are mapping out an independent reality, a reality that's 'out there', then how do we get to know about the features of this reality? By means of what weird faculty is this strange realm revealed to you?

Kraus: I still don't see the problem.

Bridie: Well, I'm a scientist. When I want knowledge of how things stand 'out there' in reality, I have to use my five senses. We scientists find out

	about the world by looking, listening, smelling, touching and sometimes even tasting. And, of course, we also use instruments, such as telescopes and microscopes, to aid our senses.
Kraus:	I know.
Bridie:	Now you say that there aren't just astronomical, geographical, physical and chemical facts 'out there' in the world waiting for us to discover them. There's also a realm of mathematical facts.
Kraus:	That's right. There is.
Bridie:	But then how do you mathematicians establish what these facts are? By which of your senses do you detect them?

This is a hard question to answer. As Bridie points out, astronomers establish the astronomical facts by observation, by using their five senses, often aided by telescopes and other devices. But how do mathematicians find out how things stand in the realm of numbers?

You might suggest that mathematicians gain knowledge in much the same way as astronomers: by using their senses. Just as observation is able to reveal that the earth revolves around the sun, so they are also able to reveal that $12 \times 12 = 144$.

But we have already seen that mathematical knowledge does *not* appear to be based on experience. That $12 \times 12 = 144$ is something known a priori. It's something that can, in principle, be worked out entirely in the head.

But if this is correct, then realists like Kraus face a problem. Our five senses appear to provide us with our *only* window on to external reality. We establish by observation what the astronomical, physical, geographical and chemical facts are. But if the mathematical facts also form part of this independent reality, and if our five senses are incapable of revealing these facts to us, then how *do* we get to know about them?

In short, realists like Kraus find it very difficult to explain how mathematical knowledge is possible.

Mathematical 'Intuition' and Plato's Solution

Some mathematical realists have tried to solve this problem by suggesting that we are equipped with an additional, sixth sense, sometimes referred to as 'intuition'. It's this additional sense – a sort of mathematical aerial – that allows us to discern the mathematical facts.

But this merely introduces another mystery: what *is* this weird faculty that connects us to the realm of numbers? How does it work? The appeal to 'intuition' succeeds only in replacing one mystery with another.

Other mathematical realists, such as Plato (c. 428–347 BC), have tried to answer the question about how we come by mathematical knowledge by suggesting that such knowledge is essentially *remembered*. In Plato's view, our immortal souls were presented with the realm of numbers prior to our birth. We were then exposed to the mathematical facts. When we now perform a calculation, we merely *remind* ourselves of the facts to which we were exposed prior to our birth.

But again, this suggestion raises at least as many difficult questions as it answers. What is a soul, and how exactly does it come by knowledge of the realm of numbers prior to becoming physically embodied? These questions are no less mystifying than the one Plato is trying to answer.

A great advantage of conventionalism, on the other hand, is that it can easily explain how we come by knowledge of mathematical truths. If $12 \times 12 = 144$ is merely 'true by convention', then there's no particular problem about our knowing that it's true: we need only to have grasped the relevant conventions in order to be able to work it out.

So the ease with which conventionalism can account for mathematical knowledge gives us a powerful reason for favouring conventionalism over realism.

Why Maths Must Be 'Out There'

So should we give up on realism and embrace conventionalism? Perhaps not. For conventionalism also faces powerful objections. In particular, the following train of thought seems to show that conventionalism can't possibly be true.

Kraus: OK, I admit it's something of a mystery how we come by mathematical knowledge. Still, we shouldn't let that drive us into embracing conventionalism. It's *obvious* that conventionalism is false.

Bridie: Why?

Kraus: Imagine an alien civilisation that calculates by *different* mathematical conventions. Instead of using the rules of multiplication, addition, subtraction, and so on, these aliens use the rules of schmultiplication and schmaddition and schubtraction. Let's call this alternative alien system of calculating *schmaths*. In schmaths, 12 schmultiplied by 12 is 150. That's 'true by convention'.

Bridie: Bizarre.

Kraus: I know. But such an alternative system of rules of calculation is at least *possible*, isn't it?

Bridie: I guess so.

Kraus: Now, you believe that 12 multiplied by 12 equals 144 is merely true by convention. Correct?

Bridie: Yes.

Kraus: But then 12 schmultiplied by 12 is 150 is also true by convention. Right?

Bridie: Yes.

OH OH!

Kraus: But if this alien civilisation calculates according to the rules of schmaths rather than the rules of maths, then they are going to *get things wrong*. Because we calculate according to the rules of maths, we can build bridges that stay up, land people on the moon and arrive in Glasgow with fuel to spare. The alien civilisation that uses schmaths, on the other hand, isn't going to have a civilisation for very long. Their bridges will collapse, their electrical appliances will be faulty and their spaceships will constantly run out of fuel. You see, unlike schmaths, *maths really does get things right*.

Bridie: I suppose that's true.

Kraus: But then it follows that, unlike schmathematical truths, mathematical truths aren't *just* 'true by convention'. The truths of mathematics *really are* true. They accurately represent how things stand out there in the world. Use schmaths rather than maths and you'll end up with *the wrong result*.

Kraus does appear to be on to something. We often use maths to predict what will happen. If Kraus had used schmaths instead of maths to predict how many tiles would be needed exactly to cover the bathroom floor, he would have ended up with six tiles too many. Unlike schmaths, maths gives the *right result*. So it seems that, unlike schmaths, maths really does somehow manage accurately to mirror the structure of the world 'out there'. But if that's so, then $12 \times 12 = 144$ is not just 'trivially' true and conventionalism must be false.

Thinking Tools: Rationalism *v.* Empiricism

Conventionalism is often closely associated with a position called *empiricism*.

Empiricists believe that all non-trivial knowledge is derived from our five senses. Rationalists deny this: they believe that at least some non-trivial knowledge can be possessed a priori. In the empiricist camp one finds philosophers such as Mill (1806–73), Locke (1632–1704), Berkeley (1685–1753), Hume (1711–76) and Quine (1908–2001). In the rationalist camp one finds Plato, Descartes (1596–1650), Leibniz (1646–1716) and Spinoza (1632–77). Descartes, for example, thought that we can know a priori that God exists: a very non-trivial piece of knowledge. Some rationalists claim not just that *some* non-trivial knowledge can be had independently of experience, but that this is the *only* route to genuine knowledge: our five senses are incapable of furnishing us with any knowledge at all. This is the view of Plato.

Mathematics has always been something of a thorn in the side of empiricism. For, as Kraus just pointed out, mathematical knowledge does seem to be non-trivial. Yet, as Bridie indicated, mathematical knowledge also appears to be a priori.

So empiricists have one of two choices: they must either deny that maths is a priori (Mill took this view, for example) or else show that mathematical knowledge is trivial after all (the strategy of Locke, Berkeley and Hume).

Conventionalism is one obvious way of trying to show that mathematical knowledge is ultimately 'trivial', which is why it has appealed to many empiricists.

Conclusion

Are mathematics and its truths our own invention? Or does mathematics describe a reality that is 'out there' independently of us? Philosophical and mathematical opinion remains divided.

On the one hand, we have seen a pretty powerful argument for conventionalism: it seems that only conventionalism, or something like it, can account for mathematical knowledge.

But, on the other hand, it seems that Kraus is right when he suggests that, unlike the truths of schmaths, the truths of maths aren't merely true by convention. The fact that maths *gets things right* seems to shows that, unlike schmaths, maths does somehow manage accurately to mirror how things stand 'out there' in external reality.

So which, if either, position is correct?

What to read next

You might find it helpful briefly to reread this chapter in conjunction with Chapter 20, Is Morality like a Pair of Spectacles?, in which I discuss another sort of realism: *moral* realism.

Just as mathematical realists believe that our mathematical judgements are made true by mathematical facts that exist 'out there' independently of us, so moral realists believe that our moral judgements are made true by moral facts that exist 'out there' independently of us.

You will find that the positions and arguments outlined in Chapter 20 mirror those outlined in this chapter.

Further reading

One of the best-known exponents of conventionalism is A. J. Ayer (1910–89). See:

A. J. Ayer, *Language, Truth and Logic* (Harmondsworth: Pelican Books, 1971), Chapter 4.

Having read both this chapter and Chapter 20, you might wish to try:

Hilary Putnam, *The Many Faces of Realism* (La Salle, IL: Open Court, 1991), which contains four accessible lectures on realism.

Kraus and Bridie both assume that there are two kinds of truth: truth by fact and truth by convention. W. O. Quine famously challenges this assumption in his immensely influential 'Two Dogmas of Empiricism', reprinted in:

Willard van O. Quine, *From a Logical Point of View*, second edition (Harvard: Harvard University Press, 1961).

19

WHAT IS
KNOWLEDGE?

We all want knowledge. We want to know when the bus is coming, what's for tea and how the economy will do next year. We respect those who have knowledge, seeking them out for advice. And yet, despite the enormous value we place on knowledge, we quickly come unstuck when we ask ourselves what it actually is. The question 'What is knowledge?' is the sort of question that we think we can answer easily – until we try. This chapter explores two competing answers.

Plato's Answer

Let's begin with Plato's (c. 428–347 BC) answer.

The scene: Pegeen and Pat are philosophy students who have decided to visit a racecourse. Pat knows absolutely nothing about horse-racing, but she decides to bet anyway. She picks her horse by sticking a pin into the list of runners. Pat guesses that the horse with the name she stuck the pin into will win. Now, by sheer chance, Pat happens to get lucky. Her horse does go on to win.

Pat: Aha! You see. I knew Black Beauty would win.
Pegeen: You did not.
Pat: But I said Black Beauty would win, didn't I? And she did. So I knew.

Did Pat *know*? Of course not. Pat simply guessed and got lucky. And a lucky guess is not knowledge. But if a lucky guess isn't knowledge, then *what else is required*?

Pegeen: You did not know that Black Beauty would win. OK, I admit that your belief was true. But that's not enough. After all, you know nothing about horse-racing, do you? It was just a *coincidence* that your belief turned out to be true.

Pat: So what else is required?

Pegeen: *Justification.* In order to *know* something, your belief must be true. But that's not enough. You must also have *pretty good grounds* for believing what you do.

In Pegeen's definition of knowledge, three things are required. For Pat to know that Black Beauty will win:

1. Pat must *believe* that Black Beauty will win.
2. Pat's belief must be *true*.
3. Pat must be *justified* in holding that belief.

In other words, knowledge is *justified true belief*. This definition of knowledge has a long pedigree running right back to Plato.

Why didn't Pat know that Black Beauty would win? The first two conditions were satisfied, but not the third. Pat wasn't *justified* in believing Black Beauty would win. That, according to Pegeen, is why Pat didn't know.

How Much Justification?

Let's get a little clearer about what Pegeen's third condition involves. What does 'justified' mean?

In fact, justification comes in degrees. You can be more or less justified in believing something. For example, if I see Jake, a formerly poor student, wearing an extremely expensive suit, then I have some grounds for believing that he has come into a lot of money (not strong grounds, though: perhaps the suit was merely a gift). If I also see him driving a new car, then my belief becomes better justified. If he tells me he has just bought a helicopter and a ten-bedroom house in Mayfair, then I am more justified still.

So what degree of justification is required for knowledge? How much evidence do I need before I can be said to *know* that Jake has come into a great deal of money? According to Pegeen, I must have *pretty good grounds* for believing what I do.

Admittedly, 'pretty good grounds' is rather vague. Exactly how much justification does one need before one possesses 'pretty good grounds'? Still, let's just set that worry to one side.

Of course, it's possible to be justified and still be mistaken. For example, if Jake goes on to give me a helicopter ride and a guided tour of a Mayfair mansion, and if he tells me he's won the lottery, then surely I have pretty good grounds for supposing he has really come into money. But I might still be wrong. Maybe Jake is lying. Maybe he's just been looking after all this stuff for his rich sister. Unlikely, perhaps, but possible.

The Regress Problem

The definition of knowledge offered by Pegeen and Plato might seem to be 'common sense'. In order to know something, you surely need some grounds – at least pretty good grounds – for supposing that your belief is true. But, as Pat now points out, this definition of knowledge immediately raises a thorny problem: *it seems to rule out the possibility of us having any knowledge at all.*

Pat: Not *all* knowledge requires justification, surely?
Pegeen: Why not?
Pat: Well, I currently have a belief: I believe that George Bush is in New
            York. Call this belief *belief A*. If my belief is to count as knowledge,
            then according to you my belief must be *justified*, right?
Pegeen: Yes.
Pat: Now, usually we justify one belief by appealing to *another*, don't we?
            For example, I might try to justify my belief that George Bush is in
            New York by appealing to my belief that it was reported on the TV
            news that he's in New York and the TV news is pretty reliable. Call
            this second belief of mine *belief B*. Now I'm only justified in appealing
            to *belief B* to justify *belief A* if *B* is *itself* justified, correct?

Pegeen: I guess so.
Pat: For example, I might justify my belief that the TV news is pretty
            reliable by appealing to my belief that, on a number of occasions
            when something was reported on TV, I knew that what was reported

was actually correct. Call this third belief *belief C*. But if *B* is to be justified, then *belief C* must *in turn* be justified, right?

BELIEF A ←――*JUSTIFIES*――― BELIEF B ←――*JUSTIFIES*――― BELIEF C

Pegeen: Yes.

Pat: But now you can see that *the chain of justifications is going to have to stretch back without end*. In order to have even *one* justified belief, I'll need an *infinite number* of justified beliefs!

Pegeen: Ah. I hadn't thought of that.

Pat: As I'm a finite being capable of having only a finite number of beliefs, it then follows that *none* of my beliefs can be justified, right?

Pegeen: I guess.

Pat: But then it follows that, in your definition of knowledge, *I don't know anything at all*!

Pat has raised a notorious difficulty with the suggestion that knowledge is justified true belief. It seems to force what's known as a *sceptical* conclusion on us – it seems to rule out the possibility of our having *any* knowledge.

Still, Pegeen is not yet convinced that there really is a problem.

Pegeen: What if the justification goes in a circle? What if we take the end of the chain of justifications and attach it to the beginning to make a loop?

Pat: That won't do. Suppose my sole justification for believing that there are fairies living at the bottom of the garden is my belief that there are fairy droppings down there. And suppose my sole justification for believing that there are fairy droppings at the bottom of the garden is my belief that there are fairies living down there. Then *neither* of these two beliefs is justified, surely? Such a circular justification is *no justification at all*, no matter how many or how few beliefs the circle happens to contain.

While Pat has raised a serious problem for the theory that knowledge is justified true belief, there may yet be a way of avoiding it.

Pegeen: H'm. OK, I agree that a circular justification is unacceptable. But what if certain beliefs are *self-justifying*? Suppose that the chain reaches back to a belief that *justifies itself*. Then there's no regress.

Pat: I can't make much sense of the claim that there are self-justifying beliefs. If a belief is used to justify itself, then the justification is *still* circular, isn't it? True, the circle has shrunk to include just the one belief. But that doesn't make the circularity any more acceptable.

Certainly, if *any* form of circular justification is unacceptable no matter what size the circle, then self-justification is unacceptable, too.

Thinking Tools: Self-Justifying Beliefs

What sort of belief might be self-justifying? Perhaps my belief that I exist. For, by believing that I exist, I demonstrate that I do. So my belief provides me with grounds for supposing that it is true.

Some philosophers have suggested that our beliefs about how things seem to us are also self-justifying. I can be mistaken in thinking that there's a tomato before me – I might be hallucinating. But I can't be mistaken in supposing that this is how things *seem* to me. So, arguably, my belief that this is how things *seem* is self-justifying (or is it merely a belief that requires no justification?).

Pat: It's pretty clear that if we're to avoid the sceptical conclusion that knowledge is impossible, not all our beliefs need be justified. *There must be at least some beliefs that qualify as knowledge despite not being justified.* So your justified true belief theory must be false.

This is a serious problem for the theory that knowledge is justified true belief: it rules out the possibility of our having any knowledge at all. I call this *the regress problem.*

Thinking Tools: Gettier's Objection to Plato's Theory

There's a second reason why one might want to reject the theory that knowledge is justified true belief. In 1963 the philosopher Edmund Gettier (*b.* 1927) published a three-page paper in which he showed that justified true belief is not enough for knowledge.* Gettier constructed some ingenious counterexamples in which, while a subject possesses a justified true belief, the subject clearly doesn't *know*.

Here's a Gettier-style counterexample:

The case of the purple Porsche. Suppose I see a purple Porsche parked in the college car park. That leads me to believe that Jennings, who I know drives a purple Porsche – a very unusual car – and who is rarely in college, is in college today. My belief that Jennings is in college is justified. However, it just so happens that the purple Porsche is not Jennings' – by sheer fluke, someone else parked one there today. But, coincidentally, Jennings is in college: his purple Porsche broke down and he caught the train. Do I know that Jennings is in college today?

In this case, I possess a true belief that is also justified. So, on Pegeen's and Plato's definition of knowledge, I know that Jennings is in college today. But it doesn't seem right to say that I know. Why not? Because my justification for believing that Jennings is in college has somehow become detached from the state of affairs that makes my belief true. The presence of a purple Porsche in the car park *actually has nothing to do with Jennings' presence in college*, despite the fact that it does justify my belief

---

* E. L. Gettier, 'Is Justified True Belief Knowledge?', *Analysis* (1963).

that he's in college. There is a sense in which, again, I merely *get lucky*: it's just a coincidence that my belief happens to be true. Here's another Gettier-style counterexample:

> *The case of the fixed race.* Suppose I'm told by someone who is usually an extremely reliable source of information that the next race has been fixed and Black Beauty will win – all the jockeys have been bribed. This leads me to believe that Black Beauty will win the race. Given what I've been told, I'm justified in believing that Black Beauty will win. But now suppose that, unbeknown to me, something goes wrong with the plan to bribe the jockeys and the horses run as usual. However, it just so happens that Black Beauty does win. Did I know Black Beauty would win?

Again, despite having a true belief that is also justified, it seems I don't know.

So to sum up: you can have a true belief, and also very good grounds for holding it, and yet *still* not know.

Causing Jim to Believe There's an Orange on the Table

We have seen that Plato's definition of knowledge results in the regress problem: it seems to entail that we can't have any knowledge at all. But surely we can and do have knowledge. So it seems that Plato's definition can't be correct. But if knowledge isn't justified true belief, then what is it?

One of the most interesting alternatives to Plato's definition of knowledge is the *causal theory of knowledge*. It's the causal theory that Pat now explains to Pegeen.

Pegeen: If knowledge isn't justified true belief, then what is it?
Pat: It seems to me that in order to *know* something, three things are required. You must believe. Your belief must be true. And your belief must be *caused* by the state of affairs that makes it true.

Pat has, in effect, replaced Pegeen's third condition concerning justification with a condition concerning causation. How might this third condition be satisfied?

Imagine you want to cause Jim to believe that there's an orange on the table in front of him. One very easy way to do this is to place an orange on the table. Assuming that Jim's eyes are open and the lights are on, the presence of the orange will cause Jim to believe that there's an orange before him. Light will bounce off the orange into Jim's eyes. This will cause an image to form on his retinas, which will in turn cause electrical impulses to be sent into his brain, which will in turn cause Jim to believe there's an orange there.

If all goes to plan and the orange really does cause Jim to believe there's an orange before him, does Jim *know* that there's an orange before him?

Yes, according to the causal theory, he does. Jim's belief that there's an orange before him is caused by the orange being there. His belief is caused by the state of affairs that makes it true.

In order to *know* that there's an orange before him, does Jim have to have any *justification* for believing there's an orange before him? No. On the causal theory, justification is unnecessary.

Are People like Thermometers?

Let's get a little clearer about how, on the causal theory, we come by knowledge of the world around us.

Jim's belief that there's an orange before him is caused via a particular perceptual mechanism: his eyes. But it's not only our eyes that make our beliefs causally sensitive to the world around us. We have not one sense but five: sight, hearing, touch, smell and taste. All five senses are pretty reliable mechanisms for producing true beliefs. (Sometimes they lead us astray, of course, but not very often.)

According to the causal theory, it's because our senses are reliable mechanisms for producing true beliefs that they are capable of furnishing us with knowledge. Our senses make us function in much the same way as do thermometers. A thermometer is a reliable indicator of temperature. Put it in a hot liquid, and the scale will indicate that the liquid is hot. Take it out and put it in a cold liquid, and the scale will indicate that the liquid is cold. The scale on the thermometer reliably reflects the temperatures of those liquids in which it's immersed.

My senses cause me to behave much like a reliable thermometer. Drive a car past my window, and my ears will cause me to believe that a car is being driven past my window. Stop the cars going by, and I will cease to believe cars are going by. Place a chocolate biscuit on my tongue and that will cause me to believe that I'm chewing on a chocolate biscuit. Take it away and I will believe the biscuit has gone.

On the causal theory, people know about the world around them precisely because they are causally hooked up to it via their senses in such a way that their beliefs are sensitive to how things stand out there in the world.

Knowledge of Dinosaurs

How, according to the causal theory, are we able to have knowledge, not just of what's immediately before us, but of what, say, happened in the distant past? Take, for example, my belief that dinosaurs roamed the earth millions of years ago. Why, according to the causal theory, does this belief qualify as a piece of knowledge? After all, I can't observe the past, can I?

The causal theorist will point out that there is still a causal link: my belief that dinosaurs roamed the earth millions of years ago is caused by the presence of dinosaurs walking the earth millions of years ago. But in this case the causal link is very indirect. The dinosaurs became fossils. Those fossils were then discovered by archaeologists, who wrote about their discoveries in journals and books. These journals and books were read by TV producers, who then made TV programmes that were then transmitted to my TV set and watched by me, resulting, finally, in my belief that dinosaurs once roamed the earth. So, while I believe that dinosaurs roamed the earth *because they did*, the causal chain linking my belief back to the state of affairs that makes it true is very long indeed. This is, of course, something the causal theory can allow.

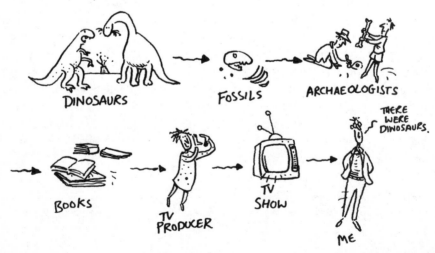

Solution to the Regress Problem

We have seen that, on the causal theory, in order for Jim's belief that there's an orange on the table in front of him to count as knowledge, all that's required is that his belief be caused by the state of affairs that makes it true. He doesn't need any *justification* for believing what he does. We have now dropped the requirement that, for knowledge, a belief must be justified. But this means that *we avoid the justificatory regress problem that plagued Plato's definition of knowledge.*

Thinking Tools: Dealing with the Purple Porsche Case

Notice that the causal theory also provides a very neat explanation of why I don't know in the two Gettier-style examples discussed in the box above. Take the purple Porsche case, for example. It's clear that, though I am justified in believing that Jennings is in college, and though my belief is true, I don't *know* he is in college. The reason I don't know, according to the causal theory, is that my belief is not caused by the state of affairs that makes it true: I don't believe Jennings is in college because he is. After all, I would still believe Jennings was in college even if he hadn't bothered to come in, because I would still have seen that purple Porsche. Gettier puzzle solved!

The Psychic Sarah Case

We've seen that, unlike Plato's justified true belief theory, the causal theory avoids the justificatory regress problem. So is the causal theory the theory we should adopt?

No. Unfortunately, there are also problems with the causal theory. Pegeen remains convinced that justification must have some role to play when it comes to defining knowledge. She illustrates why with the following thought experiment.

Pegeen: You're mistaken when you say that all that's required for knowledge is that a person's belief be caused by the state of affairs that makes it true.

Pat: Why?

Pegeen: It's clear that someone could have such a belief and yet *still* not know.

Pat:	Give me an example.
Pegeen:	Very well. Let's imagine that someone, call her 'Sarah', is psychic. She really does have psychic powers. There is, let's imagine, some as-yet-to-be-discovered 'psychic' mechanism for producing true beliefs: a 'sixth sense', if you like. And Sarah, by chance, happens to have been born with this sixth sense.
Pat:	I see.
Pegeen:	I'm not supposing the mechanism is supernatural: it could be a perfectly natural, causal mechanism, like sight or hearing. It's just a mechanism we don't yet know anything about.
Pat:	OK. So Sarah has psychic powers.
Pegeen:	Now Sarah believes that her mother is in town today. And the reason she believes this is that her psychic powers are working: her mother really is in town today. Her mother usually lives hundreds of miles away. But today she decided to pay her daughter a surprise visit. Now, on your causal theory, Sarah *knows* her mother is in town today, right?
Pat:	Yes. If her belief is caused, via this psychic mechanism, by the state of affairs that makes it true, then she knows.
Pegeen:	Right. Except she *doesn't* know. For Sarah has absolutely no reason to think she is psychic. Indeed, she possesses very good evidence that there are no such things as psychic powers. And Sarah has no reason to believe that her mother is in town. Her mother usually lives hundreds of miles away.
Pat:	Why is any of this relevant? Sarah still *knows* her mother is in town. She *is* psychic, whether or not she knows she is!
Pegeen:	She *doesn't* know her mother is coming. From Sarah's point of view, her belief *is utterly silly and irrational*. She has no reason to believe that her mother is in town. She doesn't even believe she's psychic. She just finds herself stuck with this belief that she can't shake: that her mother is in town. Given that this belief is, from her point of view, *barking mad*, how can we say she knows?
Pat:	But she does know!
Pegeen:	No, she doesn't!*

---

* This example is adapted from a famous one presented by Laurence Bonjour. See his 'Externalist Theories of Empirical Knowledge', *Midwest Studies in Philosophy*, Vol. 5 (1980).

Does Sarah know? The causal theory says she does: Sarah's psychic mechanism has produced a true belief: she is functioning in a thermometer-like way.

Yet most of us feel, at the very least, uncomfortable with the suggestion that a belief that is, from the believer's point of view, totally irrational might nevertheless count as knowledge.

Of course, we could easily fix the problem raised by the psychic Sarah case by adding on to the causal theory the requirement that the belief must also be justified. That would rule out Sarah as a knower, for, of course, Sarah is not justified in believing what she does.

But the requirement that to qualify as knowledge a belief must be justified led us into another difficulty: the justificatory regress problem. The requirement seems to rule out the possibility of our having any knowledge at all.

So we're faced with a puzzle. On the one hand, we need to avoid the justificatory regress problem. But it seems we can do so only by dropping the requirement that, to qualify as knowledge, a belief must be justified. But if we drop that requirement, then we run into the problem raised by the psychic Sarah case: that a wholly irrational belief might then count as knowledge.

In other words, we find ourselves being pulled in two different directions at once. On the one hand, it seems that justification *must* be required for knowledge. On the other hand, it seems it *cannot* be.

How do we solve this puzzle? You may have ideas of your own.

What to read next

In this chapter we have, in effect, been trying to pin down what philosophers call the *necessary and sufficient conditions* for knowledge. For both an explanation of 'necessary and sufficient conditions' and another example of how philosophers try to provide them, see Chapter 9, But Is It Art?.

Further reading

Chris Horner and Emrys Westacott, *Thinking through Philosophy* (Cambridge: Cambridge University Press, 2000), Chapter 2.

20

IS MORALITY LIKE A PAIR OF SPECTACLES?

We view certain things – people's actions – as having moral value, as being right or wrong. But according to many philosophers, this value is not intrinsic to those actions. Rather, it's rooted in our experience, in how we react emotionally to what we observe. It's as if we view the world through morality spectacles: the value that we think is objectively part of the world 'out there' is actually added by the emotional spectacles through which we're looking. If we could take off these spectacles, we would find that the world as it is 'in itself' is really value-free.

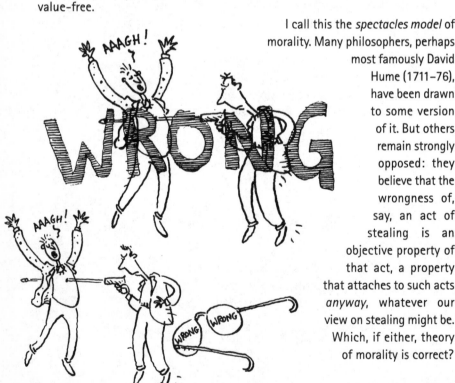

I call this the *spectacles model* of morality. Many philosophers, perhaps most famously David Hume (1711–76), have been drawn to some version of it. But others remain strongly opposed: they believe that the wrongness of, say, an act of stealing is an objective property of that act, a property that attaches to such acts *anyway*, whatever our view on stealing might be. Which, if either, theory of morality is correct?

How Do We Detect Wrongness?

Let's take a closer look at the view that moral value is *objective*, that it's 'out there' independently of us. This position is known as *moral realism*. As we're about to discover, moral realism faces a notorious difficulty: it seems to make knowledge of right and wrong impossible. This is because it appears unable to explain how we *detect* these moral properties. To see why, consider the following story.

One morning, while Virtue is hanging out the washing, an alien spacecraft lands in her back garden. The alien crew suggest that she takes a flight with them over the city. Virtue accepts their offer, and they are soon swooping above the rooftops. The aliens render their spacecraft invisible so that they don't disturb anyone in the streets below.

Then, as they pass low over a dark alley, Virtue spots a young man trying to steal a woman's purse. She points this out to the aliens. 'Look!' she says. 'We should help that woman. What that man is doing is *wrong*!'

The aliens are mystified.

'Ah. Wrong. We find your earthling talk of things being morally "wrong" deeply baffling. Most of your language we understand. But this property wrongness remains a mystery to us. We can find no trace of it. We want a complete theory of the universe. We don't want to miss anything out. Please point out the wrongness to us.'

Virtue is confused. She points out of the window and says: 'But can't you just *see* that what that man is doing is wrong?'

The aliens peer intently out of the window. Then they look back at Virtue.

'No, we can't. In fact, we find your talk of "seeing wrongness" very odd. We have five senses just like yours: sight, hearing, smell, taste and touch. But we can't find this property you call wrongness. Where is it? By which of your five senses do you detect it? You say you can *see* it?'

Virtue begins to understand why the aliens are confused. After all, it seems that our five human senses provide our only window on to the world around us. So if wrongness is an objective property – if it's part of the world 'out there' – then how do we get to know about it? How do we detect wrongness?

Virtue thinks she's spotted a confusion.

Inferring that Something Is Wrong

'Ah. I see your problem,' says Virtue. 'Wrongness isn't a property that you can *directly observe*, as you can, say, roundness. But that doesn't mean that there's a problem about establishing its existence. After all, the same is true of magnetism, isn't it? We can't see, hear, taste, touch or smell magnetism, can we?

'True.'

'Yet we still know that magnetism is out there, don't we? For we can legitimately *infer* the existence of magnetism from what we *can* directly observe: the effect it has on iron filings, for example.'

The aliens seem to be catching on. 'So you *infer* the wrongness of stealing from those features of stealing that you *can* observe?'

'Precisely.'

Is and Ought

To Virtue's surprise, the aliens remain baffled.

'You're mistaken. The inference you say you make cannot legitimately be made.'

'Why not?' asks Virtue.

'To say that something is wrong is to say we *ought not* to do it. Correct?'

Virtue nods in agreement.

'Well, the facts about what we *ought* or *ought not* to do are an entirely different sort of fact to the facts about what *is* the case.'

Virtue is confused. 'I'm not sure I follow.'

'Well, to say that something *ought not to* happen is not to say anything about what *is* happening. To say that this man *ought not to* steal that purse is not yet to say that he *is* or *isn't* stealing it, is it?'

Virtue has to agree.

'Conversely, to say that something *is* the case is not yet to say that it *ought* or *ought not to* happen.'

Virtue is not so sure. 'But what about the "is" fact that stealing causes suffering and makes people unhappy? Doesn't that immediately provide us with a rational case for not doing it?'

The aliens shake their green heads. 'No, it doesn't. Look, suppose someone delights in causing suffering and steals to make others unhappy. They actually think that it's something they *ought* to do. It won't do you one jot of good to point out to this person that stealing causes suffering and unhappiness. They will happily agree with you about that. They just disagree with you about whether stealing is something they ought to go in for.'

'I see.'

The aliens continue. 'Now, there's nothing remotely *irrational* about this cruel person's position, is there? You might think it immoral. But there's nothing you can point to by way of "is" facts that supports your contention that causing suffering is *not* something one ought to do over this person's contention that it *is* something one ought to do. You can't, simply by pointing to the "is" facts, provide any grounds for supposing that you're correct and they're mistaken.'

'H'm. Perhaps.'

'But then you can't rationally infer what ought or ought not to happen from a description of what is happening, can you?'

'Why not?'

Observation reveals only 'is' facts. It reveals only what 'is' happening. You can't directly observe the 'ought' facts. You have already admitted that the wrongness of an act of stealing is not itself directly observable.

The aliens went on. 'But we've just seen that neither can you legitimately infer the wrongness of stealing from the "is" facts that you can observe.'

'I guess you're right. They would require that I infer an "ought" from an "is". And that cannot legitimately be done.'

'Exactly.'

A Puzzle

The aliens sum up their bewilderment about this property – wrongness – that Virtue thinks is out there on the other side of the glass. 'But then how do you establish the existence of this strange property? You can't directly see it, smell it, touch it, taste it or hear it. But neither can you infer its presence from what you can observe as you can, say, magnetism. Yet you say you know it's there?'

The aliens look out of the window and raise their eyebrows. 'So how *do* you earthlings detect this "wrongness"? If it really is out there, please point it out to us.'

Virtue scratches her head and peers intently at the man still struggling to take the woman's purse. 'To be honest, I don't know. I feel sure it's out there. I feel sure that what that man is doing has the property of being wrong. But I just don't know how I detect this property.'

The aliens appear to be right: we can't directly observe wrongness. But neither can we legitimately infer its presence from what we can observe. So if the property for which the aliens are looking really is 'out there' on the other side of the glass porthole, how *does* Virtue detect it?

Hume's Solution

The spectacles model, on which moral value is added by the viewer, provides a satisfying explanation of why the aliens can't find the property for which they're looking. According to the spectacles model, by describing what the man on the other side of the glass is doing as 'wrong', Virtue is merely describing or expressing how *she feels* about what she sees. So the aliens are looking in the wrong place. To find the wrongness, the aliens need to turn around and examine *Virtue herself.*

This is precisely the view of the eighteenth-century philosopher David Hume (in fact, it's essentially Hume's argument that the aliens have just presented to Virtue). As Hume points out, a major difficulty for moral realists is to explain how we come by our knowledge of objective moral properties. If morality really were 'out there', it seems we wouldn't be able to get to know about it. Hume concludes that moral value has its origins in ourselves – in our emotions:

> Take any action allow'd to be vicious: Wilful murder, for instance. Examine it in all its lights, and see if you can find that matter of fact, or real existence, which you call vice . . . You can never find it, till you turn your reflexion into your own breast, and find a sentiment of disapprobation, which arises in you, towards this action.*

In Hume's view, the 'vice' is added by the observer.

* David Hume, *Treatise on Human Nature* (1740), Book III, Part I, Section I.

Moore and 'Intuition'

G. E. Moore (1873–1958) was a moral realist who recognised the difficulty for realism raised by Hume and proposed the following solution. Our five senses don't provide our only window on to the external world. We don't recognise the immorality of an action by ordinary observation. Rather, we are equipped with an additional, sixth sense – Moore called it 'intuition' – that allows us to discern the external moral properties. Just as you might use a radar dish to detect ships and aircraft hidden from sight, so you can use the faculty of 'intuition' to detect the moral properties that cannot be detected with your other five senses.

The reason that the aliens cannot detect the wrongness is that, unlike Virtue, they do not possess this additional, sixth sense.

Has Moore solved the puzzle of how we come by moral knowledge? Not really. For it remains utterly mysterious how our additional faculty of 'intuition' is supposed to work. Moore has dealt with one mystery only by introducing another that is no less baffling. So Hume's objection to moral realism remains: it still seems that only the spectacles model is able to account for moral knowledge.

Three Versions of the Spectacles Model

We have seen that the spectacles model of morality provides a satisfying explanation of why the aliens are unable to find the wrongness. So should we embrace the spectacles model?

In fact, there are several different versions of the spectacles model of morality from which we might choose. I shall outline three.

- *Subjectivism.* This is the simplest version of the spectacles model. According to subjectivism, to say that something is wrong is to claim that *you personally* disapprove of it. Similarly, to say that something is right is to claim that you approve.
- *Intersubjectivism.* According to intersubjectivism, to say that something is wrong is to claim that *your community* disapproves of it. Similarly, to say that something is right is to claim that your community approves.

Notice that on both these theories, to make a moral judgement is to make a *claim*. The claim, if true, is made true by a *fact*. Only the fact that makes the claim true is not 'out there' independently of us. The fact is a fact about *ourselves*.

But not all versions of the spectacles model maintain that moral talk is fact-stating. Consider a third version of the spectacles model:

* *Emotivism*. According to emotivism, to say that something is wrong *is not to make a claim at all*. Rather, it is to *express* disapproval of it. Similarly, to say that something is right is to *express* approval of it. Suppose I go to a football match. My team, Wormington Rovers, scores, so I say 'hoorah for Wormington Rovers'. Do I make a claim when I say this? No. 'Hoorah for Wormington Rovers' involves no claim. It is neither true nor false. Notice that I am *not even making a claim about how I feel*. Rather I am *expressing* how I feel. Now, according to emotivism, something similar happens when I say 'killing is wrong'. To say that killing is wrong is, in effect, to go 'boo to killing'. So 'killing is wrong' is *neither true nor false*. For, of course, 'boo to killing' is neither true nor false. But then *no fact is required* to make 'killing is wrong' true. Leading emotivist philosophers include A. J. Ayer (1910–89) and C. L. Stevenson (1908–79).

All these theories are versions of the spectacles model, because all three say that moral value is not a feature of objective reality, but rather is grounded in our subjective reactions to it. Morality has its roots in how we individually or collectively *feel* about certain actions. We individually or collectively *create* moral value by feeling as we do.

Why the Aliens Can't Find the Wrongness

All these three theories explain why the aliens can't find the wrongness, though they do so in slightly different ways.

According to subjectivism, when Virtue says 'stealing is wrong', she says that she personally happens to disapprove of it. In order to find the fact that makes her judgement true, the aliens need to turn around and examine Virtue.

According to intersubjectivism, when Virtue says 'stealing is wrong', she says that her community disapproves of it. So in order to discover whether what Virtue says is true, the aliens need to stop examining what the thief is doing and to start investigating how both Virtue and the rest of her community feel about stealing.

According to emotivism, Virtue *makes no claim at all*. But then no fact is required to make what she says true. There simply is no such fact as the 'fact' that stealing is wrong. So in searching for this 'fact' the aliens are on a wild-goose chase.

But while the spectacles model does sidestep the problem of explaining how we come by moral knowledge, there is a feature of our moral talk to which it seems it cannot do full justice. It appears that each version of the spectacles model, no matter how sophisticated, inevitably rules out the possibility of certain sorts of moral mistake – mistakes of a sort that we *can* in fact make.

Think, for example, about subjectivism. According to subjectivism, when I say 'killing is wrong', I claim that I personally disapprove of killing. But then *there's no possibility of my being mistaken about what's wrong* (other, of course, than because I am out of touch with my feelings). If I *feel* that killing is wrong, that *makes it* wrong (for me, at least). Similarly, if Max feels that killing is right, then he, too, is correct: for him killing *is* right. According to subjectivism, we're both correct.

But this is absurd, surely? It is at least *possible* for individuals to be mistaken about what's right and what's wrong. In using the moral vocabulary of 'right' and 'wrong' we take ourselves to be referring to properties that are 'there anyway', independently of how things might happen to strike us. But then the mere fact that we feel something to be wrong provides no guarantee that we are correct.

Intersubjectivism also rules out certain sorts of mistake. According to intersubjectivism, if I say 'killing is wrong', what I say is true when my community collectively feels killing to be wrong. This allows for the possibility of *me* being mistaken (I might be mistaken about what my community disapproves of), but it rules out the possibility of my community being mistaken. If my community *feels* that killing is wrong, that *makes it* wrong (for them at least).

Again, this is implausible. Surely even an entire community can be morally mistaken? The fact that the ancient Romans *felt* that watching a slave being torn apart by wild animals for their own amusement was morally acceptable did not make it acceptable.

Finally, consider emotivism. According to emotivism, when I say 'killing is wrong', I don't make any claim at all. But, as I am not making any sort of claim, it again follows that there's no possibility of my being mistaken about what's wrong. There's *nothing to be mistaken about.*

In short, the possibility of such individual and collective error seems to show that moral properties are, after all, *objective* properties.

Why Being Wrong Is Like Being Round

The following analogy may help to explain why. Being round is, presumably, an objective property. Things are round *anyway*, no matter how they might strike us. Admittedly, a round tower in the distance and in a certain light might not look round. It might seem square. But were we all to judge that the tower is square, the fact is that we would be mistaken. The tower would *still* be round.

Now, it is because shape is an *objective* property, a property that is 'there anyway', that explains why we can be both individually and collectively mistaken about whether something is round. If things were round, square, and so on only because they seemed that way, then, because the tower seemed square, that would *make it* square.

Similarly, if the spectacles model were correct and things were wrong only because they *seemed* wrong, then the possibility of our being mistaken about what's wrong couldn't arise. The fact that we *can* be both individually and collectively mistaken about what's wrong appears to show that being wrong, like being round, is an objective property.

Conclusion

We have been looking at two competing views about morality. Some adopt the spectacles model of morality on which moral value is added by the emotional spectacles through which we observe the world. Others believe that right and wrong are objective properties, properties that are 'there anyway' no matter how things might strike us.

Which position is correct? I have to admit, I'm pretty confused. On the one hand, those who believe moral value is independently 'out there' seem to face an insurmountable difficulty – that of explaining how we come by moral knowledge. On the other hand, I must also admit that the possibility of us being both individually and collectively mistaken about what's right and what's wrong does appear to show that we intend the words 'right' and 'wrong' to pick out objective properties that are 'there anyway'. The arguments pull us in opposite directions.

Where do we go from here? Some philosophers suggest that the only solution is to adopt an 'error' theory. On the one hand, our moral concepts of 'right' and 'wrong' demand that any properties worthy of these labels must be objective. But it turns out that there are no such objective properties out there. So everything we say using these terms is actually false. It's false that stealing is wrong. It's also false that it's right. We make an 'error' when we think of actions as having moral properties. Moral value is ultimately an illusion.

But this is a lot to swallow. Is the only satisfactory solution to this puzzle to admit that *there's ultimately no such thing as moral value*? Or can we come up with a more palatable answer?

What to read next

In this chapter we have looked at some of the arguments for and against *moral realism*. In Chapter 18, The Strange Realm of Numbers, I look at arguments for and against *mathematical realism*. You will discover that most of the positions and arguments in that chapter mirror those in this.

The spectacles model appears inevitably to involve a commitment to moral relativism – the view that what is right for one individual or community may be wrong for another, there being no objective fact of the matter as to which is correct. Moral relativism is discussed at some length in Chapter 5, Into the Lair of the Relativist.

Some might assume that the view that moral value is objective requires that God exists. This assumption is challenged in Chapter 10, Can We Have Morality without God and Religion?.

Further reading

Emotivism is clearly explained by one of its most important exponents in:

A. J. Ayer, *Language, Truth and Logic* (Harmondsworth: Pelican Books, 1971), Chapter 6.

A good discussion of the positions and arguments in this chapter can be found in:

J. L. Mackie, *Ethics: Inventing Right and Wrong* (Harmondsworth: Penguin Books, 1977).

Having read both this chapter and Chapter 18, you might wish to try:

Hilary Putnam, *The Many Faces of Realism* (La Salle, IL: Open Court, 1991), which contains four accessible lectures on realism.

21

SHOULD YOU BE EATING THAT?

Every year several billion animals are slaughtered in order to satisfy our taste for their flesh. I eat meat, but I have to admit that there are powerful philosophical arguments that appear to show that the slaughter of other species of creature merely to satisfy our preference for a certain sort of foodstuff is highly immoral. This chapter introduces the main arguments.

Eating Humans

The scene: a restaurant. Le Clerque is just ordering another round of pork sausages. De Selby gives him a disapproving look.

Le Clerque: Look, I *like* eating meat. Why shouldn't I eat it if I want to?

De Selby: Because it involves killing a living thing just so you can enjoy its taste.

Le Clerque: And what's wrong with that?

De Selby: Do you think it would be morally acceptable for someone to kill human beings just because they enjoyed the taste of human flesh?

Le Clerque: You mean like Hannibal Lecter? Of course not.

De Selby: Yet you think it OK to kill and eat pigs, cows and chickens?

Le Clerque: Yes.

De Selby: Then I think you need to explain *why* it's wrong to kill and eat human animals, but not these other sorts of animal. What's the difference between us and them that *justifies* us in treating them so differently?

De Selby's question is a good one. As we shall see, it's not an easy question to answer.

There's no doubt that we do quite properly morally discriminate between different kinds of being. For example, we treat children differently from adults. We restrict what they are able to do; we don't allow them to vote, and so on. But this is justified.

Children are not sufficiently rational or responsible to be able to look after themselves properly or to exercise the vote. There's a *morally relevant difference* between children and adults that warrants the difference in treatment.

But not all differences are morally relevant. Take skin colour and sex, for example. Both black people and women were at one time denied the vote. Their freedom was also heavily restricted (in some places it still is). But while black people and women have been discriminated against, the differences between them and their oppressors did not and does not justify the difference in treatment. When it comes to the right to be free and to have the vote, what's morally significant about race or sex? Nothing at all.

Those who discriminate on the basis of race or sex are guilty of *racism* and *sexism*: forms of unreasoned prejudice and bigotry against those who are different.

What de Selby is asking Le Clerque, in effect, is to point out that morally relevant difference between cows, chickens and pigs on the one hand and ourselves on the other that justifies us in treating these other species so differently. Unless Le Clerque can point up some difference, it seems that he, too, is guilty of a form of bigotry: what many now call *speciesism*.

Le Clerque: But, look, you wouldn't extend moral consideration to a rock, a cloud or a blade of grass, would you?
De Selby: I guess not.
Le Clerque: So why do you give such consideration to other sorts of animal? Like rocks or blades of grass, they are *also* very different from us. Surely the onus is on *you* to explain why we *should* extend moral consideration to them?
De Selby: Well, in many ways we *are* similar. A pig, for example, is capable – in an admittedly rather limited way – of enjoying life. While the range of pleasures and achievements open to a pig is fairly restricted compared with those open to the average human, still, a pig can, as a famous saying testifies, be happy. A rock can't.
Le Clerque: That's true.
De Selby: Now, shouldn't the happiness and suffering of other creatures be of moral concern to us? Of course, almost everyone thinks it should – even you. Hardly anyone thinks that torturing a pig to death with a hot poker for fun is morally acceptable. Do you?
Le Clerque: No.

SHOULD YOU BE EATING THAT? **231**

De Selby: In fact, you probably think that someone who tortures animals in this way should be prosecuted, perhaps even jailed. Yet most people, while quite happy about extending *this* much moral and legal consideration to a pig, are quite comfortable with the thought that this same pig might be slaughtered simply to satisfy our taste for its flesh. You are, aren't you? Why is that?

'Animals Are Stupid'

In fact, as Le Clerque now points out, there is a fairly obvious difference between ourselves and other species that, on the face of it, might seem to justify the difference in treatment.

Le Clerque: OK, I admit that we do extend moral consideration to other animals. But obviously we shouldn't extend to them *the same* moral consideration that we extend to humans. For they *are* relevantly different from us. For example, animals are pretty *stupid*, aren't they? Take pigs, for example. They can't talk, write or hold down a job. They don't know right from wrong. They are capable of only fairly basic pleasures. These are important differences between ourselves and pigs. They're what justifies us in treating pigs differently.

De Selby: You think it's the fact that pigs are comparatively stupid that justifies our killing and eating them?

Le Clerque: Yes.

De Selby: Then consider this case. Perhaps because of a disease that affects babies in the womb, some children are born that are fairly unintelligent. They are unable to learn language. Indeed, they are capable of enjoying only fairly crude sensory pleasures. They will never be any more emotionally, intellectually or morally sophisticated than is, say, the average pig.

Le Clerque: That would be tragic.

De Selby: I agree. But, look, how do you think we ought to *treat* these individuals?

Le Clerque: I guess we would build special centres and employ people to look after them, to give them the best quality of life possible.

De Selby: But why not *kill and eat them*? After all, in your view that should be perfectly OK!

De Selby is right. If Le Clerque's defence of killing for meat were adequate, it would also justify killing and eating such unsophisticated humans. Yet most of us would be morally outraged at the suggestion.

De Selby: It seems to me that you are simply prejudiced against other species.
Le Clerque: Why?
De Selby: You must either say that it *is* morally acceptable to kill and eat such unintelligent humans or else you must say that it is no less morally wrong to kill and eat pigs. Yet you do neither. You think you're justified in treating other species differently, but it turns out you have no justification. You're just a bigot.

'Most People Think It Morally Acceptable to Eat Meat'

Le Clerque is outraged at De Selby's suggestion that he is a bigot.

Le Clerque: But *most* people think it OK to kill and eat pigs, cows, and so on. How can all these millions of people be wrong?
De Selby: Just because most people think something is morally acceptable doesn't mean that it is. Only a few hundred years ago most Westerners deemed it morally proper to hold those of other races as slaves. They were simply blind to the immorality of what they were doing. Because almost everyone thought the same way, and because slavery was sanctioned by the authorities, hardly anyone questioned it. Looking back, we *now* recognise that what was done was very wrong indeed. But people couldn't see that at the time. Perhaps we are in a similar situation now. Maybe in a few hundred years' time people will look back at the way we currently treat other species and be horrified.

'Animals Are Bred to Be Eaten'

Le Clerque still thinks it is obvious that meat-eating is morally acceptable. He starts to run through some of the most popular justifications, beginning with the observation that cows, pigs, sheep and so on are, after all, bred for human consumption.

Le Clerque: But animals are *bred* to be eaten. That makes killing and eating them morally acceptable, surely? After all, if we didn't eat them, they wouldn't exist, would they?

De Selby: True. But that doesn't justify what we do. Consider those mentally impaired children we discussed a minute ago. Suppose that their disability is inherited, so that their children and their children's children also suffer similar impairments. Then, by your reasoning, it would be morally acceptable for us to breed these humans for the dinner table.

'We *Need* Meat'

Le Clerque: OK, I admit you're right: the fact that animals are bred to be eaten doesn't justify our eating them. But we need meat to remain healthy.

De Selby: Why?

Le Clerque: There are various vitamins and minerals present in meat that it can be hard to get elsewhere. And meat is a rich source of protein.

De Selby: There are millions of Buddhists, Hindus and Jains who eat no meat at all and who remain perfectly healthy. Meat is *not* essential for a healthy diet. Ask any dietary expert. You just need to be careful to eat sensibly. We can all do that.

'It Comes Naturally to Us to Eat Meat'

Undeterred, Le Clerque tries a different tack.

Le Clerque: All right, here's a better argument. Human beings have *evolved* to be omnivores, haven't they? We are *supposed* to eat meat. It comes naturally to us. That's why it's morally acceptable.

De Selby: All sorts of behaviour comes naturally to us that very clearly isn't morally acceptable. It seems that a tendency towards violence is to some extent genetically programmed into man. Does that make violent behaviour morally acceptable?

Le Clerque: Obviously not.

De Selby: Similarly, just because eating meat comes naturally to us – we may even, if you like, be 'designed' that way – doesn't make it right.

'But Animals Eat Animals'

Le Clerque tries yet another popular justification.

Le Clerque: Animals eat other animals. It's not wrong for them to do so. So why shouldn't we eat them?

De Selby: But other animals have no sense of right or wrong. Nor can they help themselves. So of course it's not 'wrong' for other animals to kill each other. But we're different. We *do* know right from wrong. We've no excuse. After all, you wouldn't try to excuse murder or stealing on the grounds that animals do it, would you?

Le Clerque: No.

De Selby: Then why do you try to excuse eating meat in the same way?

Le Clerque: Good question.

De Selby: Also, suppose that some of those mentally impaired children we were talking about killed and ate each other. If it's OK for us to kill and eat those who kill and eat each other, then it would then be OK for us to kill and eat those children. But it *wouldn't* be OK, would it?

Le Clerque: I guess not.

De Selby: So you *agree* with me, then?

Le Clerque certainly didn't agree.

Le Clerque: Absolutely not! It's *just obvious* to me that there *is* a morally relevant difference between humans and other species that justifies our killing and eating them. I'm merely finding myself a little hard pressed to specify exactly what that difference is.

De Selby: Hah! You sound like the slave owner who thought it 'just obvious' that there's a morally relevant difference between whites and blacks but found himself 'a little hard pressed' to say what it is.

Le Clerque: I'm no bigot!

De Selby: Then explain to me *why* you're not a bigot. It seems to me that you are.

'It's the *Potential* to Be Smart that Matters'

Le Clerque suddenly has a brainwave: it's not what a mentally impaired child *is* that's important, but what he or she *might have been*.

Le Clerque: Actually, there *is* a morally significant difference between those mentally impaired children and pigs, a difference we've overlooked.

De Selby: What difference?

Le Clerque: Even those children *start out with the potential* to be smart, sophisticated beings like ourselves. It's just that something goes wrong with their development in the womb. On the other hand, no pig has, or was ever going to have, that sort of potential. So it's the *potential* that counts, what a creature *might have* been. Those kids *would have been* smart had disaster not struck. That's why, unlike pigs, they still deserve our full moral respect.

Some philosophers have attempted to defend discrimination against other animals in just this sort of way. But de Selby is not convinced.

De Selby: OK, then, consider this case. It turns out that humans originated on another planet. We represent a particular line of evolution that has taken place on earth from 'dumb' human stock brought here by an alien civilisation many thousands of years ago. Luckily, our minds have been honed by the intervening years of evolution.

Le Clerque: Bizarre.

De Selby: I know. But just *suppose* this turns out to be true. Also, it turns out that, on the other planet from which we came, this other line of 'dumb' humans still survives. But they haven't evolved as we have. They are as dim as they ever were.

Le Clerque: The poor things.

De Selby: Right. Now imagine that *half* the mentally impaired children we are talking about are a result of a recent alien experiment: dastardly aliens implanted into the wombs of earthling women fertilised eggs recently taken from their 'dumb' human counterparts on the other planet.

Le Clerque: I see. So half these kids are biologically the children of this parallel, 'dumb' human race?

De Selby: *Half* of them are, yes. *Half* have this extraterrestrial ancestry.

Le Clerque: So what about the other half?

De Selby: Well, the other half are regular, terrestrial human kids. Their mental impairment is due to a nuclear accident. Their fathers were accidentally irradiated, resulting in damage to the genetic code handed down to them. So these children *would have been smart* had their fathers not been involved in a nuclear accident. The *potential* was there.

Le Clerque: I see. But these two groups of children are otherwise identical?

De Selby: Right. Neither group is very bright, and for the very same reason: they don't have the right sort of genes to be smart. Were you to examine their genetic codes, you would find them indistinguishable. However, while the terrestrial group possesses this 'dumb' genetic code due to an unfortunate nuclear accident, the extraterrestrial group possesses it because of a failure to evolve as we terrestrial humans have.

Le Clerque: I see.

De Selby: Now, should we morally discriminate between these two groups of children? In particular, would it be right to kill and eat one group but not the other?

Le Clerque: Obviously not.

De Selby: Ah! But now you're in trouble. You suggested that it would be OK to kill and eat pigs but not the equally dumb humans because the dumb humans at least once had the *potential* to be smart. But then it follows that we *should* discriminate between these two groups of children. Yes, they're genetically identical. But while the children of terrestrial origin once had the potential to be smart, the children of extraterrestrial origin did not. So, if you're right, while it would be wrong to kill the former children, there would be nothing wrong with killing and eating the latter. Like pigs, they were *never going to be anything other than dumb*!

Le Clerque: OK. I agree it would be morally wrong to discriminate between these two groups of children. Let's drop that suggestion.

'Is Killing a Fly Morally Wrong?'

Le Clerque pauses for a moment to chew on some sausage.

Le Clerque: I admit you've presented what *seems* like a pretty powerful argument for it being highly immoral to kill and eat pigs. But, frankly, your conclusion is ridiculous.

De Selby: Why?

Le Clerque: You're suggesting that ants and flies deserve our moral respect!

De Selby: Actually, I'm not saying that. It's unclear to me whether flies can really be said to suffer or be happy. So it's unclear to me whether they qualify for moral consideration. But when it comes to a creature like a pig, it's very obvious that it can both suffer and be happy. So it does deserve moral respect.

Le Clerque: The same degree of respect as a human? Imagine there are four people and a pig stuck in a boat. There's only enough drinking water for four of them. Who do they throw out? It seems obvious to me that they should throw out the pig.

De Selby: You know, that seems obvious to me, too. I don't think pigs *are* as important as humans. Their happiness, suffering, and so on counts for less. It's the pig that should go.

Le Clerque: Right.

De Selby: So we agree about that. But think: *why* is it right to throw the pig out?

Le Clerque: Because it's a pig.

De Selby: That's no reason: a racist could similarly say the reason it's right to throw a black person out is that he is black.

Le Clerque: True. Very well, it is, again, because *pigs aren't as smart as us.* They don't have the same range of emotions. They have no sense of right and wrong.

De Selby: Actually, I agree. But then suppose that there are five humans in the boat, one of whom is one of the mentally impaired children we discussed earlier. Who, if anyone, should be thrown out?

Le Clerque: I don't know: all human life is of equal value. Perhaps they should flip a coin.

De Selby: But, *by your own reasoning*, it's the mentally impaired child who should be thrown out. For, like the pig, it's not as smart as us.

Le Clerque: You're a Nazi! You think this poor, unfortunate child is morally no more important *than a pig*?

De Selby: I'm just pointing out what follows *by your own argument*. In fact, my point is that pigs *are* morally very important indeed. But not as important as is a typical human. For the typical human is, as you say, more morally, intellectually and emotionally sophisticated than is a pig.

'Animals Lack Souls'

Le Clerque now decides to try a quite different sort of justification for meat-eating: a *religious* justification.

Le Clerque: I've changed my mind. It's not the fact that we are smarter and more sophisticated than other species that justifies the difference in treatment. It's the fact that we have *souls*, and they don't.

De Selby: What is a soul?

Le Clerque: A person's essential character – what they're like. Their personality.

De Selby: But then even a pig can have a soul of sorts. Ask anyone who has kept one as a pet – each has its own distinctive character. They are much like dogs in that respect. So at least some other species of animal *do* have souls.

Le Clerque: But dogs and pigs don't have *much* of a personality, do they?

De Selby: That's debatable. Ask an animal lover. But look, your point is, in any case, irrelevant. Consider those mentally impaired children we talked about earlier. They are no more sophisticated – have no more personality – than does a pig or a dog. So again, by your own reasoning, it should be OK to kill and eat them!

Le Clerque: No, those poor children do have souls. You see, by a soul I really mean something capable of floating free of a physical body and existing independently. According to many religions, each person has such an immortal soul. Animals don't. *That's* what justifies us in treating them differently.

De Selby: Well, that may be your *opinion*, but in order for it to be a *rational* thing to believe, you are going to have to come up with some *reason* to suppose that humans – even very mentally impaired ones – have souls and animals don't.

Le Clerque: It says so in the Bible.

De Selby: Does it? Are you sure? But, look, even if it does, *so what*? What reason have you to suppose that everything in the Bible is true? After all,

Leviticus xxv, 44 states that you may own slaves, just so long as they come from neighbouring nations. You don't believe, I take it, that US citizens have a moral right to enslave Canadians?

Le Clerque: Of course not.

De Selby: But then what reason have you to trust what it says in the Bible about animal souls or the morality of eating meat? The fact is, you are just using the Bible to prop up your own particular prejudices, aren't you, in just the same way that slave owners used to quote Leviticus in defence of slavery? And you don't endorse slavery, I take it?

The Sanctimonious Reply

Le Clerque is becoming increasingly irritated. He has tried to defend meat-eating but failed miserably. So he decides to go on the offensive.

Le Clerque: It seems to me that by worrying about cows, pigs, chickens and sheep when there are famines and earthquakes killing millions of humans, you get your priorities all wrong. *How dare you* bang on about animals when babies are starving to death.

De Selby: That's a popular reply to those who question the morality of eating meat. But it is hardly a good reply, is it?

Le Clerque: Why not?

De Selby: Just because I'm concerned about the welfare of other animals doesn't mean I can't also be concerned about human welfare, does it? I am. In fact, I do believe that human beings are generally speaking more important than non-humans. It's just that I *also* believe that our treatment of other species is very wrong. And, in fact, you haven't given me a single reason to suppose that I'm mistaken about this. You haven't given me any reason to suppose that it isn't as wrong as murdering and eating those children we were talking about. And you do think that would be very wrong indeed.

Le Clerque: I still think you have your priorities all wrong.

De Selby: Suppose I pointed out that it's wrong that a certain company is stealing the pensions of its employees. You wouldn't turn round and say: '*How dare you* bang on about pensions when there's mass murder going on in Rwanda! That's *much* worse!' You wouldn't insist that everyone forget about the pension-stealing and focus on the situation in Rwanda instead.

Le Clerque: I guess not.

De Selby: Right. Yet you sanctimoniously accuse me of getting my priorities all wrong when I raise the issue of animal welfare. I find that odd.

Conclusion

Many of us think it 'just obvious' that it's morally acceptable to kill and eat other species of animal. I did until I started reading philosophy. But I'm now finding it increasingly difficult to defend my meat-eating lifestyle. If, like me, you eat meat, then you should take the arguments in this chapter seriously. Perhaps our meat-eating can be defended. But the onus is surely on us omnivores to show how.

What to read next

This chapter looks at one particular moral issue: is it right to kill animals simply to satisfy our taste for their flesh? In Chapter 20, Is Morality like a Pair of Spectacles?, I ask a rather different and more fundamental sort of question: what *is* morality, and where does it come from?

Further reading

The essential read, both accessible and gripping, is:

Peter Singer, *Animal Liberation* (London: Pimlico, 1995).

A short overview of many of the key arguments is provided by:

David DeGrazia, *Animal Rights* (Oxford: Oxford University Press, 2002).

2 2

BRAIN TRANSPLANTS, 'TELEPORTATION' AND THE PUZZLE OF PERSONAL IDENTITY

I was leafing through an old photograph album the other day. As I flicked through the photos, I saw pictures of myself at different stages of my life. There I was at graduation, in my first school uniform and in my cot. I was struck by how much I have changed over the years, both physically and psychologically. My body has become much bigger, for example, and my store of memories has massively increased. And yet it was still myself that I saw in each photo, despite all these changes. What was it, I wondered, about each of the people I saw in the photographs that *made them* all me? What connected all these individuals together as a single person. What's essential so far as *being me* is concerned?

The Animal Theory

Here's a seemingly plausible answer to my question. When I look at the photographs in my album, I see the same *living organism* each time: a member of the species *Homo sapiens*. I don't mean that it's the same lump of matter in each case. The material out of which my body is made is constantly being replaced, so that only a small fraction of the atoms that went to make up my two-year-old body form part of my body as it is today. What I see in each photograph is rather *the same living creature*, the same *animal*, at different stages of its development. So perhaps what each person is, in essence, is an animal. If that's true, then necessarily each person ends up wherever the relevant animal ends up.

Let's call this theory about what people are and where they end up *the animal theory*. As I say, prima facie, the animal theory does sound pretty sensible. At least, that is, until you start thinking about the following sort of case.

The Brain Transplant Case

One night, while Freyja and Ferne are sleeping, aliens sweep down and land their flying saucer outside Freyja's and Ferne's house. The aliens creep into the two humans' bedrooms, where they perform a complex surgical procedure. They open up Freyja's and Ferne's skullcaps and carefully remove their living brains. With their advanced technology, the aliens then reinstall each brain in the other human's body, taking great care to reconnect all the nerves and other plumbing. They then replace the two skullcaps and use a special technique they have developed to heal all the scars invisibly. Finally, the aliens leave.

Next morning, two people awake. The human in Freyja's bed jumps out of bed and looks down. Her body seems to her to have changed. And when she looks in the mirror she gets a shock. For she sees Ferne's face staring back at her, not the face she remembers. Then she sees what appears to be herself walk in through the door. 'What's going on?' she says. 'Why do you look like me, and I look like you?'

Of course, the kind of operation described in the above story is not yet a medical possibility. Nevertheless, there seems no reason *in principle* why a human brain might not come to be housed in a different animal body. We already transplant organs and limbs. Why not a whole body?

Now ask yourself: where do Freyja and Ferne end up? Most of us, when asked to test our intuitions on this sort of case, say that *the two people involved have swapped bodies*. Freyja now has Ferne's body and Ferne has Freyja's.

Why is this? After all, if some other organ – the liver, say, or the heart – were switched round, the person would not go with it. What's different about the brain?

The answer, of course, is that it's primarily the brain that determines what a person is like *psychologically*. Your memories, abilities and various personality traits, for example, are largely a product of how your brain is put together – how the neurons are spliced, how the chemicals are balanced, and so on. So when Ferne's brain is transferred to Freyja's body, so, too, are these psychological properties. Ask the person with Freyja's body who they are and she will say 'Ferne'. For she has all Ferne's memories and various other personality traits. But then surely she has everything that's essential so far as being Ferne is concerned, despite the fact that she now has Freyja's body. That, at least, is how the situation strikes me.

A Problem for the Animal Theory

But if my intuitions are correct and Freyja and Ferne have swapped bodies, then the animal theory is mistaken. While each of us might happen to stick with the same animal body throughout our existence, it's not *necessary* that we do so. In which case it cannot be correct simply to identify the person with their animal body. You happen to have a particular body, but you could in principle part company with it.

The Brain Theory

So it appears that the animal theory is false. But what if we were to revise the theory slightly? What if we claim, not that it is the *whole* animal body that is relevant to the identity of a person, but merely a *part* of it: the brain. Our intuitions about the brain swap case don't contradict this revised theory, for, of course, in the brain swap case each person does end up where her brain ends up. So perhaps the theory that you are, essentially, your brain is the right one. Let's call this *the brain theory*.

Few philosophers are prepared to embrace the brain theory. One of the most obvious problems with it is raised by the following tale.

The Case of the Brain Recorder

This is the *brain recorder*. Place it on someone's head and flip the 'on' switch, and it then scans exactly how that person's brain is put together: how the neurons are intertwined, how the chemicals are balanced, and so on. All this information is then stored. Place the helmet on a *second* person's head and flip the appropriate switch and the recorder then reconfigures this second brain exactly as the first was configured. The neurons in the second brain are re-spliced so as to match exactly the way they are spliced in the first brain. The glands

are re-balanced so as to function in just the same manner, and so on. The result is that the second body ends up with the psychological properties previously associated with the first.

Of course, such a device is currently a technological impossibility. But there seems no reason in principle why such a machine should not be developed.

Now suppose that instead of swapping Freyja's and Ferne's brains round, we use the brain recorder instead. We use it to move Freyja's psychological properties over to Ferne's body, and Ferne's over to Freyja's. The question is: where do Freyja and Ferne now end up?

Intuitively, it seems to me that the right answer is that Freyja ends up with Ferne's body and Ferne ends up with Freyja's. They swap bodies. After all, the person that now has Freyja's body will think she is called 'Ferne'. She will have all Ferne's memories, mental ticks and foibles. But then surely she will have everything that's essential so far as being Ferne is concerned.

And yet notice that no *physical part* of Ferne was moved over to Freyja's body, *not even her brain.* So it seems the brain theory cannot be correct either. It is in principle possible for a person to part company not only with their original body, but also with their original brain.

Thinking Tools: Philosophy and Science Fiction

At this point you may be wondering about the use of science fiction stories to draw philosophical conclusions. 'Surely', you may argue, 'such stories can't tell us anything. After all, they are *not even true.* How can you gain any genuine philosophical insight simply by making up some fantastic tale?'

Here is one traditional answer to this question (I shall leave you to decide whether or not it is adequate). As philosophers, we are interested not just in what happens to be the case, but in what is essential. Scientists investigate how things actually stand – about what the laws of nature are, about how matter is actually arranged, and so on. As philosophers, however, we are interested not merely in what happens to be the case, but in what must be the case no matter what. We want to establish what is *true in principle.*

Now, we can test a given claim about what is true in principle by constructing a science fiction scenario. Consider, for example, the philosophical claim that each person is essentially a particular living body, so that it is in principle impossible for a person and their body to come apart. It's enough to refute this claim that we can come up with a situation that is *in principle* possible in which a person and their body part company. Whether or not the situation described happens to be a medical or technological or scientific possibility is quite beside the point.

The Stream Theory

We have seen that while each person has a particular animal body, their identity does not appear to be essentially bound up with that body. Rather, each of us seems essentially tied to various psychological *properties*, properties that could, in principle, pass from one body to another.

Of course, a person's psychological properties can change. Take memory, for example. My store of memories has been added to over the years. And there are plenty of things I have forgotten. In fact, I have no memory at all of when I was two. My personality traits and abilities have also changed dramatically since then. Yet I remain the same person as that two-year-old. Why?

According to many philosophers, the reason I am one and the same person as that two-year-old is not that we are psychologically exactly alike – we aren't – but that we are *psychologically continuous*.

Here's an example of psychological continuity. I can remember nothing of when I was two. But suppose I can remember when I was ten. And suppose that when I was ten I could remember being five. Suppose also that when I was five I could remember being two. Then there is an overlapping series of memories linking me as I am today back to that two-year-old. Psychologically, I'm not exactly like that two-year-old. But we are psychologically continuous.

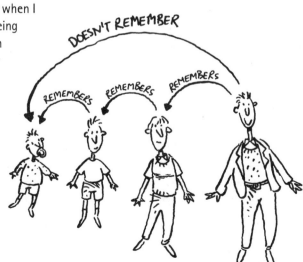

Let's refer to the theory that it is psychological continuity that determines personal identity as *the stream theory*. We can think of the identity of a person as residing in a stream of properties, a stream that might, in principle, flow from one animal body to another.

Of course, I'm not suggesting that people do swap bodies. I rather doubt that has ever happened. My point is simply that, on the stream theory, it *could* happen.

Making Two of 'You'

We have seen that, so far, the stream theory seems rather more plausible than either the animal theory or the brain theory, for it gives intuitively the right result in the brain swap and brain transplant cases.

But there is a notorious difficulty with the stream theory. This difficulty is called *the reduplication problem*, and it's nicely illustrated by another imaginary case.

Suppose a machine is developed that can duplicate physical objects. Let's call this machine *the object copier*. Place an object – a vase of flowers, say – in cubicle A, press the 'start' button and after a short pause there is a flash and a fizzing noise. A perfect atom-for-atom replica of the vase is created in cubicle B.

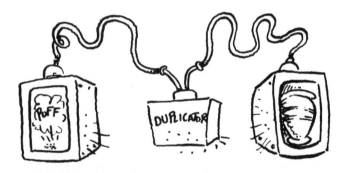

Unfortunately, in the process of creating the duplicate vase (which is put together out of a store of brand-new molecules), the original vase is instantaneously vaporised, leaving a small heap of ash on the floor of cubicle A.

Now suppose we put *you* inside cubicle A and press the 'start' button. What happens next? On the animal theory, you are killed. For the original animal with which you are supposed to be identical is reduced to a heap of grey ash. It is merely someone *just like you* that materialises in cubicle B.

But on the stream theory we get a different result. The machine doesn't *kill* you; it *transports* you from cubicle A to cubicle B. It is not merely a copy of you, but you yourself that appears in cubicle B. True, you no longer have your original animal body. It's a duplicate body that materialises in cubicle B. But on the stream theory that doesn't matter. As the person that appears in cubicle B possesses all the right psychological properties, they are you. This machine only copies physical objects, but it *transports* people.

Perhaps this strikes you as the right way to describe what occurs: you really do get transported from cubicle A to cubicle B. But now suppose this happens. An additional cubicle, C, is added to the duplicator machine so that, rather than one duplicate body being produced, two now appear. You step into cubicle A and press the 'start' button. Where, if anywhere, do you end up?

We now face a problem. For on the stream theory, as both these future individuals are psychologically exactly like you, it follows that both *are* you. But that is impossible, for it would follow from the fact that they are both identical with you *that they are also identical with each other*, which clearly they are not: there are *two* of them.

This is the reduplication problem, and it constitutes perhaps the most serious difficulty facing the stream theory.

Thinking Tools: Muddling Two Sorts of 'Identity'

Philosophy undergraduates often become confused at this point in the debate. They say something like the following.

> You said to begin with that the object copier produces exact duplicates. So the people that get out after the button is pressed will be exactly the same – they will be identical in every way, both physically and psychologically. Yet now you say that these two individuals are *not* identical – they are *not* the same person. So you have contradicted yourself. In fact, I don't see why we can't say that the two people who get out of the machine *are* both me. What's the problem with that?

This is an understandable confusion. It arises because the expressions 'identical' and 'the same' are used in two quite different ways. Suppose two steel balls are manufactured. These balls are, let's suppose, exactly similar in all their qualities, right down to the last atom. So there is a sense in which they are 'identical' and 'the same'. But there is also a sense in which they aren't. For the number of balls is two, not one. They are not identical in that sense of 'identity' that requires they be *one and the same ball*. Philosophers distinguish these two senses of 'identical' by calling the first *qualitative identity* and the second *numerical identity*.

Now it's clear that our interest in this chapter is in *numerical* identity. The question we asked right at the beginning was: what makes each of the people I see in my photo album *one and the same person* despite the difference in their *qualities*. And the stream theory is supposed to answer this question. It says that it is sufficient for the *numerical* identity of people that they be connected by a flow of psychological properties. But then it follows, on the stream theory, that the people created in cubicles B and C aren't just qualitatively identical, they are numerically identical, too. As these individuals clearly aren't numerically identical (the number of people is two, not one), it follows that the stream theory is false.

Adding to the Stream Theory

Can the reduplication problem be dealt with? Perhaps. Some philosophers insist that we need make only a slight modification to the stream theory in order to salvage it. All we need do, they say, is to add the following condition:

> If *two* later individuals, who exist at the same time, are *both* psychologically continuous with an earlier individual, then *neither* of those later individuals is numerically identical with the earlier.

How does this condition help solve the reduplication problem? It allows that, in the situation where only *one* person is produced by the object copier, that later individual is identical with the person that entered cubicle A. So far, so good. However, if *two* people are produced, then the above clause kicks in, with the result that neither is identical with the person that stepped into cubicle A. The original person has ceased to exist, and we now have two brand-new people before us. So the reduplication problem is dealt with. For the stream theory, now modified, no longer entails what is patently false: that the two people who step out of cubicles B and C are one and the same person.

Let's call this amended version of the stream theory *the modified stream theory*.

The modification may deal with the reduplication problem. But our troubles aren't over. For the modified stream theory produces highly counter-intuitive results of its own, as the following story illustrates.

The Duplicator Gun

Suppose that the CIA develop a gun-like machine that is capable of producing a perfect physical atom-for-atom duplicate of whatever object it is pointed at. Point the gun at a glass of water, pull the trigger and an exact atom-for-atom copy of that glass of water immediately materialises in a cubicle attached to the gun. However, unlike the object copier described earlier, the duplicator gun does *not* destroy the object it duplicates. The duplicate and the original both continue to exist.

Suppose that, as you leave home one morning, a CIA operative secretly points the duplicator gun at you from a van parked across the street. The operative pulls the trigger. As she does so, an exact physical duplicate of you is produced inside the van (of course, this person wonders how he just ended up inside a van – he believes that but a second ago he was locking his front door). Unaware of what has happened, the person with your original body wanders off down the street and turns the corner.

Now ask yourself: where, if anywhere, do *you* end up?

According to the modified stream theory, by pointing the duplicator gun at you and pulling the trigger, the CIA operative brings your existence to an end. For there are now *two* individuals around who are exactly like the one that stepped out of the door. At this point, then, the new clause that we just added to the stream theory kicks in, with the result that *neither* of these people count as you.

But this is wrong, surely? Intuitively, it seems right to me to say that it's *you* that walks off down the street and turns the corner, and not merely someone just like you. How can it make any difference to whether or not it's you that some CIA agent has secretly run off a copy of you in the meantime? I don't see how it can. Yet that is what the modified stream theory entails.

Let's now consider a slightly different scenario. Suppose that, just as the copy of you materialises in the van, a piano falls out of a window and squashes you flat. Where do you end up now?

According to the modified stream theory, you are transported to the van. It's not merely someone just like you that materialises in the van, but you yourself. For in this case there is only one person around psychologically continuous with the person that stepped out of your front door.

But again, this seems wrong. Surely you're dead. For the animal that stepped out of your front door has been squashed flat. The fact that the CIA have produced someone *just like you* in the van doesn't alter this fact.

These two cases pull us strongly back in the direction of the theory with which we started: the animal theory. For, unlike both the stream and the modified stream theory, the animal theory actually gives the *right* verdict in both cases. In the first story, as it is the *same animal* that walks down the street and turns the corner, so it *is* the same person. In the second story, as that animal is killed, so, too, are you. The fact that a second, duplicate animal is produced elsewhere is quite beside the point.

A Puzzle

So we find ourselves being pulled in two directions at once. On the one hand, when we consider the brain transplant and brain recorder cases, our intuitions very strongly support the conclusion that the body is irrelevant so far as the identity of the person is concerned. You could, in principle, swap bodies with someone.

But the duplicator gun cases draw out a contrary intuition: that that particular animal body is very relevant indeed to your identity. If we haven't got that particular animal body – the one you have now – then we haven't got you. We have, at best, merely got someone *just like you*.

So which intuition are we to trust? And why? That is a problem with which philosophers are still struggling.

The problem raised in this chapter is brought into sharp focus by my last story. I shall leave you to decide what the narrator should do.

The year is 3222, and I am Joe Jones. At least, I think I am. Let me explain.

The Tifrap Deep Space Mining Corporation introduced the tele-matic three years ago. They use it to 'teleport' employees to and from work here on Borax3 on a daily basis. It would take hundreds of years to reach Borax3 from earth by spacecraft. The tele-matic was developed to allow Tifrap Corp's employees to travel here in a matter of minutes.

Then, today, there was a revelation. It turns out Tifrap Corp has been deceiving its employees. The management originally told us that the tele-matic transports people to and from Borax3 by flinging their bodies through space at fantastic speed. But they lied. What really happens is this. You get up in the morning and step into a tele-matic machine back on earth. It scans your body. The tele-matic records exactly how your body is put together. This information is then transmitted to Borax3, where a perfect atom-for-atom duplicate body is created. Your original body is then instantaneously vaporised. The person who steps out of the tele-matic on Borax3 is in every respect exactly like the person who stepped into the machine on earth. But they have a brand-new body.

When we were told this morning about how the tele-matic really works, I wasn't too bothered. 'Sure,' I thought. 'Each time I use the tele-matic, I get a new body. But so what? No one gets killed. I might have some sentimental attachment to my original body, but what's the big deal if it did get incinerated? The important thing is that I've survived, isn't it? In fact, I wouldn't even have noticed that my body had been replaced if Tifrap Corp hadn't admitted it.'

But then a worrying thought started to nag at me. Was I Joe Jones? Maybe not. Perhaps I have existed only since this morning when I stepped out of that tele-matic machine over there. Maybe Joe Jones was incinerated when he first stepped into the tele-matic three years ago. Maybe I'm merely someone *just like* Joe Jones. Maybe there's merely been a series of Joe Jones-like people created and then killed by the tele-matic. If so, then Mrs Jones has been a widow these last three years and she never even knew. In fact, I've never even met Mrs Jones. My memories of her are the memories of a dead man.

Tifrap Corp has given all its employees here on Borax3 the option of using the tele-matic to take one last 'return' trip back to earth. In fact, that's the only way we can get home. Travelling by spaceship would take us hundreds of years to get back, by which time we would all be dead.

I miss Mrs Jones. I miss my children – if they are my children. But I don't want to die. So what should I do? Do I step into the tele-matic over there and press the red button? If I do, will I be transported back to earth? Or will I be killed? Will it be me that appears on earth and gets to return to the family of whom I seem to have all these fond memories? Or will I be incinerated, to be replaced by someone merely just like me?

What would you do?

What to read next

Other philosophical problems concerning the mind can be found in Chapter 8, The Strange Case of the Rational Dentist, Chapter 6, Could a Machine Think?, and Chapter 13, The Consciousness Conundrum.

Further reading

A clear introduction to the issues raised here can be found in:

Keith Maslin, *An Introduction to the Philosophy of Mind* (Cambridge: Polity, 2001), Chapter 9.

An entertaining discussion of many of the same issues can also be found in Daniel Dennett's paper, 'Where Am I?', which appears as Chapter 39 of:

Nigel Warburton (ed.), *Philosophy: Basic Readings* (London: Routledge, 1999).

23

MIRACLES AND
THE SUPERNATURAL

PHILOSOPHY GYM CATEGORY

WARM-UP

MODERATE

MORE CHALLENGING

Every age has its reports of miracles and the supernatural. Even today, witnesses are rife. Almost everyone knows someone who claims to have witnessed a miraculous happening – a ghostly visitation, a vivid and highly prophetic dream, objects that appear to have moved by themselves. Given the sheer quantity of evidence provided by such testimony, you might think that there's got to be *something* to it.

Or has there? This chapter introduces some of David Hume's (1711–76) key arguments on the miraculous.

A Visit to the Psychic

Pat has been to see his psychic.

Pat: The Great Mystica really is psychic.
Bridie: How do you know?
Pat: Well, for a start, there's the testimony of her many satisfied customers. She has hundreds of thank-you letters on her walls.
Bridie: The testimony of gullible fools.
Pat: You can't seriously maintain it's *all* rubbish, can you? Shouldn't you be more open-minded? There's *so much* evidence concerning the amazing powers of psychics, miracle healers and other supernatural goings-on.

A Sense in Which 'Miracles Happen'

In fact, as Bridie now points out, there's at least one sense in which we can all agree that 'miracles happen'.

Bridie: I don't wish to deny that miracles can and do occur.
Pat: Really?

Bridie:	Yes. For there are such things as *fortuitous coincidences.*
Pat:	What do you mean?
Bridie:	Let me give you an example. In a lottery, each of the million tickets is sold to a different person. Fred purchases one of these tickets and happens to win. In a sense, this is, from Fred's perspective, a 'miracle'. It was *extraordinarily unlikely* that he should win. His chances of winning were one in a million. Fred has been the recipient of fantastic good fortune. But while Fred's winning is, in *this* sense, a 'miracle', his winning doesn't require any explanation, let alone any sort of *supernatural* explanation. After all, *someone* had to win.

Bridie is right that the occurrence of Fred's 'miracle' is something even the staunchest sceptic about the supernatural can allow.

Pat:	I see that. But what's your point?
Bridie:	Well, similarly, as billions of humans go through the lottery of life, some of them are inevitably going to get spectacularly lucky. Again, this is just what we should expect.
Pat:	I'm not sure I follow.
Bridie:	Here's an example. A child runs on to a railway line moments before a train is about to pass by. It seems she must be killed. However, the points directly in front of the child develop a fault, resulting in the train being diverted on to a parallel track at the last moment. We would no doubt say that the child's survival is 'miraculous', meaning by this that she is extraordinarily lucky not to have been killed.
Pat:	Of course.
Bridie:	So, in a sense, a 'miracle' occurs.
Pat:	But what if the parents want to claim *more* than this? Suppose they insist that some sort of supernatural agent – God, perhaps – must have intervened to save their child? Wouldn't that be a rational thing for them to believe under the circumstances?
Bridie:	No. You see, that a certain number of such 'miracles' will happen is itself overwhelmingly probable. In fact, what would be *genuinely* weird is if they *didn't* happen now and then. So I'm afraid the fact that such unlikely events occur gives us no reason at all to believe in either God or supernatural intervention.

Bridie is correct that we should actually expect reports, entirely accurate reports, of extremely improbable things happening occasionally, whatever the truth about the supernatural.

Supernatural Miracles

But, as Pat now points out, it won't do to try to dismiss all reports of miracles on the grounds that 'coincidences happen'.

Pat: Very well. We can agree that 'miracles happen' in the sense that extraordinarily unlikely and fortuitous things happen. But there's a great deal of testimony about events that aren't just unlikely but actually *impossible*, given the laws of nature.

Bridie: For example?

Pat: Lots of people recently reported some very peculiar events during an evangelical church service in the United States: amalgam dental fillings spontaneously turned themselves to gold right there in people's mouths! That such a thing should happen isn't just fantastically unlikely, it's impossible. The *laws of nature* prohibit amalgam fillings turning themselves to gold.

Pat is right: this case differs from Bridie's railway example because what is supposedly witnessed cannot be dismissed as a result of mere chance.

Pat: Surely the only plausible explanation of what these people saw is that something supernatural went on behind the scenes to *overturn* natural law? *That's* what I mean by a 'miracle' – something from 'beyond' the natural order intervenes to alter how things turn out.

Our Fascination with the Miraculous

Does the wealth of testimony of the sort to which Pat appeals give us good grounds for supposing that such supernatural miracles (and, from now on, by 'miracles' I shall mean just the supernatural variety) occur? Bridie still thinks not.

Bridie: I agree there's a great deal of testimony concerning things that are not just unlikely but actually impossible, given the laws of nature: people report seeing long-dead relatives; people claim to have had out-of-body experiences; psychics appear to know things that only some sort of supernatural faculty could reveal. But there are good reasons why we should be highly distrustful of all such testimony.

Pat: What reasons?

Bridie: It's a fact of human psychology that we find ourselves drawn to tales of the supernatural. Every age and culture has its myths and legends of fantastical beings and supernatural happenings. Many of our most popular films and TV shows continue to be dominated by supernatural themes. We desperately *want* to hear and believe such stories.

One of the most famous discussions of the miraculous can be found in David Hume's *Enquiry Concerning Human Understanding.* Hume was highly sceptical about the occurrence of miracles. His discussion includes much the same point as that just made by Bridie:

The passion of *surprise* and *wonder*, arising from miracles, being an agreeable emotion, gives a sensible tendency towards the belief of those events, from which it is derived. And this goes so far, that even those who cannot enjoy this pleasure immediately, nor can believe those miraculous events, of which they are informed, yet love to partake of the satisfaction at second-hand or by rebound, and place a pride and delight in exciting the admiration of others.

With what greediness are the miraculous accounts of travellers received, their descriptions of sea and land monsters, their relations of wonderful adventures, strange men, and uncouth manners . . .*

Hume also points out that people often have a *strong personal interest* in propagating such reports. There's sometimes a financial motive. Reports of weeping statues and miracle cures sell newspapers and help television programmes gain high ratings. The media have a strong interest in presenting such reports in the most favourable light, focusing on what lends the reports credibility and ignoring what doesn't. TV shows about the supernatural, while purporting to be 'balanced', tend to consist for the most part of interviews with psychics and witnesses to paranormal events interspersed with dramatised reconstructions of allegedly supernatural happenings.

* David Hume, *An Enquiry Concerning Human Understanding* (1777), Section X, Part II, p. 93.

Fakery

There are other reasons why we should treat reports of the miraculous with caution. Because of our fascination with the supernatural, it's hardly surprising that many charlatans are prepared to take advantage. Given the number of easily mastered illusions that can be used to dupe people into thinking they are witnessing a miracle, we should, again, expect a great many false reports.

The Techniques of the 'Psychic'

What of the seemingly miraculous powers of Pat's psychic? Doesn't the uncanny accuracy of her predictions demonstrate that she must possess some supernatural ability? Pat claims that his psychic 'knew' all sorts of things about him that she couldn't possibly have known except by supernatural means.

Pat: The Great Mystica knew my uncle was called 'George'. She also knew that he died of a heart attack and had a slipped disc. Yet I didn't tell her anything, not a word! How do you explain that?

Bridie: H'm. I'm not sure I can. But I'm not sure I need to. Think about it – did she *really* know all this stuff about you? What *really* happened?

In fact, what actually happened was this:

The Great Mystica: I'm ready to begin. Let me see. I am sensing a presence.
Pat: A presence?
The Great Mystica: I'm getting a name. George. Or is it Gerald?
Pat: George! My dead uncle!
The Great Mystica: Yes, that's right. It is George. I knew he was a close relative.

This snippet of conversation illustrates a few of the many ways in which psychics regularly convince their clients of their powers. Notice that:

- The psychic gave two names, not one. Both names are common to people of a certain age, particularly in the UK. Ask any British person of around sixty-five – Pat's age – whether they know someone with either of these two names, and the chances are that they will. Even if Pat didn't happen to know someone called George or Gerald, the psychic can still say: 'There will be someone called George who will play a part in your life, perhaps in a year or two.' Or the psychic can claim that a George who is unknown to Pat is attempting to relay a message from someone else in the spirit world.

- The psychic did not say George was dead. Pat gave her that information. In fact, if Pat knew someone alive called either George or Gerald, the psychic would still have scored a 'hit' and could then suggest that the message from beyond *concerned* someone called George or Gerald.

- The psychic never said George was a relative of Pat's, let alone his uncle. Again, Pat provided all that information.

The session continued:

The Great Mystica: Ah. He had trouble here (pointing to the middle of her torso), didn't he?
Pat: That's right! A heart attack! That's how he died!

Notice that the psychic did not say George died of a heart attack. Psychics often claim that a deceased person had trouble in their torso. In fact, almost everyone who dies ultimately does so because of the failure of an organ in the torso – most often the heart. Even cancer affecting the head or a limb usually kills by spreading to organs in the abdomen. But even if George had died from being shot in the head, the psychic would *still* score a 'hit' if George had ever had *any* sort of trouble in the region of his torso – if George had occasionally suffered from bad indigestion, for example.

The Great Mystica: Did he have trouble with his back?
Pat: Wow! Right, again! He had a slipped disc.

Notice that the psychic didn't say that George had a slipped disc. Pat supplied that information. In fact, the psychic didn't even claim that George had trouble with his back. She merely *asked* if he did. So if the answer to her question is 'no', the psychic cannot be accused of having made a mistake. However, as almost everyone does have some back trouble at some point, the probability again is that she will be perceived to have scored a 'hit'.

So while Pat might *think* that his psychic knew that his Uncle George had a slipped disc and died of a heart attack, the fact is she knew no such thing.

Psychics regularly use these and numerous other techniques to generate the illusion that they possess supernatural powers. They tend to ask questions rather than make claims. And they tend to speak in very vague and general terms about the sort of thing that applies to a great many people. Everyone knows someone who is thinking of changing job; every parent argues with their child occasionally; everyone has difficulties with a close relative. It's the detail that is invariably and unwittingly filled in by the client.

Even when psychics do stick their necks out and make clear, unequivocal claims, there remains a powerful and well-documented mechanism operating in their favour. Because of our fascination with the extraordinary and the miraculous, human beings have a powerful tendency to forget the 'misses' among such claims and focus only on the 'hits'. You're likely to be so impressed by the fact that the psychic guessed your exact age that you immediately forget the ten other things about which she was wrong.

I should stress that not all the psychic's techniques involve deliberate trickery. There's little doubt that many psychics genuinely believe themselves to be psychic. They don't *intend* to deceive. Yet they do.[*]

Thinking Tools: Clever Hans

Humans and other creatures can learn to read extremely subtle changes in people's behaviour, changes by which we can unwittingly give away information. One of the most dramatic examples is provided by the horse Clever Hans. In 1888 Hans's owner set about teaching his horse maths. After much painstaking training, Hans was finally able to give the correct answers to mathematical questions by tapping his hoof. For example, if someone were to ask, 'What is the square root of sixteen?', Hans would tap his hoof four times. Hans could perform even without his trainer present. There was no deliberate trickery involved: Hans's owner believed his horse really could perform mathematical calculations.

Clever Hans become world-famous, his abilities baffling both scientists and public audiences alike. Until, that is, a young psychologist tested whether Hans could still perform if asked questions by someone who didn't know the answers. It turned out he couldn't. Somehow, Hans was reading almost imperceptible changes in the behaviour of his questioners, tapping

---

[*] I have adapted some of my examples of how psychics can fool both us and themselves from examples provided by Tony Youens of the Association for Skeptical Enquiry. For more information, see www.aske.org.uk. Incidentally, Tony regularly takes part in events where the public are asked to judge whether or not he has psychic powers. He usually manages to fool them.

his foot until some unconscious behavioural cue – such as an almost imperceptible tensing of the body – told him when to stop. Someone who didn't know the answers was unable to supply Hans with the appropriate cues, which is why he then lost his mathematical powers. Eventually, these cues were identified.

If a horse can learn to read such subtle, unconsciously given signals, then no doubt a psychic can, too. It may be that one of the techniques used by psychics is to read (if only subliminally) these same behavioural clues. Of course, there would be nothing remotely supernatural about such an ability.

Hypnotism

False miracles aren't just conjured up through trickery. We are now more aware than was Hume of the power of hypnotic suggestion. Hypnotism is a perfectly natural if not particularly well-understood phenomenon. The use of hypnotic techniques can lead people to believe that they are witnessing what they are not. Stage hypnotists regularly convince people of ridiculous things: that they are presenting a TV show, or flying through the air, for example. Hypnotism can also produce astonishing physiological effects, such as a blister on the arm of someone hypnotised to believe they have been scalded. But hypnotism can also be used in more subtle ways. Usually, where something miraculous has supposedly been witnessed by a large group of people, it turns out that it was witnessed on an ashram, in a church or at some other religious site where, perhaps through a combination of chanting, candles, incense and music, believers are likely to have been lulled into a highly suggestible state. A mesmeric leader would not find it particularly difficult to convince such an audience that they were witnessing something miraculous. Rarely does one hear of a miracle being witnessed by several hundred people at, say, a busy supermarket.

Self–Deception and the Power of Suggestion

Human beings are notoriously prone to self-deception, and this also accounts for much testimony concerning the supernatural. Consider Pat's example of the evangelists who reported that their amalgam fillings had spontaneously turned to gold. Perhaps what happened is this. A member of the congregation who had some dental work done that morning attends church under the impression that he has been given an amalgam filling. But there was a mix-up and, unbeknown to him, he received a gold filling instead. He shows his new filling to someone in church, and it's discovered that the filling has 'turned to gold'. Considerable excitement is generated as other members of the congregation begin to hear about the 'miracle' that has occurred in their midst. They start to look in each other's mouths. There is increasing hysteria as more gold fillings are discovered. Now, suppose that you are a member of this congregation and that your friend asks you to look in his mouth to check if his filling has also turned to gold. It's pretty dark in there, so you can't see the filling too well. Maybe what indoor light there is also has a yellowish hue. At this point the psychological pressure on you to 'see' a gold-coloured filling is going to be very strong indeed. For you are aware, of course, that if you say the filling is amalgam, your friend is going to be extremely disappointed. There will also be the suggestion that your friend is not quite 'good enough' to have received one of the miraculous fillings. So you 'see' a gold filling. You don't lie, exactly. Rather, you unconsciously tailor your perception a little to make it accord with what you strongly hope and expect to see. You engage in a kind of self-deception.

I do not claim that this actually happened, of course. But the suggestion is surely not that absurd.

In fact, our tendency to 'see' whatever we strongly want or expect to see is well documented. Flying saucers were first reported back in 1947. Pilot Kenneth Arnold reported seeing nine flying objects, and the newspapers immediately printed reports of 'flying saucers'. Unfortunately, in the excitement that followed, one important piece of information was lost: Arnold didn't actually report seeing saucers. In fact, he said that the objects looked like *boomerangs*, but that they flew 'like a saucer if you skip it across the water'. Yet UFO reports have been dominated by the saucer theme ever since. It seems that either our alien visitors coincidentally happened to redesign their craft back in 1947, changing the shape from boomerang to saucer, or else the many thousands of saucer reports since have largely been a result of the power of suggestion.

Bridie concludes that the amount of testimony concerning miraculous happenings is about *what one should expect anyway*, even if miracles don't happen.

Bridie: It's hardly surprising that there are so many reports of seemingly impossible things happening. It's exactly what one would anticipate, given the extraordinary fascination we have with the supernatural and the ease with which the appearance of such events can be generated through fakery, hypnotism, self-deception, the power of suggestion, and so on. *That's* why I dismiss this testimony – including even your testimony about your psychic. I am *not* being cynical and closed-minded.

Miracles and God

Hume was particularly concerned with the suggestion that miracles provide us with good evidence of the existence of God. Jesus, for example, is said to have performed a number of miracles, including making blind people see and raising the dead. Even today, religious miracles are regularly reported. Do these reports give us good grounds for believing in God?

Hume thought not. He points out that there are many religions, all of which claim to have their own miracles. As each religion makes claims incompatible with those made by other religions, they cannot all be true (for example, some religions say there are hundreds of gods, others claim there is just one, while Buddhists do without God altogether). But as each religion has its own store of miracles to which it can appeal, so all these miracles cancel each other out.

One might also wonder why, if God is in the habit of making miracles happen, He chooses to perform what are, for the most part, such trivial examples. Rather than turning people's dental fillings to gold or making statues weep, why doesn't He give us a cure for cancer or conjure up food where there is a famine? Surely, if the Almighty really were to go in for miracles, He wouldn't bother with the sort of trivial music-hall fare with which He so often gets credited.

Extremely unlikely and fortuitous events are often cited as evidence of God's intervention. The parents of the child saved by the faulty railway points may well believe that God intervened. But, as I say, one should expect such fortuitous coincidences to happen from time to time. You should also bear in mind that for every happy coincidence there is an unhappy one. For every train that is safely diverted at the last moment, another train is disastrously rerouted right into a crowd of people. Consistency requires that, if we count the former coincidence as evidence of the existence of a loving and benevolent God, then we ought to count the latter coincidence as equally good evidence of the existence of a bitter and malignant God. We don't, of course.

One of Hume's Main Arguments Concerning Miracles
Bridie now sums up her position on miracles.

Pat: I still think you're too quick to reject all testimony of miracles.

Bridie: OK, let's put it this way. Suppose a friend whom I consider to be a generally reliable witness tells me that she has observed a supernatural event – she sees her dead mother materialise for a few seconds in the middle of her living room. I now have two hypotheses to consider. First, there's the hypothesis that my friend is either lying or else has – through some combination of fakery, hypnotism, self-deception and illusion – herself been deceived. Secondly, there's the hypothesis that the supernatural event in question really did occur. Correct?

Pat: Correct.

Bridie: So I must weigh up the evidence on either side. I must consider which hypothesis is more likely to be true. Now, it seems pretty clear to me that, in every case, the probability that the witness is either deceived or a deceiver will always be equal to or greater than the probability that something genuinely supernatural has occurred.

Pat: Why?

Bridie: Because on one side we have very strong evidence that the universe is governed by laws that *don't* allow dead people spontaneously to appear in people's living rooms. We also have strong evidence that human beings nevertheless very much want this sort of thing to happen, that people lie, and that there exist many mechanisms by which we're actually *very likely* to be deceived about this sort of thing every now and then. On the other side, we have my friend's testimony.

Pat: I see. If you put it like that, I suppose the evidence does tend to point towards your friend's testimony being unreliable.

Bridie: Exactly. No doubt she had a vivid dream or is having some kind of mental breakdown. We know that this sort of thing happens, don't we?

Pat: I suppose so.

Bridie: So the rational thing to believe is that my friend's testimony is, on this occasion, unreliable.

What Bridie has just presented is one of Hume's main arguments against accepting testimony of the miraculous.

> When anyone tells me, that he saw a dead man restored to life, I immediately consider it in myself, whether it be more probable, that this person should either deceive or be deceived, or that fact, which he relates, should have happened. I weigh one miracle against the other; and according to the superiority, which I discover, I pronounce my decision, and always reject the greater miracle. If the falsehood of his testimony would be more miraculous than the event which he relates; then, and not till then, can he pretend to command my belief or opinion.*

As Hume points out, as the available evidence invariably points more strongly towards the conclusion that the person is a deceiver or was deceived, that is the rational thing to believe.

Bridie: So, to repeat, I am *not* being cynical and closed-minded. I am not saying that it's *impossible* for miracles to occur. Perhaps they do. My point is that there's nothing like the kind of evidence required to support belief in miracles. I'm simply proportioning my belief to the available evidence, as any rational person should.

Pat: But there's not just *this one person's* testimony concerning supernatural events. There's a *great deal* of such testimony.

Bridie: The fact remains that all this testimony is precisely what we should expect even if supernatural events don't occur. We also have considerable evidence supporting the hypothesis that nature is governed by strict laws that prevent such things from happening. So surely a sceptical attitude *is* the rational attitude to take?

Pat is still not prepared to admit defeat.

Pat: OK, suppose that I accept it would be irrational of me to believe that miracles happen simply on the basis of the available testimony. Still, *I don't need to rely on that testimony.* For I have *myself* witnessed my psychic's miraculous abilities. She is able to come up with amazingly accurate information about me, information she couldn't possibly

---

* David Hume, *An Enquiry Concerning Human Understanding* (1777), Section X, Part I, p. 91

have come by except by the exercise of some sort of supernatural power. Surely I'm justified in believing what *I have experienced for myself?*

Bridie: No, not in this case, you're not. You may *choose* to believe that she has supernatural powers if you want. But your belief is neither justified nor rational. For again, what is more probable: that, on the one hand, you have been tricked, hypnotised or deceived in some way, or, on the other hand, that your psychic has genuinely miraculous powers? Given the overwhelming evidence that people do *not* have such powers, and given that there are many techniques that psychics regularly use to dupe people, surely it's rational for you to be sceptical.

Conclusion

Is Bridie right? I believe she is. Yes, it's *possible* that miracles occur. In fact, I would rather like to believe that they do occur. But there isn't the kind of evidence needed to make belief in their occurrence rational. Admittedly, there exists a great deal of testimony concerning the supernatural. But when we take a step back and survey the evidence more coolly, it turns out to fall a long way short of the standards required for sensible belief.

What to read next

This chapter contains an argument for the existence of God – the 'argument from miracles'. Other arguments for God's existence can be found in Chapter 7, Does God Exist?, and Chapter 1, Where Did the Universe Come From?.

Further reading

An excellent discussion of miracles, the supernatural and all things weird is provided by:

Theodore Schick Jr and Lewis Vaughn, *How to Think about Weird Things*, second edition (California: Mayfield, 1999).

Simon Blackburn provides a succinct introduction to Hume's thinking on miracles in:

Simon Blackburn, *Think* (Oxford: Oxford University Press, 1999), Chapter 5.

24

HOW TO SPOT

EIGHT EVERYDAY

REASONING ERRORS

PHILOSOPHY GYM CATEGORY

WARM-UP

MODERATE

MORE CHALLENGING

A fallacy is an error in reasoning. Reason – the use of argument – is the main tool of the philosopher. But, of course, we also depend on reason in our everyday lives. So it's important that we can spot a logical howler when we come across it.

This chapter will help you to identify eight common reasoning errors (errors that, very probably, you sometimes make, too).

1. The Post Hoc Fallacy (a Fallacy of the Superstitious)

I had been worried about my exams. So Jill bought me a rabbit's foot to take with me for luck. I took the foot, and I passed the first exam. So, you see, the rabbit's foot worked! I shall take it to all my other exams, and it will make me pass them, too.

This is an example of the post hoc fallacy. Here are two more examples:

- John's psychic told him she would send positive psychic vibes when he tried to climb Everest. And he succeeded! So, you see, his psychic really does have miraculous powers! From now on he's always going to ask her for help in climbing mountains.
- Local taxes went up. And, look, the crime figures went up. So higher local taxes cause crime. Local taxes should never have been raised!

Examine all three examples and you will find that someone concludes that, because one event occurred *after* another, therefore the first event must have *caused* the second.

This is clearly flawed reasoning. Usually, when one event occurs after another, there is no causal connection between them. Suppose, for example, that I plug in the kettle. Immediately after, a comet crashes into Jupiter. Did I cause the comet's impact? Obviously not.

Of course, there *may* be a causal connection between two events that occur one after the other. Perhaps the rise in taxes really did cause a rise in crime. Perhaps John's psychic really did cause him to succeed. The point is that such 'one-off' observations do not remotely *justify* the claim that the first event caused the second.

The moral is: *don't leap to conclusions.* Noticing that one event occurs immediately after another might give one grounds for investigating whether two events are causally connected. But it does not, by itself, make it rational to believe that there is any such connection.

Unfortunately, superstitious people are very prone to the post hoc fallacy, and the unscrupulous can and do take advantage. Point out that just after someone bought one of your lucky rabbit's feet they immediately won some money on a scratch card and you will soon find gullible customers beating a path to your rabbit's foot store.

2. Argument from Authority (a Favourite of Celebrity Advertisers)

- 'I'm going to find my perfect partner soon.' 'How do you know?' 'I consulted the fortune-telling machine on the pier, and it said so.'
- 'Blancmange face packs are an effective beauty treatment.' 'How do you know?' 'All the celebrities are using them – Anita Sopwith Camel, actress and pop star, even advertises them on TV.'
- 'Genetic engineering is always morally wrong; it should never be carried out.' 'Why do you believe that?' 'Because Dr Bits told me.' 'Is Dr Bits an expert in ethics and genetic techniques?' 'No, he's a professor of mathematics.'
- 'I believe that Brand X washes whiter than any other brand.' 'Why?' 'Because scientists working for the Brand X corporation say so.'

Sometimes we're justified in believing something because an authority on the subject tells us that it is true. If a professor of chemistry warns you not to drop a lump of phosphorus into a sink full of water, I would follow her advice.

But often such 'appeals to authority' are fallacious.

In the first two examples, the 'authorities' in question are highly dubious. Why should a celebrity be any better informed about the efficacy of blancmange face packs than anyone else?

In the third, while Dr Bits really is an authority, he is not an authority on the issue in question. There is no reason to suppose that his opinion on the ethics of genetic engineering is any more reliable than anyone else's.

In the fourth example, the authority in question may be biased. To what extent can we trust scientists working for a particular company to give impartial advice about its products?

When appealing to a supposed 'authority', you must be warranted in supposing that it really is an authority on the issue in question, that there aren't many other authorities on the issue holding an opposing view, that the authority is not significantly biased, and so on. *Only then* is it sensible to place your trust in the authority in question.

3. Slippery Slope (the Miser's Favourite)

- If I lend you one pound today, tomorrow it will be two pounds, then ten pounds. Pretty soon you will owe me thousands!

This is an example of the slippery slope fallacy. It occurs when someone argues that one thing will inevitably follow from another but without providing any justification for supposing that 'slide' from one thing to the other is likely to happen. Usually, there are a number of intermediate steps involved in the 'slide'.

Is the following an example of the fallacy?

- If we allow someone to select the sex of their baby today, tomorrow we will have to allow selection for eye and hair colour. Pretty soon, we will have to allow 'designer babies'.

Yes, it is, if no reason is given for supposing that we cannot or will not simply stop at some point along the 'slide'.

4. False Dilemma (the Salesperson's Favourite)

It is common to argue like this:

- Either *A* or *B*. Not *A*. Therefore *B*.

This is often a perfectly acceptable form of argument, as in this case:

- Either John has a driving licence or else John is not permitted to drive. John has not got a driving licence. Therefore John is not permitted to drive.

This argument, on the other hand, is not acceptable:

- Either 1 + 1 = 5 or 2 + 2 = 5. It is not true that 1 + 1 = 5. Therefore 2 + 2 = 5.

Why not? Because, unlike in the first argument, the alternatives presented in the either/or premise could *both* be false. People often construct such arguments without registering that there might be other alternatives, as in this example:

- Either we cut welfare or the government goes into the red. We cannot allow the government to go into the red. Therefore we must cut welfare.

In this case, there are other options not mentioned, such as raising taxes. Customers are often railroaded into making bad decisions by a salesperson's use of false dilemma:

- Either you give a substantial donation to the Blue Meanie cult or you will have an unhappy life. You don't want an unhappy life, do you? So make that donation!
- Either you buy the Kawazuki K1000 for great home sound entertainment, or else you make do with second-rate rubbish. Are you really prepared to accept second-rate rubbish? I thought not. So you have no choice, do you? You have to buy the Kawazuki K1000!

Be cautious when salespeople appear to offer you an inescapable either/or decision. As often as not they are using false dilemma.

5. Trying Only to Confirm
(a Favourite of Politicians the World Over)

Suppose I show you four cards, each of which has a letter on one side and a number on the other. An 'E', 'F', '2' and '5' are visible, like this:

Now suppose I ask you what is the quickest way of establishing that the following is true: *of the four cards shown, those with vowels on one side have even numbers on the other.* Which cards do you need to turn over to establish that the hypothesis is true? Take a moment to think about it . . . Probably you think the E and 2 cards should be flipped. In fact, that's actually the wrong combination of cards to turn over. Yet *most people* believe that E and 2 are the cards to examine (so did I when I first saw this test).

So what cards should you flip? The answer is E and 5. Why?

You need to turn the E card over to check that there is an even number on the reverse. If there isn't, the hypothesis is false. You also need to turn the 5 card to check that it doesn't have a vowel on the reverse. If it does, the hypothesis is false. As long as E has an even number and 5 doesn't have a vowel, the hypothesis is true. It doesn't matter what's on the reverse of the F and the 2.

So why are we led astray? Why do we tend to turn the 2 and not the 5? It seems *we have an in-built tendency to try to confirm such hypotheses rather than disconfirm them.* We turn the 2 because we are searching only for positive instances of the hypothesis, not negative ones. We tend to look for confirming evidence, even when a search for disconfirming evidence might be far more telling. This tendency can lead us into serious trouble. Here's another example.

A politician believes that cutting local taxes will cause the crime rate to drop. So she asks her researchers to look for examples of situations where local taxes were cut and the crime rate fell. They find that there are a hundred such examples. So the politician concludes that she is justified in supposing that by lowering local taxes she can cut crime.

The politician sought only to confirm her hypothesis, not disconfirm it. That may have led her astray. Had her researchers bothered to look, they might have found *two* hundred cases in which the crime rate went up after local taxes were cut.

The moral is: when testing a hypothesis, make sure you look not just for confirming evidence, but also for disconfirming evidence.

6. The Gambler's Fallacy

Here are two examples of the gambler's fallacy.

Simon: Still buying those scratch cards?
Stan: Yes. I've been playing for three years and I haven't won yet.
Simon: So why do you bother?
Stan: Well, as I haven't won yet, I must be due for a win fairly shortly!

Tracey: Did you win anything at the dogs last night?
Bob: No. I bet on Rover Dover three times in a row and he lost each time.

Tracey: So you won't bother betting on him again, I guess?

Bob: I shall definitely bet on him again! You see, his record shows that he wins fifty per cent of his races. As he has lost the last three, it follows that he *must* win the next three to even things up! Rover Dover is now a dead cert!

In each case, someone takes the probability of an event A happening over a period of time, notices that, over the first part of that period, the actual incidence of A is much lower than what is probable, and then concludes that A must be much more probable over the rest of the period. They predict a short-term increase in the probability of A to 'even things up' over the longer term.

The fallacy can also work the other way: someone might suppose that a higher-than-expected incidence of A must result in a short-term lowering in the probability of A to 'even things up', as in this case.

Ruth: Doing the lottery again this week?

John: Yes. What numbers are you going to pick?

Ruth: H'm. Well, the numbers that have come up most are 3, 7 and 28. So I certainly shan't be choosing them. As they have come up a lot recently, they are bound not to come up again for a quite a while.

The gambler's fallacy is extremely common. Wait a few minutes around any lottery or scratch card outlet and it won't be long before you hear someone saying that they are 'due' a win, that they won't make the mistake of picking the same numbers that won last week, and so on.

The truth, of course, is that it makes not one jot of difference what has happened up to now. Each week, the probability of any particular sequence of numbers coming up in the UK lottery is always exactly the same: about 14 million to one.

Interestingly, I recently saw a news reporter commit just this fallacy on TV. A couple who chose the same numbers week after week in the UK lottery forgot to buy a ticket the very week that those numbers came up. The couple were devastated, but insisted they would keep on choosing the same numbers in future. The reporter concluded that, sadly, the couple were now far less likely to win with those numbers.

7. Circular Justification
(also Known as 'Begging the Question')

Tom: The Great Mystica is a reliable source of information.
Sarah: How do you know?
Tom: She told me so herself.

Bert: God must exist.
Ernie: Why?
Bert: It says so in the Bible.
Ernie: How do you know the Bible is reliable?
Bert: Because it is the word of God.

Violet: John is honest.
William: How do you know?
Violet: Tom told me.
William: How do you know Tom is honest?
Violet: Jane told me.
William: How do you know Jane is honest?
Violet: John told me.

Each of these justifications runs in a circle. In each case, the truth of the claim that is supposed to be justified is actually *assumed* by that justification. Such circular justifications are unacceptable: you can't justify a claim simply by assuming it to be true.

8. The Fallacy of Affirming the Consequent

Take a look at the following argument:

• If I am a man, then I am mortal. I am a man. Therefore I am mortal.

There's nothing wrong with this argument. It has two premises, both of which are true. And the conclusion follows. Now look at these arguments:

• If John is happy, then John is playing football. John is playing football. Therefore John is happy.

- If I am taller than Sue, then Sue is short. Sue is short. Therefore I am taller than Sue.

Are these arguments acceptable? Interestingly, a study of people who had no training in logic found that *over two-thirds believed arguments of this form to be acceptable.* Yet both arguments are faulty. Each resembles the first argument we looked at, but differs from it in an important way. The first argument has this form:

- If A, then B. A. Therefore B.

The faulty arguments have this form:

- If A, then B. B. Therefore A.

It is known as the fallacy of *affirming the consequent.* To work through a concrete example, look again at my first illustration of the fallacy above. It is true that if John is happy, then John is playing football. Football is the only thing that makes John happy. Does it follow that if John is playing football, then he is happy? No. For while John may be happy only when playing football, it may also be that he is often unhappy even when he *is* playing football.

Here, finally, are a couple of philosophical examples of affirming the consequent:

- If God exists, then there is good in the world. There is good in the world. Therefore God exists.
- If other humans feel pain, then they will cry out when injured. Other humans will cry out when injured. Therefore other humans feel pain.

Further reading

This chapter provides just a few examples of fallacies. For more examples, see:

Nigel Warburton, *Thinking from A to Z* (London: Routledge, 1996).

There is a useful list of fallacies with both explanation and examples at:

www.nizkor.org/features/fallacies/

25

SEVEN PARADOXES

This chapter contains seven of the most famous, fascinating and infuriating paradoxes. All the examples in this chapter take the form of seemingly plausible arguments leading to seemingly implausible conclusions. They leave us flummoxed because, while we are unwilling to accept the conclusion, we can't see anything wrong with the reasoning that leads us to the conclusion.

See if you can figure out solutions to the following seven examples. But be warned: some of the world's greatest minds have tried and failed. Indeed, the first of our paradoxes is alleged to have caused the early death of Philetas of Kos.

Many readers will be content to dip into my seven examples just for fun: they are curiously entertaining. Others may wish to pursue things further. For the second group, I have included some further hints and comments at the end.

Paradox 1: The Man who Spoke the Truth but Didn't

A traveller was walking one day when he met an old man sitting beside the road smoking a pipe.

'The first thing said to you by the first person you meet today will not be true,' said the old man. 'Trust me – don't believe what he says!'

'OK,' said the traveller. 'But hang on a minute: *you're* the first person I've met today.'

'Exactly!' said the old man.

You may have spotted something funny going on here. If the old man speaks the truth, then the first thing he says is not true. But if the first thing he says is not true, then the first thing he says is true.

This is a version of the famous *liar paradox*, a paradox first formulated in ancient Greece over 2,000 years ago.

The traveller thought he saw a way out of the paradox: claim that what the old man first said is *neither true nor not true*. After all, why *does* every such sentence have to be either true or not true?

'Old man, you're trying to trick me,' said the traveller. 'It's obvious that what you said is *neither* true nor not true.'

'Aha,' said the old man. 'You're suggesting that it is not true that what I said is true, and also not true that what I said is not true?'

'That's exactly right,' said the traveller.

'Well, then, if it's not true that what I said is true, then what I said *is* not true!'

The traveller was starting to get a headache. The old man continued: 'And if it's not true that what I said is not true, then what I said *is* true! For what I said is precisely that what I said is not true!'

The traveller was starting to feel like ramming the old man's pipe down his throat.

'So you see,' said the old man, 'your suggestion is wrong: it's *not* true that what I said is neither true nor not true. In fact, it's *both* true and not true!'

But that's impossible. Isn't it?

Paradox 2: The Sorites Paradox

Here are two versions of this ancient paradox.

Jenny's Sandpit

Jenny is tidying her sandpit while Jim looks on.

'You know, the ants from that ants' nest over there keep stealing grains of your sand.'

Jenny looked down at the line of ants. Each marched up to her heap, took a single grain of sand between its mandibles and carried it off down the garden.

Jenny didn't seem much bothered.

'But they'll never be able to remove this heap of sand, will they?' she replied.

'Why not? Look, if they keep on removing those grains one by one, then eventually there will be just a single grain left, won't there? It might take weeks, but eventually you'll have just a single grain of sand left at the bottom of your pit. Then you won't have a heap of sand any more, will you?'

Jenny scratched her head. 'But look, *by removing a single grain of sand from a heap, you can't turn it into a non-heap, can you?'*

'No, obviously not,' replied Jim. 'For example, if I have 1,000 grains, and I remove one grain, giving me 999 grains, I still have a heap. Correct?'

'Right,' said Jenny. But then, no matter how many grains are removed by those ants, they will *never* succeed in turning my heap into a non-heap.'

Jim was now very confused. 'But if that's true, then a single grain of sand *is* a heap!'

'Precisely!' said Jenny. 'In fact, even *no* grains of sand is a heap!'

But it's surely false that no grains of sand is a heap. So where did Jenny go wrong?

Bob's Balding Spot

Bob was looking forlornly into the bathroom mirror while holding a pocket mirror up to the back of his head.

'There goes another hair,' he said sadly.

'Stop worrying,' replied Sarah. 'You can't turn from being not bald to being bald with the loss of a single hair, can you?'

'I guess not,' said Bob.

'So you're still not bald, are you?' said Sarah.

'I suppose not. But hang on! If what you say is true, then, no matter how many hairs fall out of my head, I will never be bald!'

'Er. I didn't say that.'

'But it does *follow* from what you said, doesn't it? Suppose there are exactly a million hairs on my head now, and I'm not bald. If one hair is removed, and you're right that removing a single hair can't transform a non-bald person into a bald one, then I still won't be bald. Remove another hair, and I still won't be bald. Remove yet another, and I still won't be bald. And so on, until there are no hairs left. I still won't be bald! But clearly I *will* be bald! So it follows that your principle that, by removing a single hair from his head, you can't turn a person from being not bald into being bald, must be false!'

'You're mad.'

'But it follows! In fact, there must come a point where, by losing just a *single hair*, I'll turn from being bald into being not bald!'

'But that's absurd. There's not a precise number of hairs that marks the boundary between being bald and being not bald.'

'But there must be!'

'But then *what is* that number of hairs?'

'I don't know. Maybe it's 10,027. Maybe it's 799. But there must be such a number.'

'That's just plain silly.'

'Actually, it *must* be true! In fact, perhaps the hair that just fell out was the one that turned me from being not bald into being bald!'

Paradox 3: The Boastful Barber

Luigi, the barber of Seville, was proudly boasting of his success. 'You know, I'm the man who shaves all and only those men in Seville who don't shave themselves!'

'I can't believe that,' says Franco.

'Why not?'

'Well, do you shave yourself? If you do, then, from what you just said, it follows that you *don't* shave yourself. For you said you shave all *and only* those who don't shave themselves. Right?'

'Right. But what if I tell you that I don't shave myself – my wife does the job for me?'

'Well, if you don't shave yourself, then it follows that you do. For you said you shave *all* and only those who don't shave themselves. Right?'

'Er. Right.'

So does Luigi just shave those who don't shave themselves? Or doesn't he?

Paradox 4: Achilles and Tortoise

Achilles rides a huge motorbike. Tortoise has a little moped. They decide to have a race. But as his motorbike is much faster than Tortoise's moped, Achilles decides to give Tortoise a head start.

Achilles starts at A. Tortoise starts at B. By the time Achilles has made up the distance to B, Tortoise has moved forward to C. By the time Achilles reaches C,

A   B   C   D

Tortoise has got to D. Every time Achilles manages to close the gap between where he is and where Tortoise is, Tortoise has moved forward a bit more. But there are going to be an infinite number of such gaps to close before Achilles finally catches up with Tortoise. But one can never travel across an *infinite* number of gaps, for no matter how many gaps one travels across there will always be an infinite number yet to travel. There's no last gap. *So Achilles can never catch Tortoise.*

Yet, of course, he can. How come?

Paradox 5: The Ravens

Pluck is asking Bridie, a scientist, what it is that scientists do.

Pluck: How does science work?

Bridie: Well, scientists construct theories that are confirmed by observation.

Pluck: Give me an example.

Bridie: Very well. Take the generalisation that all ravens are black. Now *all generalisations are confirmed by their instances*. So, for example, an observation of a black raven, being an instance of the generalisation that all ravens are black, confirms that generalisation. Each black raven one sees confirms the hypothesis that all ravens are black a little more.

Pluck: I see. But look, it's true, is it not, that if two hypotheses are logically equivalent, then whatever confirms one hypothesis should confirm the other?

Bridie: That must be true. Logically equivalent hypotheses are really just two different ways of saying the same thing. So whatever confirms one hypothesis should confirm the other.

Pluck: Right. But the hypothesis that *all ravens are black* is logically equivalent to the hypothesis that *all non-black things are non-ravens.*

Bridie: True. In effect, they say the same thing.

Pluck: But then if all generalisations are confirmed by their instances, then a non-black non-raven confirms that all non-black things are non-ravens, right?

Bridie: True.

Pluck: But then a non-black non-raven confirms that all ravens are black, true?

Bridie: Er. True, I suppose.

Pluck: So white shoes, red poppies and blue skies – being non-black non-ravens – all confirm the hypothesis that all ravens are black.

Bridie: But that's absurd!

Pluck: But *it follows from what you agreed before.* My observation of this pink blancmange confirms that all ravens are black!

Pluck is right: if everything Bridie agreed to is correct, then a pink blancmange really does confirm that all ravens are black. But that's absurd. Or is it?

Paradox 6: The Unexpected Examination

The teacher tells her students that they should expect an exam some time during the next week. But she does not say when. The exam is to be unexpected.

But will it be unexpected?

Can the teacher give the exam on Friday? No, for if she gives it on Friday, then on Friday morning her students, knowing that they hadn't had the exam earlier in the week, will expect it.

What about Thursday? Well, as her students know that the exam cannot be on Friday, if she leaves it till Thursday, the exam will again be expected. So Thursday is out, too.

What about Wednesday? That, again, is ruled out. Her students know the exam cannot be on either Thursday or Friday, so if the teacher leaves it until Wednesday, the exam will again be expected.

But then Tuesday and Monday are also out, and for the same reason.

In short, *the teacher cannot give an unexpected examination.*

Yet, of course, she can. Can't she?

Paradox 7: 'Santa Claus Doesn't Exist'

Little Brian is reading an English grammar book.

'Dad. Names are used as labels for people and other things, aren't they?'

'That's right. The job of a name within a sentence is always to pick out someone or something so that you can then go on to say something about it.'

'Right. So if I say "Jack is tall", what I say is true when the person the name "Jack" refers to has the property of being tall, and false otherwise.'

'You've got it.'

'But wait a second. Yesterday you said "Santa Claus doesn't exist", right?'

'I did, yes.'

'And what you said is true?'

'Of course.'

'But how *can* it be true? You said the job of a name in a sentence is to pick out an object so that one can then go on to say something about it. But the name "Santa Claus" doesn't pick out anyone, does it?'

'Er, no.'

'But then "Santa Claus" cannot do its job within the sentence, can it? In which case, the sentence "Santa Claus doesn't exist" cannot be true, can it?'

'H'm. I guess not.'

'But you just said it *is* true.'

Little Brian's question is a good one. How can 'Santa Claus doesn't exist' be true if the job of the name 'Santa Claus' within a sentence is to refer?

General Advice for Solving Paradoxes

Here's a hint on how to solve paradoxes. All the paradoxes in this chapter take the form of *arguments*. An argument is made up of one or more claims or *premises* and a *conclusion*. The premises are supposed to *support* the conclusion.

These arguments are paradoxical because the premises are plausible, the conclusion implausible, yet the reasoning apparently cogent.

When faced with such a paradox, you always have three options:

- Explain why at least one of the premises of the argument seems true but is false.
- Explain why the conclusion of the argument seems false but is true.
- Expose some logical flaw in the reasoning.

Before you do any of these things, however, it often helps to identify and set out the argument clearly. This is not always as easy as it sounds.

Here, by way of illustration, is the sandpit version of the sorites paradox set out in more formal style (I assume, for the sake of argument, that Jenny's sandpit contains a heap of 100,000 grains).

- If n number of grains is a heap, then so is $n-1$ grains. 100,000 grains of sand is a heap. Therefore, 99,999 grains is also a heap.

This same form of reasoning is then reapplied over and over again (dropping the figures in the middle premise and conclusion by one each time) until you reach the conclusion that zero grains of sand is a heap.

Your options are: 1. to accept the conclusion, 2. to reject the reasoning, or 3. to reject one of the premises.

Here are some further tips and comments on the seven paradoxes we have looked at.

Paradox 1

There's no consensus on how this paradox should be solved. You might, perhaps, be tempted just to bite the bullet and say: 'OK, so what the old man says is both true and not true. It's a contradiction. What's the problem with admitting the existence of contradictions?'

This strategy won't work. Not only are there plenty of problems with admitting contradictions (which I won't go into here), but we can in any case rework the paradox so that admitting contradictions doesn't help.

Here's how. Suppose we introduce the prefix 'UN-P' in such a way that 'UN-P' applies to all and only those things to which the term 'P' applies. That's just stipulated. So, for example, 'UN-horse' applies to all and only those things that aren't horses. Now consider this sentence:

This sentence is UN-true.

It follows that this sentence is both true and UN-true. But we just defined 'UN-' in such a way that, *by stipulation*, nothing can be both true and UN-true. Admitting contradictions does nothing to solve *this* version of the paradox.

Paradox 2

Again, there's no agreement about how to solve this paradox. Some philosophers insist that there must be a precise number of grains of sands marking the boundary between a heap and a non-heap. So it's not true that removing a single grain will never turn a heap into a non-heap. It's just that we don't know what this precise number is.

But the suggestion that there is such a precise boundary is a lot to swallow. Surely, it is *we* who determine what our concepts are and where their boundaries lie. So how could our concept of a heap come to have a precise boundary of which we are ignorant?

Paradox 3

This paradox is fairly easy to solve: deny that there is any such person as Luigi, the barber who shaves all and only those who don't shave themselves. So the sentence 'Luigi shaves just those who don't shave themselves' is neither true nor false.

Paradox 4

Here's a similar paradox.

Movement is impossible. For suppose I wish to move one yard. In order to move one yard, I must move half that distance: half a yard. But to move half a yard I must move a quarter-yard, and so on ad infinitum. So I must make an infinite number of movements before I can move a yard. But I cannot make an infinite number of movements, for an infinite number of movements can never be completed. Therefore, I cannot move one yard (or even a bit of a yard).

Paradox 5

One of the more popular strategies here is to deny the principle that all generalisations are confirmed by their instances. And in fact there are other counter-examples to this principle. Take the generalisation that *all snakes are located outside Ireland*. An instance of this would be: *Fred is a snake and Fred is located outside Ireland*. But the more such instances one accumulates – the more snakes outside Ireland one observes – surely the more likely it is that there *are* snakes in Ireland. So our generalisation about snakes is actually *disconfirmed* by its instances!

Paradox 6

You should assume two things for this paradox to work: that the students can be pretty sure there will be an exam (otherwise even on Friday the exam might be unexpected: they might believe the teacher to have forgotten all about it, and when she doesn't forget that might come as a surprise), and that the students are rational and have good memories (they won't simply forget about the exam, or get confused, so that it does come as a surprise).

Paradox 7

This paradox continues to perplex philosophers of language. Note that it won't do to say that the name 'Santa Claus' *doesn't* refer to a *person* but *does* refer to *something*: it refers to our *concept* of Santa Claus. The reason this won't do is that it would then follow that, as our *concept* of Santa Claus *does* exist, so 'Santa Claus does not exist' would be false.

Further reading

For a clear, rigorous and entertaining introduction to paradoxes, I recommend:

Michael Clark,
Paradoxes from A to Z
(London: Routledge, 2002).

INDEX

Note: the letter *n* appended to a page number indicates a footnote.